DATE DUE

WITHDRAWN

Get Lucky

THOR MULLER LANE BECKER

GET LUCKY

How to Put PLANNED SERENDIPITY to Work for You and Your Business

JOSSEY-BASS
A Wiley Imprint
www.josseybass.com

Published by Jossey-Bass
A Wiley Imprint

One Montgomery Street, Suite 1200, San Francisco, CA 94104-4594—www.josseybass.com

Cover photograph by Steve Allen | Brand X | Getty (RF)

Jossey-Bass books and products are available through most bookstores. To contact Jossey-Bass directly call our Customer Care Department within the U.S. at 800-956-7739, outside the U.S. at 317-572-3986, or fax 317-572-4002.

Wiley publishes in a variety of print and electronic formats and by print-on-demand. Some material included with standard print versions of this book may not be included in e-books or in print-on-demand. If this book refers to media such as a CD or DVD that is not included in the version you purchased, you may download this material at **http://booksupport.wiley.com**. For more information about Wiley products, visit **www.wiley.com**.

Library of Congress Cataloging-in-Publication Data

Muller, Thor, 1971-
    Get lucky : how to put planned serendipity to work for you and your business /
Thor Muller, Lane Becker. – 1st ed.
        p. cm.
    Includes bibliographical references and index.
    ISBN 978-1-118-24975-8 (cloth), ISBN 978-1-118-27647-1 (ebk), 978-1-118-27693-8 (ebk),
978-1-118-27694-5 (ebk)
    1. Success in business.   2. Creative ability in business.   I. Becker, Lane, 1973-
II. Title.
    HF5386.M828 2012
    650.1–dc23

                                                                        2012001579

Printed in the United States of America

FIRST EDITION

HB Printing 10 9 8 7 6 5 4 3 2 1

Contents

For those who accept what we are, and celebrate what we aren't—Courtney, Amy, Quinn, and Tesla.

"The world is much larger than you can imagine right now. Which means, you are much larger than you can imagine."

—WILLIAM DERESIEWICZ

Get Lucky

1

Prepare for the Unpreparable

"Luck is merely an illusion, trusted by the ignorant and chased by the foolish."
— Timothy Zahn

"I'm a great believer in luck, and I find the harder I work, the more I have of it."
— Thomas Jefferson

The audience greeted the young entrepreneur with a hero's welcome. He walked out onto the stage of the conference hall and looked out into the audience. The applause was deafening.

It was the fall of 2005, the last day of the Web 2.0 Summit in San Francisco. Sergey Brin, the 32-year-old cofounder of Google, was making a surprise on-stage appearance with John Battelle, the conference host.

Though it's hard to believe now, in this era of a new wave of Internet success stories such as Facebook, Twitter, Zynga, and Pandora, back in 2005 most of the world still thought of the Internet as a financial sinkhole whose moment had permanently passed after the technology stock bubble burst in 2000. The several hundred people at this conference, true believers in the business potential of the Web, knew otherwise. All the proof they needed was standing right there in front of them.

Brin, along with his cofounder Larry Page, had started, built, and taken public a company that had managed in just five years to become the greatest engine of wealth creation the world had ever seen. At a time when people were still scoffing at the idea of building a real business on the Internet, Brin and Page had not only done that, but had done it in a way that had made both of them, and several others, billionaires in the process.

The audience quickly fell silent as Brin sat down. What would he say? What secrets would he reveal? What would he explain to the audience that would help them emulate or understand his unbelievable achievement? Battelle's first question cut straight to the heart of the matter: "What," he asked Brin, "do you attribute Google's incredible success to?"

Brin responded confidently, as if this was just a run-of-the-mill engineering question. "The number one factor that contributed to our success was *luck*."

Silence from the audience. Was that really his answer? Could that possibly be true? He and Page had just blindly stumbled into their fortune? That didn't make any sense. Surely it must have been their superior intellect, their foresight, their dedication and perseverance that led to their success.

Realizing that his answer begged for an explanation, Brin continued: "We followed our hearts in terms of research areas, and eventually found we had something pretty useful, and wanted to make an impact with it."

This was a strange kind of luck. He wasn't talking about random interventions or being at the right place at the right time. No, he was talking about motivation, instinct, accidental discoveries, and passion. How was this luck?

If anybody in the audience was disappointed by that answer, they shouldn't have been. Brin was not just being humble. He was sharing a crucial insight: that for something to succeed with the kind of scale and speed that Google did, it requires more to happen than any one person, or even a team of people, can ever fully take responsibility for. This insight was central to how Google's founding team built the company.

By crediting his fortunes (and his fortune) to good luck, Brin wasn't abdicating responsibility for his success. He was acknowledging the creative tension between his personal goals and a world utterly out of his control. Miraculously, Google seemed to have turned this tension into an actual business practice. A practice that changed the world.

Luck Is a Four-Letter Word

It's easy for us to dismiss "luck" as mere superstition.

When we hear the word, we're likely to picture a gambler on a winning streak, sitting on a stool at a Vegas blackjack table, taking another swig from a glass of whiskey. He has an impressive stack of chips on the table in front of him. At his elbows are the envious faces of his fellow players, and in front of him, the impassive face of a dealer preparing to deal the next hand.

Our gambler knows in his bones that he is on a lucky streak. His confidence has swelled, it seems as if nothing can stand in his way, and his next move is clear: he'll double down at his first opportunity.

We pity the poor gambler, for we know what he seems to have forgotten: that this is a carefully calibrated game designed to deliver just enough of this intoxicating feeling to keep him playing. And play on he does. By the time the dealer is finished with him, he'll give up not just his winnings, but dig himself a hole trying to recover his streak. The gambler will continue on, sure that his luck will return, and may end up pawning his wedding ring a few hours later once he hits his credit limit.

Looked at through this lens, there is no luck, only probability and human frailty. In fact, the reliability of the casino coming out on top is so complete that it stands as a counter-argument to the existence of luck at all. Luck, like the cocktails that lubricate its appearance, is a cleverly crafted mirage, in the form of lotteries, slot machines, and reality TV shows, fodder for the desperate and undereducated.

Or we hurl the word "lucky" as a kind of insult at people we look down on. How many of us, upon seeing someone achieve notable success, haven't said to the person next to us, "Well, *she* certainly got lucky." The intimation is that when luck does strike, it is random, without rhyme or reason. What better way to imply that someone didn't actually *deserve* their success?

But these views of luck detract from just how audacious the idea of luck really is. When we look at luck closely, it is a direct challenge to the logic of modern society. For hundreds of years we have built institutions based on reason and the inexorable advance of our machines. We've engineered career paths, industries, schools, markets, and political systems in ways that banish the role of chance brick by brick, rule by rule. The benefits of progress, we've been told, are available to everyone with machine-like regularity by dint of hard work and applied learning.

Our schools recoil at the suggestion that a student was a success, or that a professor gained tenure, because of luck. Executive boards would never admit that its officers held position by chance. Athletic teams and their fans rarely suggest that their winning records can be boiled down to happy accidents. Each of these, we're told, is a formal system that produces results, based on individual hard work and well designed processes. Any suggestion otherwise would be heresy.

And yet . . .

Stickier Than It Looks

There are many popular stories in which luck plays a central role, like the tale of Isaac Newton discovering gravity after being hit by an apple falling from a tree, or Ben Franklin encountering electricity while flying his kite. But most of these are dumbed down, just-so tales. The truth behind most creation myths is almost always more complicated—and more interesting. What follows is one of the most commonly cited examples of luck leading to massive business success: the story of the invention of the Post-it note. And yet, even though many know the basic details of how Post-it notes were born, few draw the right conclusions from this luck-drenched story. For those of us looking to get as lucky with our next creation as 3M did, it's worth re-examining the story in full detail.

It was 1968, and a young chemist named Dr. Spence Silver had taken his first job at the Minnesota Mining & Manufacturing Company. He was working as part of a five-person research team trying to develop stronger adhesives for use in aircraft manufacturing.

"Adhesives are not to be confused with your everyday glue," Dr. Silver says. To make glue, you just "boil animal bones down and make sure it's something that sticks when it dries." Adhesives, by contrast, require real chemical engineering. They are delicate constructions built on complex molecules called polymers. By changing the structure of a polymer, chemists can affect an adhesive's qualities like stickiness, elasticity, and durability.

Working on his own one afternoon, Dr. Silver experimented with adding more chemical reactant to his polymer recipe than was considered safe. The results were astonishing: his mixture produced tiny bubbles that kept the adhesive from bonding firmly. This was not what he had expected.

Before long his experiments led to something very unusual but considered useless by most others. Rather than make a stronger adhesive, as was the goal, he had created one that had "high tack" but "low peel" adhesion, the latter being the measure of how easily it can be removed from items it is stuck to. Put simply, it was a magical adhesive that could be endlessly reused.

Silver was proud of his invention and began evangelizing its qualities. His colleagues didn't care. The adhesive was not relevant to the tasks they were working on. Eventually, Silver managed to convince the New Products lab manager, Dr. Geoff Nicholson, to make a prototype of a permanently sticky bulletin board that would allow papers to be attached and detached easily. But the product concept floundered. No one was interested.

Silver was frustrated. "I felt my adhesive was so obviously unique that I began to give seminars throughout the company in the hope I would spark an idea among its product developers," he said.

Four long years later, an inventor named Art Fry from the Tape Division Lab attended one of the seminars Silver was still tirelessly delivering. Fry's job was to propose new product ideas for the Tape Division and build them into businesses—for instance, tape for skis or for sticking books to shelves. But Fry didn't have an immediate use for Silver's unique adhesive, so he filed the information away in his brain.

Even more months passed. And then one day, while sitting in church choir practice, Fry became frustrated with his hymnal bookmark. It kept falling out, and he would lose his place. At that moment the memory of Silver's novel adhesive flashed into his mind. The next morning he tracked down Silver to get a sample of the adhesive and used it to make a prototype of a sticky bookmark.

After several trials and errors, Fry successfully created a sticky bookmark that could be removed from a page without leaving adhesive behind. It was just what he needed to solve his choir practice problem, but the test users he gave them to just weren't using them up very fast. It turned out people didn't need that many bookmarks. As clever as his invention was, Fry needed people to use more of them on a regular basis to justify producing it commercially. The product didn't appear viable after all.

Sometime later, while writing a report, Fry had a question he wanted to set aside for later investigation. Seeing one of his leftover sticky bookmarks on his desk, he cut off a piece, wrote his question on it, and attached it to the front of the report, which he then passed on to his supervisor.

"My supervisor wrote his answer on the same paper, re-stuck it to the front, and returned it to me," Art explains. "It was a eureka, head-flapping moment—I can still feel the excitement. I had my product: a sticky note."

He called in his boss, Nicholson, whose backing he would need to turn his idea into a product. The two immediately began to work on a prototype together. They needed paper, and the lab next door happened to have yellow scrap paper. They used it to make their first sticky notepads.

Early test users were ecstatic. Executives would march through knee-deep snow in the dead of winter to get replacement notepads. The yellow color of the pads, in particular, was a hit. People assumed the color had been selected after much research and retrospectively attached significance to the choice. "The yellow was chosen to evoke a strong emotional response," they would say, or "they're designed to match yellow legal pads."

"To me it was another one of those incredible accidents," says Nicholson. "It was not thought out; nobody said they'd better be yellow rather than white because they would blend in—it was a pure accident."

Accident after accident, through an accumulation of chance and circumstance spanning many people and multiple years, the Post-it Note was born. This $100 million-a-year product line now includes pads in dozens of colors, sizes, and as of 2007, a super-sticky version for more demanding surfaces.

Yet there was nothing accidental about the way 3M, as the company is known today, created the conditions for the Post-it Notes—and over 55,000 other products across a range of categories—to emerge and make it to market successfully. Quite the contrary. Dozens of things had to go right inside the organization for the accidents to morph into creative inspiration and from there into business opportunities. 3M has found ways to harness chance occurrences over and over again. The company has, in a very real sense, discovered how to create its own luck.

Good Luck Is Hard Work

Google and 3M are by no means the only companies that have figured out that luck is a crucial factor of their mojo, and that they can design their businesses to harness it. Your organization can plan to get lucky just as much as they have. What you're holding is a manual to help you do just that, a manual for luck: what it is, how it works, and how to put it to work for you.

Let's be honest, though: for most of us harnessing luck sounds as bizarre as strategy planning with Tarot cards and palm reading. Yet what we've found is that the ability to harness unexpected discoveries is not just an actual practice; it is rather the *essential* practice for building a business in a time of accelerating, vertigo-inducing change. Making ventures work in a world as interconnected, complex, and unpredictable as ours requires engaging with the full scope of that complexity even though we can't see, model, or even imagine all that much of it. No matter how smart we are, or how big our idea, the world is always bigger. No matter how many of the possibilities we can see, there will always be factors outside our sight and beyond our control.

Many of us live with a daily background terror. We see industries failing, jobs disappearing, populations shifting, governments falling, currencies collapsing. This can't help but sow confusion and self-doubt, and the idea of putting our fate in the hands of chance may seem like the worst idea for calming jittery nerves and setting ourselves up for success.

The good news is that what worked for the characters we've met so far—that combination of hard work, personal vision, and unplanned good fortune—can work for you, too. Luck, it turns out, doesn't just happen by chance. Rather, the best kind of luck—that creative force known as *serendipity*—is the luck that we attract to ourselves. Because even if we can't predict it, we can court it and prepare for it, so that we know what to do with it when it shows up. And when it does, thanks to this book, you will know what to do.

OK, but wait a minute: who are we, exactly, and what do we know about luck in business?

For the past decade we have been in a remarkable position to witness the kinds of practices that power the most innovative companies in the world. We've worked with big companies as diverse as Google, Procter & Gamble, Zynga, Facebook, and Walmart, as well as countless startups and mom-and-pop operations. These companies couldn't be more different in terms of their purposes and their products, but over the years we began to see unmistakable patterns in the companies that have successfully adapted to the breakneck pace of change our modern world demands.

Much of our insight came to us courtesy of the online service we founded with two other partners in 2007, Get Satisfaction, which has helped almost a hundred thousand organizations increase the role of happy accidents and unplanned information in their everyday operations. It's a community platform that lets companies of every size engage in open conversations with their customers—something like a Web forum, but one that plugs into all those life-or-death internal business processes that companies depend on.

From a simple idea—getting people inside and outside of an organization to talk to each other like human beings—we've seen all kinds of age-old assumptions get turned on their heads: customer service has become a new kind of marketing instead of just an after-the-sale cost center, organizations now materially benefit from responding and adapting to the needs of individual customers, and openness has become a virtue even in companies that previously thrived on secrecy.

Here are some of the amazing things we've seen through the eyes of Get Satisfaction customers:

- **Timbuk2**, a fashionable messenger bag company, discovered that its customers wanted a diaper bag, and that they could offer one simply by adding a set of accessories from other manufacturers.
- **Tide**, the detergent brand, found that the free samples they were giving out at events were often thrown away by people who didn't want to carry them around. A side-comment from a consumer was overheard by a product manager, giving rise to a redemption code innovation that both saved the company money and spared the landfill.
- **TechSmith**, a software maker, collected input about what customers wanted from a new version of their product. One suggestion about the user interface seemed straightforward until other customers responded, exposing surprising counterpoints that caused the company to rethink their entire approach to the product.

This new openness between companies and customers is a big change. Pundits are talking about how we're witnessing the rise of something new: the social business. Management consultants are getting paid truckloads of money to present graphs and buzzwords depicting "radical operational efficiencies," "friction-free communication," and "low-cost marketing" made possible by these new social tools. But what gets us excited isn't repackaging tired old business clichés in a fancy new wrapper. Instead, what's amazing is that truly social businesses are inviting the unexpected to intervene in their everyday functions. These businesses are letting go of much of the control they have traditionally hoarded in order to gain the huge benefits that can arise through chance interactions with their customers. Our goal in founding Get Satisfaction was precisely to help organizations make the transition into a new business environment filled with less certainty but more opportunity.

That same year we started Get Satisfaction, we also came across a blog post called "Luck and the Entrepreneur," by Netscape founder turned rock star venture capitalist Marc Andreessen, a Silicon Valley legend. His post described the work of American neurologist Dr. James H. Austin, who dissects the ins-and-outs of serendipity in his book, *Chase, Chance, and Creativity*. In the book, Austin recounts his early days as a medical resident accidentally stumbling into the clinical cases that would define his research, through the long and winding path of experimentation in the lab, to India where he forms some of his most important collaborations. Looking back on his career, Austin marvels at the consistent role chance has played throughout his career and proposes a formal model for understanding how luck works.

We were deeply impressed with the idea that luck is something that can be broken apart, studied, and perhaps even directed. Andreessen noticed this as well, and he ended his post with a bold statement that has rattled around in our heads ever since: "I think there is a roadmap to getting luck on our side."

This started us down our own path to understanding how these fortuitous accidents come about. What are people doing when they make these discoveries that change their lives? Where does the surprise come from, and how does one recognize it when it arrives? Why are some environments more conducive to serendipitous discoveries? In other words, what makes some organizations luckier than others?

Our goal was to create a toolkit that would allow any organization to do what 3M or Google does so well—foster the conditions for serendipity to work its magic. We found that by breaking luck down into its component parts, by building on the research and insights of scientists as well as the behaviors of the smartest entrepreneurs we knew, we were able to demystify it. We surprised even ourselves when we uncovered a framework that makes sense of it all.

But hold on. Even in explaining our story we're making it sound like our path to writing this book was linear and intentional. This is the trap we humans often fall into—we all love a good story, after all, even when it isn't entirely true. (Just ask Ben Franklin.) The reality is that our path from Andreessen's post to observing the behaviors of so many companies to a coherent insight to an actual framework makes sense only in reverse. In fact, most of this happened as a subconscious background process while we started companies, raised families, and hosted cocktail parties. In retrospect—for instance, when we revisit presentations we made at conferences five years ago—we knew we were on the trail of a big idea, but at the time it looked like something else entirely. We could never have predicted all the unexpected encounters and surprising connections that finally brought us to this place where we now find ourselves sharing our ideas with you.

This book is itself, then, a product of serendipity.

Science Gets Lucky

As it turns out, we're in excellent company. Luck isn't just for search engines and paper products—many if not most of the giant leaps forward in science are rooted in accident and only seem obvious after the fact.

You might think that science would be hostile to anything as seemingly impenetrable as luck. "It is never entirely in fashion to

mention luck in the same breath as science," as Dr. Austin wrote
in his book on the subject. If we can't measure it or even agree on
basic definitions, how can it possibly be science? It may be surprising,
then, that luck, this most slippery of ideas, has been treated with
great interest and even academic rigor, not just by Dr. Austin but by
many of the world's brightest scientific minds. A 1996 academic survey
showed that almost 10 percent of the most cited scholarly articles include
serendipity as a factor in discovery.

Turns out luck is more measurable and definable than it appears
at first.

The scientific community's interest in luck is by no means a new
phenomenon. The mother of all "a-ha!" stories is the tale of Archimedes,
the Greek physicist who lived three centuries before Christ. His story
begins with King Hiero hiring a goldsmith to manufacture a gold
crown. The King was pleased with the beautiful crown until his advisors
suggested to him that the gold might be impure because it had been
diluted with silver. Still, nobody was able to provide proof of the crime.
Incensed, the King pleaded with his most trusted sage, Archimedes, to
figure out a way to determine whether he had been swindled.

Archimedes was in a tough spot. He had to solve the problem
definitively or he'd be shamed in the eyes of the court. He spent
many hours in contemplation but was simply unable to come up
with a workable solution. Eventually he decided to give up the chase
for the evening and take a bath. He cleared his head and immersed
himself in the tub. As he did so the water began spilling over the edge.
This unrelated event spurred his mind to make the critical leap. He
jumped out of the tub and began running through his home shouting
the phrase that would be forever linked with serendipitous discovery,
"Eureka! Eureka!"

Thanks to the overflowing tub, Archimedes's mind was drawn to
understand the relationship between relative displacement and specific
gravity. He knew at that moment that by measuring the water displaced
by equal weights of gold and silver he'd be able to prove whether or
not the crown displaced too much water to be pure gold. He brought

his experiment to the court, where he demonstrated the crime to the approval of all—except, of course, the lying goldsmith.

Fast forward a few centuries and we find Joseph Priestley, the discoverer of oxygen, waxing eloquent on the theme: "More is owing to what we call chance . . . than to any proper design, or preconceived theory in this business."

Priestley very well may have had in mind the accidental path that led him to soda water, which he invented in 1767. After moving to Leeds, England, to take a position with the clergy, he noticed the haze rising from the vats of beer at the brewery next to his temporary housing. This was a curious situation, so Priestley devised an experiment: he suspended bowls of water above the vats. When he tasted the water days later he found that it had a delightful effervescence. Indeed, the carbon dioxide released in the fermentation process had infused the water, a process we today call "carbonation" (though it took the business-minded J. J. Schweppe to turn Priestley's Eureka moment into the business that continues to this day).

Chance has always played a significant role in science, but scholarly interest in it exploded in the last hundred years. Its star has risen in tandem with two of the biggest scientific ideas of the twentieth century: quantum physics and modern evolutionary theory.

In just the last hundred years we've seen the foundations of science upended: since the seventeenth century Newton's "celestial clockwork" had dominated the imagination of investigators with the idea that they were studying a structured universe that was fundamentally deterministic. It was believed that the entire character of the world could be inferred from Natural Law; truths such as "an object in motion stays in motion" and "what goes up must come down" describe a machine-like universe, a well-oiled contraption of valves, levers, and ball bearings.

Quantum physics didn't exactly contradict this idea, but it added a massive twist. Starting in the 1920s, physicists including Niels Bohr and Werner Heisenberg began to tell us that reality at the smallest level of matter—particles like atoms, electrons, gluons, and neutrinos—operates *very* differently indeed. They taught us that rather than thinking of sub-atomic particles such as electrons as behaving like billiard balls moving from one position to another, we need to think of them as behaving "probabilistically." An electron is only more or less likely to move from one position to another based on its position and velocity in space. It could, if the mood struck, jump suddenly to another part of the universe. Or it could spawn a doppelganger version of itself and exist in multiple places at once. Probabilities! Uncertainty! It turned out the physical world was not as consistent as we had once thought, and in fact our heretofore reliable Laws of Nature were actually built on a platform of chance.

But, in science as well as business, it's not always easy to buy into the idea of such grand uncertainty as a key component of the way the world functions. Even Albert Einstein, who had contributed to the field of quantum physics, did not like its implications—that the world was not as deterministic as he personally believed it was. "I, at any rate, am convinced that He [God] does not throw dice," he famously wrote in a letter to a colleague. But the math behind the science worked, and decade after decade the experimental results confirmed the new model, much to Einstein's chagrin.

Meanwhile, a revolution of equal scale was occurring in biology as well. Charles Darwin had already transformed the field with the introduction of natural selection: the idea of "descent with modifications," the straightforward concept that only those species that survive get the chance to pass down their traits to their offspring. Darwin, though, was haunted until the day he died by a question he could never answer: where did these "modifications" come from? Though evolution became widely accepted by the early twentieth century, biologists still squabbled over *how* evolution happens.

The answers came during the first half of the twentieth century, when Francis Crick and James D. Watson, building on a century's worth of work regarding the nature of genetic inheritance, cracked the code that was the human genome. It was the discovery of DNA—the means of coding and replicating inherited traits—that brought the answer to light: random mutations in DNA and genetic recombination accounted for all the necessary variation in the gene pool. The big surprise of what became known as the "neo-darwinian synthesis" was this: the only known source of biological innovation in life on our planet is chance. Combining the random input of genetic mutation with the sorting process enabled by natural selection creates evolution.

You could say, stretching the definition just a bit, that this is serendipity by another name. It appears as if luck is embedded deep, both within our genes and in the fabric of the universe.

Spinning a Rattleback in Rotterdam

Until now we've used the words *luck* and *serendipity* almost inter-changeably, but not just anything can be called serendipity. It's this peculiar sub-species of luck that we're really interested in.

Serendipity is a coined word, made up out of whole cloth in 1754 by the English wit Horace Walpole. The word has exploded in popu-larity only in the last fifty years or so, and still has no translation in many other languages. Its sudden ubiquity is stunning; there were a mere 135 mentions in print before 1958, but by 2000 the word had appeared in the titles of fifty-seven books, was the name of a 2001 major motion picture starring John Cusack, appeared in 13,000 news articles, and produced 23 million Google search results. Facebook's CEO Mark Zuckerberg announced in 2011 that his social network was being designed to enable "real-time serendipity."

Still, most people are confused about what the word actually *means*. It has been used to describe everything from "a witty writing style" to "destiny with a sense of humor," and the word famously appeared, without explanation, on the cover of a women's underwear catalog in 1992. In fact, the definition of "serendipity" has been consuming scholars ever since the word was invented. This presents a challenge for those of us looking to better plan our own serendipity, as it's only with a sturdy and concise definition of this concept that we can hope to understand what makes it work. That's where Pek van Andel comes in.

Van Andel is a medical researcher at the University of Groningen, two hours outside of Amsterdam, but the title he prefers these days is "serendipitologist." He's also completely, *madly,* in love with the word serendipity. He's become famous for his epic collection of thousands of examples of the phenomenon, and his personal history is a living example of the word.

In 1992 Van Andel and his colleague Jan Worst won a Dutch Innovation Prize for the invention of a low-cost artificial cornea, making eyesight a possibility for millions of low-income cornea-blind people throughout the world. A few years later he made headlines for his groundbreaking research on sexuality, having visualized human intercourse through live MRI scans. The idea for the project came about by chance after he stumbled upon MRI scans of a singing human larynx. Afterwards, the YouTube video of the not-safe-to-watch-at-work MRI scan was seen by over a million people, and received an international award (the Ig Nobel Prize) for "research that makes people laugh and then think."

With a disarming smile, bushy mad scientist eyebrows, and lengthy hair suggesting an artist's temperament, he is just what you would imagine a serendipitologist to look like, wry humor etched deeply into his face. Listening to Van Andel talk about his work suggests there may be another reason why scientists are so willing to embrace the role of chance. Science is a madcap endeavor, littered with wacky personalities whose obsessions and unconventional paths are the stuff of legend: Tycho Brahe's gold prosthetic nose and pet moose, Gregor Mendel's obsession with peas, Richard Feynman's safe-cracking, Stephen Hawking's scientific wagers. The best scientists treasure the unexpected because it's a natural extension of their idiosyncrasies. Van Andel is no exception.

Thor got a chance to experience Van Andel's passion for the subject of serendipity in person while visiting Rotterdam, The Netherlands, for a conference, where Van Andel shared with him the story of how Horace Walpole originally coined the term. Walpole based the word on a Persian fairy tale, *The Three Princes of Serendip,* referencing it in one of his eighteen hundred letters to his friend, the diplomat Horace Mann. Mann had given Walpole a portrait of a duchess, and Walpole had stumbled upon her family's coat of arms in a book. In describing his delight at his finding, Walpole wrote:

> *This discovery indeed is almost of that kind which I call* serendip- *ity, a very expressive word . . . I once read a silly fairy tale, called* The Three Princes of Serendip: *as their highness travelled, they were always making discoveries, by accidents & sagacity, of things which they were not in quest of [emphasis ours] . . . No discovery of a thing you are looking for comes under this description.*

Walpole's new word captured the spirit of the phenomenon brilliantly. Pek van Andel suggests the succinct modern definition is "the art of making an unsought finding." Or as the old saw goes, "looking for a needle in a haystack and coming out with the farmer's daughter."

What becomes clear when you spend some time with Pek van Andel is the depth of thinking on the phenomenon of serendipity that has occurred over the last hundred years—it's verging on a proper discipline. It's been exhaustively picked apart and analyzed by sociologists, mathematicians, inventors, creativity gurus, and everyone in between. Van Andel believes fervently in the importance of understanding the role serendipity plays in the world, and when he travels across Europe to give master classes on the subject he often carries with him a suitcase full of books as physical proof of the righteousness of his cause.

During Thor's visit, Van Andel opened his case up for Thor to see, pulling out book after book, each one a treatise on the role of accident in the creative process: French philosophers, German epistemologists, mathematicians and linguists, among others (a full list of his suitcase books is listed in the notes). Several times Van Andel paused to crack one of these well-worn books and point out an underlined quote, usually in a language Thor couldn't read. He was like a wizard in a sacred order with his magical scrolls, the dog-eared secrets of serendipity ready at his fingertips.

With his prized books stacked in small towers scattered across the table, Van Andel announced he would now share the physical embodiment of serendipity: the ancient "Rattleback" Celtic Stone. "I can explain serendipity to a person without saying a single word by showing them this stone," he said, removing a small wooden box from his bag. Nestled inside was a surfboard-shaped plastic form, flat on one side, curved on the other. With a mischievous grin he placed the Rattleback on the table, curved side down and flicked it into a spin with his index finger. Around and around it glided, eventually slowing towards a stop, when it suddenly reversed itself, accelerating its spin in the opposite direction!

"It's much like a boomerang, you see. But it must have been discovered by accident. It *had* to—nobody would have spun the stone expecting this to occur. Someone thousands of years ago discovered what seemed like a magic stone, and then they turned it into this toy. We're still playing with it thousands of years later. You can buy them on eBay."

Serendipity at Work

In all those books Van Andel carries with him, however, there are few that tackle the thorny subject of the role of serendipity in organizations. The scholarly literature on serendipity is overwhelmingly focused on the experience of the individual creative mind. While it's true that businesses are made up of many different individual minds, anyone who has been employed in one can tell you the sum total of all those people working in concert is an entirely different beast—one that doesn't often place much value on making room for chance.

It's the rare organization that goes out of its way to open up space for serendipity, and yet, in business as in science, the big breakthroughs and mammoth successes always contain a significant element of luck. Consider our Post-it creation story. So many things had to go right for 3M to bring Post-it Notes to market, over the course of many, many years. How many companies would have tolerated that level of uncertainty for that long? Not only that, 3M had to create an environment that allowed researchers to follow their instincts, even when they led away from corporate expectations. It had to abide intellectual wild goose chases, even when they seemed distracting or pointless. It had to encourage unplanned interactions between employees from different areas of the organization, often with varying goals and without knowing where, exactly, those encounters would lead. Management had to provide air cover when someone thought they'd discovered the "next big thing," so that their invention wouldn't get prematurely snuffed out before its value was fully understood, and the company needed a highly improvisational relationship with potential users in order to eventually discover the best possible use for the product.

One place in the business landscape we can look to in order to better understand how to embrace the kind of uncertainty that 3M embedded into its organization is the world of technology startups. At companies like our own Get Satisfaction and many other startups, the important leaps of discovery, though unplanned and surprising, are anything but random—they are the result of consistent focus, a sense of purpose, and just enough of the right kind of structure to fertilize the appearance of chance.

Founders of early stage startups tend to be naturals at many of these practices. It's the price of admission in an environment where, with a little luck, you might get the opportunity to invent an entirely new market. Speaking from our own experience, we know that startup founders begin with only an idea (or ten) and then use their raw instincts as a guide, relying on imagination and agility to tease a new business into its earliest shape. Startup founders don't know exactly how their product will work, or where (or even if) it will find a huge market. Their companies don't start out with formal sales and HR processes. Instead, they work tirelessly to attract initial customers and skilled employees by shamelessly networking and by talking the ears off anybody who will listen. They build business habits that not only accept the unknowns surrounding their business but learn to use them to their advantage. The uncertain environment becomes a spur to work harder and keep going.

But even with a startup, this often changes as the business grows up. Success means scale, and scale means adding layers of business processes that allow us to expand the number of employees and customers. We strategize with twelve-month plans and start reading books about "managing innovation." Hierarchy and process replace agility and intuition. All of these things are designed to help grow a sustainable business—and they may work. But they alienate us from the skills that got us into the game in the first place.

Bringing Lucky Back

It's a classic conundrum: the things that make us successful are the things that get stripped away once we've made it. It's the rare company that manages to maintain these habits of luck as the organization scales. And yet as we've seen with 3M and Google (and will see many more times throughout this book), it's exactly this embrace of chance, especially as a business grows, that creates the conditions for companies to maximize their opportunities for success.

This is where *Get Lucky* comes to the rescue. We're bringing lucky back. Small company or large, it doesn't matter: we will show you discrete skills you can develop to re-introduce serendipity into your work life.

We call our approach "planned serendipity." It's a set of concrete, attainable business skills that cultivate the conditions for chance encounters to generate new opportunities. Planned serendipity also provides you with the ability to recognize and put these opportunities to good use by showing you how to create and maintain the kinds of work environments, cultural attitudes, and business relationships that value and reward serendipitous occurrences.

To explain how planned serendipity works, we need to start with our own simple definition of serendipity, which we'll use from this point forward: *serendipity is chance interacting with creativity*.

Here's what it means: although we all recognize that chance is, by definition, inherently unpredictable, our actions—which embody our creativity, our ability to create something new and valuable that didn't exist before—can have a massive impact on what's possible. Spence Silver's adhesive never would have become Post-it Notes had he not spent years scattering his discovery across the company. The actions he took, and his willingness to explore creative possibilities and make connections beyond those that were obvious to everyone else around him, increased the likelihood that he would serendipitously stumble onto something that worked—and he did. Chance is highly sensitive to the actions we take.

Spence Silver was a natural practitioner of planned serendipity. So was Sergey Brin, the cofounder of Google. So was Archimedes. And so are many others about whom you've ever thought "Wow, that person sure is lucky." Each of these individuals practiced a specific set of skills that maximized the likelihood that good things would happen to them (and, by extension, to their businesses).

We have identified eight such skills, each of which represents a different facet of how luck works. Each skill will contribute to making your life luckier, and taken together they bring new meaning to the phrase "You lucky bastard." Every skill gets its own chapter in this book, but first let's take a brief tour of all of them.

Skill 1: Motion

Motion is the most basic element of planned serendipity. To move is to shake things up, to break out of your routine, to find ways to consistently meet new people and run into new ideas. Motion does not discriminate based on experience, IQ, or educational background—it simply rewards energetic, spontaneous action. But it's not always so simple: we organize our lives and businesses to be orderly, measured, and respectful of others' spaces to a fault. We encourage immobility in our environments, making free movement far too rare.

Skill 2: Preparation

Preparation is the ability to link together seemingly unconnected events, information, and people. Each of us is naturally capable of doing this to a greater or lesser degree, but the structures and roles we've grown up with—from the requirement to declare a major in college to the ubiquitous organizational chart that governs the daily interactions in most companies—have encouraged us to compartmentalize everything. Understanding preparation can have a massive impact on how organizations model, hire, and develop roles, employees, and teams.

Skill 3: Divergence

Divergence is the ability to recognize and explore alternative paths spurred by chance encounters, some of which may challenge our current thinking. It is the natural domain of scenario planners and futurists, and for people and organizations that have mastered divergence it is a means of sustained innovation. As a certain poet once pointed out, taking the road less traveled often makes all the difference.

Skill 4: Commitment

Commitment is the ability to choose, from among the ever-widening set of options in front of us, the right ones to focus on. When we commit, we reveal ourselves publicly in the pursuit of our goals, and by exposing a strong point of view we transform the environment around us. We create awareness of our intentions in others, which often stirs up latent desires in them as well. By connecting our inner world to everything happening outside of it, we explode the likelihood of new and unexpected combinations of events and opportunities.

Skill 5: Activation

To managers it seems obvious that high performance comes from keeping the team "on task," and while this approach enforces focus, it also results in a loss of spontaneity. The way to balance these competing priorities is, somewhat paradoxically, to develop new constraints that release people from their rote behaviors. Activation is about designing experiences that foster serendipity—friendly impulses in our day-to-day lives and work situations. The best organizations are able to develop an institutional "muscle memory" that makes it more likely they'll notice and act on the unexpected.

Skill 6: Connection

The network age presents us with limitless opportunities to connect with the world at large in entirely unplanned, unexpected ways. The ability to optimize the number and quality of connections with others is one of the strongest factors in amplifying the opportunities for serendipity to happen early and often.

Skill 7: Permeability

The best way to adapt to a world of accelerating change is to replace the rigid walls most organizations put up to keep themselves separate from the outside world with something more like a semi-permeable membrane. To do so, we need to develop techniques and tools that allow for the free exchange of information as well as the development of meaningful relationships between employees inside and customers and partners outside of the company. It's not just designated representatives who should be part of this exchange. For serendipity to happen frequently, everyone inside the organization should be part of this open, ongoing conversation.

Skill 8: Attraction

Some people have the ability to attract serendipity to themselves. Unexpectedly, good things erupt around them at an uncommon rate. These are individuals who have mastered attraction, bringing to bear the full set of skills described above to project their purpose out into the world in a way guaranteed to draw the best and most valuable events, people, ideas, and opportunities towards them.

Understanding these eight skills will help us to think differently about many assumptions we take for granted in business. There's often a giant gap between the free spirits that thrive in the absence of structure and the planners who crave it. These eight skills offer a way to bridge this gap.

Caught in a Double Bind

A word of caution before we dive in. If it's true that through the practice of planned serendipity we can directly increase the role of serendipity in our endeavors, then the opposite is equally true. We can develop attitudes and behaviors that smother it—and smother it we often do, with fervor.

As we've already begun to demonstrate, the normal function of most businesses is designed to squelch serendipity, not to encourage it. There's a simple reason: companies are structured to deliver predictability and reduce risk. It's an almost pathological compulsion of businesses to excise the role of chance from their routine operations, whether through quarterly revenue commitments, management by objectives, value chain engineering, or a thousand other things. We simply do not want to be surprised. It threatens our jobs and our market position, and what's worse, it upsets our comforting (and often delusional) sense of control.

When we add into this mix a mandate to foster serendipity, to be *creative* in ways that expose control as a myth, we find ourselves ensnared in a trap. It's called "the double bind" and it hovers over every one of these skills as you seek to develop them. It's a trap we saw unfold on a grand scale just a few years ago, on the occasion of the fortieth anniversary celebration of the Republic of Singapore.

Singapore is the tiny city-state that floats, like the dot on an exclamation point, off the southern tip of Malaysia. The ruling political party, the People's Action Party, had led its country to hyper-efficiency and growth, and had governed unchallenged since the country's founding in 1965. For its fortieth anniversary, the party now rallied its five million citizens with a wide-ranging new ad campaign to promote the country's achievements: *"The future is ours to make."* There was a great deal to celebrate—in the previous four decades they had created one of the indisputable economic miracles of Southeast Asia, with the nation's gross domestic product (GDP) growing an average of over 7.5 percent every year. The young city-state was admired around the world not just for its commercial gains, but for its low crime, clean streets, and high-tech infrastructure.

Singapore was equally well-known for its draconian rule, with strict speech policies on what its citizens could or could not do and say and severe punishment for disobedience. The author William Gibson once described the country as "Disneyland with the Death Penalty" in a 1993 article for *WIRED*. "You come to suspect that the reason you see so few actual police," he wrote, "is that people here all have 'the policeman inside.' Conformity here is the prime directive, and the fuzzier brands of creativity are in extremely short supply."

It was therefore widely noted when Singapore launched a campaign that included a message, which was, essentially, "*Be Spontaneous!*"

Indeed, by 2004 the government had recognized the limits that such strict social controls were placing on the nation's potential and was making changes to encourage a cultural vibrancy to match its famed efficiency. The prime minister announced without irony, "If we are to encourage a derring-do society, we must allow some risk-taking and a little excitement," adding, somewhat amusingly, "So changed is our mind-set that we will even allow reverse bungee jumping." *The New York Times* duly noted that the country's infamous ban on chewing gum would be "relaxed for people with medical prescriptions."

However, forty years of authoritarian rule leaves a deep mark on a society. The embedded response of Singapore's citizens was, as always, to obey. Except that in this case the imperative, to follow their impulses, ran directly against the grain of every other constraint imposed by their obsessively ordered culture. The two messages—be spontaneous, but make sure you don't do anything unexpected or out of line—couldn't be more contradictory.

This is a classic double bind.

The *double bind* is a term often used by psychologists and systems thinkers to describe this particular kind of crazy-making scenario. An authority makes two demands, one of which contradicts the other, on two different logical levels. Whichever instruction the victim follows, the other instruction becomes impossible. Making matters worse, the victim is usually unable to communicate the dilemma. They often aren't aware that it exists at all, just that they are overtaken by a profound uneasiness. We see echoes of this dysfunction in many of the companies we've worked within. As employees we are expected to be candid but then are chastised for being impolitic. We're told to be authentic but are chided for being frivolous. We're encouraged to "think outside the box" but are held to aggressive schedules and narrow business requirements.

Singapore may yet escape its double bind. Six years after the "be spontaneous" campaign, a new Singapore—one with more personality, verve, and, yes, even a bit of spontaneity—is emerging. The prime minister's progressive policies have helped, but what is really making it a reality is a new generation that thinks differently about their choices and the range of what's available to them. No longer constrained by the need to conform completely, the younger generation of Singaporeans looks into the world and sees a broader set of opportunities than their parents' generation was able to imagine. A decade ago prospects were poor for an eclectic fashion designer in Singapore, but today that's changed. Jo Soh, 35, started a label called Hansel that has not only thrived but gone international. "When I'm 60 and look back on this time, I will see that I was part of a pioneering group that helped to change society," he says. Evidence of this cultural thaw is appearing all over the city.

Psychologists believe this is the way to untie a double bind: we have to change the basic rules under which we function and replace the logic that created the dilemma in the first place. First, by acknowledging it, putting names to the contradictory messages that form the straitjacket and creating conscious awareness of it, then by embracing a new way of thinking that resolves the conflict.

Planned serendipity serves just this purpose for us. Taken literally, it is a contradiction, of course. It is impossible to plan something that, by definition, is unplannable. Yet organizations are planning machines. The only way for them to embrace the unexpected is to find a space for it within these plans. In the chapters that follow we'll see how this seeming paradox opens up a middle path, so that we no longer have to choose between lame predictability and chaos. Planned serendipity gives you and your business a way to actively, methodically engage the unknown.

Loving the unknown is the key, because if we want to succeed in today's frantically paced business environment, none of us has any choice but to face up to the uncertainties that lurk around every corner. And while we stand on the shoulders of giants in our endeavor to unlock the mechanics of chance—renowned businessmen, philosophers, scientists, inventors, and artists all make appearances on the pages of this book—it is more than anything a product of the hyper-accelerated Internet-era marketplace that surrounds us. In a world that changes as quickly as ours now does, where the pace of this change only seems to increase and where so much of what we need is as unpredictable as it is critical to our success, luck is the best ally we have.

2

Skill: Motion
Breaking Out

"Life is about moving, it's about change. And when things stop doing that, they're dead."
—Twyla Tharp

If you were to ask yourself what has made Pixar, the computer graphics motion picture studio that's responsible for a long string of blockbuster movies including *Toy Story*, *The Incredibles*, and *Finding Nemo*, so incredibly successful, odds are good that you would be able to come up with a wide range of answers: fantastic artistry, amazing storytelling, or an obvious dedication to the craft of computer animation, just to name a few.

But if you had asked that same question of Steve Jobs, Pixar's founder and one of the people most responsible for the existence of all those wildly successful films, he might have given you a different response. He might have said it was all because of the atrium in the middle of their office.

Here's why: back in 2000, just as Pixar was beginning its long and successful animated run, Jobs went looking for a place to house the growing pool of talent he knew he would need to turn his organization into a world-class movie studio. He and his colleagues Ed Catmull and John Lasseter, ended up purchasing an old Del Monte factory in Emeryville, a tiny town scrunched between Berkeley and Oakland in northern California, right across the bay from San Francisco. Their plan was to remodel it into a world-class campus in which his rapidly growing crew of designers, programmers, and animators could do their best work.

Jobs firmly believed that the most important activity that took place at Pixar was not the work of any one individual but rather the thousands of interactions that took place every day between different employees within the organization. After all, a two-hour computer animated movie was a much bigger endeavor than anything one person could do on her own. To maintain the level of craft and artistry that Pixar was already recognized for, Jobs knew he needed an office that would encourage and facilitate these interactions.

Science columnist Jonah Lehrer, writing in *The New Yorker* about Job's process for designing a building to achieve this goal, explained: "Jobs realized that it wasn't enough to simply create a space: he needed to make people go there. As he saw it, the main challenge for Pixar was getting its different cultures to work together, forcing the computer geeks and cartoonists to collaborate. Jobs insisted that the best creations occurred when people from disparate fields were connected together, when our distinct ways of seeing the world were brought to bear on a singular problem."

The first architectural design Jobs was presented with, however, fell far short of his vision for a place where this kind of creative work could happen. It consisted of three separate buildings, each intended to house a different set of workers—computer scientists in one, executives in another, and designers in the third—and Jobs flat out rejected this approach. A design with separate buildings for different job types would actively discourage interactivity. He wanted something better.

The revised plan, developed by Jobs himself, dropped the three separate spaces in favor of one large, spacious, open-aired building. To achieve his goal of actively encouraging all kinds of employee interactions, Jobs made an unusual but extraordinarily effective design decision: he chose to locate most of the company's essential services—those services employees might need several times a day—in the main atrium in the center of the building, in order to force every employee to get up and away from their desk on a regular basis. He placed the meeting rooms, the cafeteria, the coffee bar, the staff mailboxes, and even the gift shop all in the same space, right smack in the middle of the office. As the story goes, he even tried to put all the bathrooms there (although for practical reasons that plan was quickly vetoed.)

The new design had the intended effect. Forced to the center of the building several times a day, individual workers frequently bumped into coworkers from all different divisions of the organization and levels of the org chart. Often nothing came of those interactions, but occasionally one of them would bear fruit. Almost every employee at Pixar has at least one story about a chance encounter that ended up being valuable: a random encounter with an individual in line for lunch or while picking up paper in the supply room who was able to help solve a particular problem, or a conversation unexpectedly overheard by a nearby coworker who was then able to contribute a valuable piece of information. Reflecting on the Emeryville campus design to Jobs' biographer Walter Isaacson, Pixar's creative mastermind John Lasseter marveled at how effective this approach was: "Steve's theory worked from day one," he said. "I kept running into people I hadn't seen in months. I've never seen a building that promoted collaboration and creativity as well as this one."

These sorts of things happen in office environments all the time, of course. Most of us have at one time or another benefited from just this kind of serendipitous interaction. The difference in Pixar's case, though, is that the random occurrences weren't entirely random; instead, they were the result of a building designed to move people in unexpectedly valuable ways—a building built for serendipity.

Creative Collisions

Serendipity is the set of positive outcomes that lie at the intersection of chance and creativity:

Serendipity = chance + creativity

Baked into this definition is our belief that you have agency when it comes to making your own luck—that you can significantly increase the amount of serendipity in your own life. When setting out to make that happen, it's easy to assume that you can only affect the creativity part of that equation—that the hard work of being creative is the only way to increase your luck. This might seem daunting at first, but the good news is that you don't have to be a creative genius to bring serendipity into your life. You have the ability to affect the chance part of the equation just as much.

Consider how most of us spend our workdays. We follow predictable patterns: we get up, eat breakfast, head to work, arrive at our desk, get some work done, maybe attend a few meetings, and go home around the same time every day. We work mostly with the same people, in the same place, and do much the same thing, day in and day out. That's our work life, as we live it and as the companies we work in expect us to: consistently, reliably, necessarily routine.

If you're trying to get lucky, however, routine can really get in the way. Doing the same thing, seeing the same people, experiencing the same environment without change—this is no recipe for accidentally encountering something new and important. As Charles Kettering, the American inventor responsible for, among other things, the modern electrical motor, leaded gasoline, the refrigerator, and air conditioning, once put it: "Keep on going and chances are you will stumble onto something, perhaps when you are least expecting it. I have never heard of anyone stumbling on something sitting down."

What Kettering means when he says "keep on going" is what we refer to as motion, the most basic of the core skills of planned serendipity. Motion is the raw material of luck, and being in motion is the essential skill you need to develop to foster serendipity. We define "being in motion" as the act of putting yourself in unfamiliar situations, but within familiar environments. The key to this definition is "familiar environments"—putting yourself in motion is not about movement without purpose. We don't mean just randomly dropping into any new situation but instead mixing it up with previously unfamiliar people and ideas adjacent to your job, your projects, or your interests. Being in motion is about greatly increasing the likelihood that you will encounter new experiences, opportunities, and information that are relevant to you and your work by actively inserting yourself into new situations in which they *might* exist.

As with all our serendipity skills, it's important to remember that serendipity is about finding what you *aren't* looking for. When you're in motion you're not actively looking for any one *specific* experience, opportunity, or piece of information. A Pixar employee who finds the exact person she needs to talk to while standing in line for lunch didn't get in that line expecting that person to be there—she was just hungry! Motion is about finding what you need without knowing from whom or where or when, exactly, you will find it—or even, sometimes, without knowing that you even need it in the first place.

In short, motion is all about breaking out of routine by knowingly seeking out the unknown. By looking for new people, places, or experiences that are relevant but outside of your normal everyday activities—or, even better, by making room and time in your work life to move around every day in new and different ways—you're giving those experiences, opportunities, and information the chance to find you. Some of these will have value for you, and some of them won't. The key is to put yourself in a position to expose yourself to them so that you can be the judge of what's important to you and what isn't (and there are ways to improve your judgment, too, which we'll discuss in later chapters). Motion increases your chances of running into the good stuff.

This is the key benefit of motion—not the act of moving itself but instead the unexpected, creative collisions that are the natural result of being on the move. We move because we're going somewhere or trying to accomplish something, and along the way we hope to collide with unsought ideas, directions, and clues that end up mattering to us. But we can't do this if we never actually expose ourselves to environments and situations where these kinds of collisions might occur.

Let's Get Moving

When it comes to developing the skill of motion it's pretty easy to take the first step. In fact, odds are good that you're already putting yourself in motion, at least in small doses. Especially if you're a smoker.

Smoking, though deleterious to your personal health, turns out to be surprisingly valuable to the health of many organizations for a very simple reason: rules and regulations that forbid smoking in the workplace end up driving most smokers in a particular office building to the closest convenient spot to feed their habit—often the area right outside the front of the building. There, in a common environment and with a forced timeframe—the five minutes or so it takes to smoke a cigarette—any number of conversations between people from different departments and different levels in the organizational hierarchy take place. A couple of times a day, smokers get a chance to genuinely interact with other smokers—a slightly different mix of people and personalities every time—and while many of those interactions come to nothing, occasionally a new idea, a new concept, a new answer, or a new direction results. And all it took was a short walk to the front of the building.

Getting in motion is really that simple, at least to start. But you don't have to sacrifice your future health just to bring a little more luck into your life. There are plenty of opportunities besides going for a smoke that you can use to "move" more inside your work environment. Attending events and seminars put on by different departments in your organization, joining extracurricular activities where other employees are also participating, even sitting with new people in the cafeteria at lunch are all ways to bring a little motion into your day.

And yet, though they might sound easy, those activities can be challenging to implement consistently. We know from our own experiences in the corporate world how difficult it can be to achieve perpetual motion within an office environment. The siren song of our daily routine is powerful in its familiarity and comfort, and the idea of making time and space at work to experience the unknown can be more than a little intimidating. You have to put yourself directly in the path of the unfamiliar—people you don't know, places you're not normally in—which is never that easy. Not to mention that the goal of doing so is by definition fuzzy in the first place, since it's never clear beforehand how these activities will benefit you or what kind of outcomes could result. This lack of clarity kills motivation. And besides, there's all this other important—and familiar—everyday work to get done!

It gets worse. Beyond the personal challenges we encounter in getting motivated to move, most of us don't work for organizations that go out of their way to encourage motion like Pixar does either. Plenty of organizations, sad to say, actually create physical environments that are just plain hostile to the whole idea of motion. And how can we tell? Well, if we survey the structures that surround us in any given office space, what we actually see is an environment filled with obstacles to getting in motion. We call these obstacles "cubicles."

Oh, the cubicle. Those boxy workspaces have become a ubiquitous set piece in modern office life. Since being introduced in the late 1960s, the cubicle has taken over as the standard way we partition our daily work lives—so much so that according to Steelcase, a major U.S. office furniture manufacturer, 70 percent of all office work in the U.S. now takes place surrounded on three sides by those just-over-half-height walls.

And yet despite their ubiquity, as anyone who has ever read the comic strip "Dilbert" knows, the cubicle is also one of the most maligned aspects of modern office life. Omnipresent, isolating, and usually way too grey, cubicles have come to represent the triumph of efficiency over individuality, conformity over character, and process over people. When Mike Judge, director of the cult favorite movie *Office Space,* wanted to showcase a character's escape from the tyranny of his menial office job, he did it by having him attack and destroy his cubicle, knocking over one of its walls as if he were breaking out of a prison. (That was a guy ready to get moving!)

Which is why it's all the more curious that, believe it or not, the original design of the cubicle was actually intended to *create* movement. Its creators believed that the cubicle would actually liberate office workers from their previous life of isolation and drudgery. So how did we get from there to Dilbert? A quick peek into the history of the cubicle helps to illuminate why so many organizations are so allergic to movement.

The original design of the cubicle came primarily from the minds of two men: Max De Pree, an executive with the Herman Miller corporation, another major U.S. office furniture maker, and Robert Propst, their Head of Research. De Pree and Propst's first version of the cubicle—branded the "Action Office" and sold starting in 1968—was based on an amalgamation of theories about office management proposed by various architects, designers, and business writers over the previous decades, and represented what was for De Pree in particular the beginning of a new era of open, effective, and more humane office life.

De Pree and Propst (and many architects and designers of that era) had come to believe that traditional corporate environments, with their narrow hallways and enclosed offices, were a relic of a rigid, bureaucratic corporate past that wasn't prepared for the future of work. This future required an entirely new kind of office design—a design that would allow individuals to focus and work to get done, of course, but also one that would allow the "free flow of ideas" they believed was critical to business success in the late twentieth century. These were ideas that couldn't find their way through a closed office door.

Hard though it might be to imagine now, De Pree and Propst believed that cubicles, with their wide, doorless openings and low-sitting walls, would allow workers to see each other and thereby connect.

Employees would stand, acknowledge each other, and thus interact openly and unencumbered. Cubicles would remove barriers between people at different levels of the corporate hierarchy: there could be no corner offices for executives in a world where the boss's cubicle looked and worked exactly like yours. Instead of isolating workers, cubicles would unite them; instead of hindering communication, cubicles would encourage it; instead of restricting knowledge, cubicles would allow information and knowledge to flow to whoever needed it, even from a low-level employee all the way up to the head of the company. Cubicles would shepherd us into a bright new era of openness and information.

Well, the information economy has certainly descended upon us, but nobody's thanking the cubicle for it. Rather than uniting workers, cubicles now stand as testament to how far you can feel from someone who's sitting only a few feet away when there's a flimsy wall between the two of you.

Horrified by how far from its original intention the cubicle had wandered, Propst came to openly lament the "monolithic insanity" he had brought into the world. The fact that even one of the cubicle's original designers now believes his Frankenstein creation has come to personify oppression instead of openness and flexibility suggests that there were larger forces at work against this noble idea.

So why didn't it work out the way De Pree and Propst intended?

The most obvious culprit is money, which deserves a big chunk of the blame. The Action Office was originally designed as a modular system, because Propst wanted to ensure that the environment could be completely customized to the work being done and the workers doing it. But for many companies, the value of this modular design wasn't customization but simply that it took up less space. Modularity allowed businesses to cram a larger number of office workers in one open-floor room than they could in traditional offices, which meant less square footage to pay for per worker. The cubicle farm was born.

Money wasn't the only thing corporations believed space-efficient cubicles would save. "Efficiency" and "time-savings" were considered equally valuable outputs of cubicles, as more people in less space also meant less time they needed to spend actually moving.

Putting everything closer together naturally shortened the distance that workers had to travel to get something done. This meant less time spent getting up, locating coworkers, or walking to the printer. In theory at least, less movement means more time for actual work, though admittedly only by a very narrow definition of what constitutes work.

Ruthless efficiency and presumptive time-saving were, in a way, the biggest blow to De Pree and Propst's grand vision: not only did the cubicle fail to connect workers in a way that would correct for the flaws of traditional office design, but it actually made the situation worse than before by making it even *less* likely that employees would interact with each other. Closed office doors might have accidentally restricted the movement of workers and information, but cubicles, in farm formation, were now actively designed to thwart it. Because if you're not in motion, you're never going to run into anybody.

With the benefit of hindsight, we can look back and see how surprisingly accurate De Pree, Propst, and their contemporaries were in their predictions about where modern business was headed, but how wrong they were about the best way to get there. The free flow of information has indeed become critical to modern business life and huge efficiencies have been realized since the late '60s almost entirely because of it. Computer networks and the Internet, of course, have far more to do with this development than the cubicle ever did. Today we have whole classes of office workers that exist to do nothing but efficiently route information from one place to another. Great fortunes have been made by individuals and organizations that have the right information in the right place at the right time. And yet, while our information shoots around the world at the speed of light, most of us are still stuck sitting in our damn cubicles.

The organizations we work for made the assumption that economy of time and motion—less time spent moving—meant better focus and greater productivity for each individual worker. Whether or not that's true—an iffy proposition, at best—those benefits are far outweighed by the negative consequences of isolation and inertia.

The skill of motion—moving around, inserting yourself into unfamiliar situations within familiar contexts in order to reliably generate chance collisions—is hugely important to us as individuals. But it is equally important to the organizations that we work for. Companies as a whole do their best work when, like Pixar, they have made room for the kind of unexpected encounters and opportunities that motion is likely to produce. It's not enough for any one individual in a business to start getting lucky through motion—the whole organization needs to get moving in a consistent and reliable way. And that requires not just individual motivation, but as De Pree, Propst, and Jobs all recognized, collective action and an organization that marshals the resources to support it. For you and your organization to get lucky, everybody needs to get moving.

This is the fundamental issue De Pree and Propst were trying to address when they invented the cubicle, even though their original intention was subverted. But several decades later, and with a better understanding of what was required to truly embrace the planned serendipity of motion and collision, Jobs pulled it off. With better results than the cubicle, too, as this tactic has definitely worked for Pixar—its recent film, *Cars 2*, released in 2011, was another wildly successful box office hit.

In *The New Yorker* article about Jobs and Pixar, Lehrer refers to the Pixar approach—motion by design, bringing disparate ideas and concepts together in environments outside of strict plans and traditional hierarchies—as one of "consilience." *Consilience* means, literally, "a jumping together," and refers to the unexpectedly generative effect that emerges when independent fields of knowledge and inquiry—or the people who inhabit this knowledge—collide in ways that create whole new areas of invention and discovery.

Recent research explains why consilience works to produce better results. In his book *The Difference: How the Power of Diversity Creates Better Groups, Firms, Schools, and Societies,* Dr. Scott E. Page, a professor of political science and economics at the University of Michigan, lays out empirical evidence for the value of bringing vastly different (but always relevant) perspectives to bear on problems.

Page has pioneered the use of computational models to demonstrate that diversity is not just better than homogeneity; it often trumps the raw ability of individuals when it comes to solving complex problems. He puts it bluntly: "Random collections of intelligent problem solvers can outperform collections of the best individual problem solvers."

In an interview with *The New York Times*, Dr. Page explains why this is: "The problems we face in the world are very complicated. Any one . . . can get stuck. If we're in an organization where everyone thinks in the same way, everyone will get stuck in the same place. But if we have people with diverse tools, they'll get stuck in different places."

According to Dr. Page, the value we as individuals bring to problem-solving is amplified in an appropriately diverse setting, because we are able to pair our unique perspective with those of others in order to widen the range of answers available to us. Or as he puts, it, "As individuals we can accomplish only so much. We're limited in our abilities . . . . Collectively, we face no such constraint. We possess incredible capacity to think differently. These differences can provide the seeds of innovation, progress, and understanding."

Dr. Page's models only go so far, though—they don't provide a recipe for *how* to harness diversity for these results. The skill of motion is one answer: *stir the pot*. What Jobs recognized about Pixar is that this diversity of perspective was inherent in his organization, but the walls and routines that separated people were suppressing it. He knew that there were latent combinations of ideas and experiences across the Pixar staff that could represent the next big breakthrough, but no amount of planning could pre-determine which ones. The potential of his employees' collective perspectives—focused as they were on related but varying projects and tasks—could never be fully realized unless people's knowledge and instincts were brought together in consistently new and serendipitous ways.

Jobs' architectural design stirred his well-stocked pot containing a richly diverse set of individuals from unrelated backgrounds and departments who had wide-ranging approaches to their work and different ways of seeing the world. The space itself made these chance collisions a routine part of every employee's day.

Process and routine are necessary activities for managing business, but they're not sufficient. Truly great organizations like Pixar understand the need to create space for the unexpected—to make room for serendipity. While a company certainly can function without space for motion and chance collision, as so many do, we would argue that the best companies are those that have figured out how, like Pixar did, to bake motion into their space—to make it an automatic part of everyone's day. Companies that make this effort to create motion definitely reap the benefits.

Motion by Design

In case you're getting worried: no, you don't have to raze your building or add an atrium to it in order to increase motion in your professional life or organization. But if the space where you do your work is not designed to make motion an integral and effortless part of your everyday activities, then it's time to find alternative ways of making movement a regular part of your daily routine. Anyone can learn to stir the pot, no matter where you are on the totem pole.

Though it can be challenging to get moving while lacking institutional support and while plowing through the daily grind of work, there are some simple steps you can take to get started. The easiest way we know to begin doesn't even involve moving a single piece of furniture. Instead, it's about getting yourself *out* of the office on a routine basis. Conferences in your area of expertise, collaborative meet-ups, seminars, networking events, or other smaller get-togethers with like-minded individuals are all terrific ways to put yourself in an unfamiliar situation within a familiar environment. Whether it's an idea you get from a presentation by a colleague from another company or a conversation with a stranger in the lobby outside, these activities may spark a new way of seeing things you hadn't previously considered. The more you can open up space in your schedule to attend events as frequently as time allows, and to attend as wide a range as possible as opposed to just the same old conference circuit, the more likely you are to have exactly that serendipitous encounter you didn't even know you needed. As with everything about motion, the more routinely you can break out of your regular routine, the luckier you get.

Attending conferences or meet-ups is an easy form of motion for most organizations to embrace, because it's common for companies to support some form of career development for their employees. It's a type of motion they're comfortable with, and it is always easier to get moving when the organization you work for encourages it. Companies can take this a step further by creating structured opportunities for these kinds of events on a regular and recurring basis inside the organization as well.

Pixar has embraced event-based as well as structural opportunities for serendipity with Pixar University, a professional-development program that goes far beyond traditional employee education. Along with the usual employee training seminars, Pixar University's roster of classes includes improvisational theater, drawing, and screenwriting as well as classes on every aspect of computerized filmmaking, and classes are open to all employees at every level. Besides allowing its employees to experience and appreciate other aspects of the business, this professional development program, like Pixar's building, allows employees from all levels and parts of the organization to interact with each other in an environment where distinctions between roles and departments have been removed. Performing improv or learning the basics of lighting design together puts coworkers at Pixar in a different relationship to each other than they normally have during the workday. This allows for all kinds of creative collisions.

"During 90 percent of your workday, you're in this box—you get to do only certain things," says Bill Polson, Pixar's Director of Industry Strategy. "At Pixar University, all the boxes get removed. All the walls come down, and you get to be the director of your own creative idea."

Companies that are inclined to embrace rather than reduce motion seek out multiple ways to structure the work environment to encourage serendipitous behavior. The specific techniques used to create motion differ from business to business, but in general three set elements must be always present to make motion happen: a structure that allows for it, a ritual that enforces it, and a culture that encourages it. While implementing any one of these three will improve your odds for getting a company moving, it's the combination of all three that really fosters motion and, thus, serendipity.

Writ large, as in the case of Pixar, this combination is clear: structure (the design of the entire building), ritual (the central, daily activities, like picking up mail or eating lunch), and culture (top-down, as decreed by Jobs). Combine these with a bunch of talented, focused, attentive workers and out comes *Wall-E*. On a smaller scale, consider what's going on with our smoking colleagues: a combination of structure (a convenient space in front of the building), ritual (the need to light up and stand around for five minutes, puffing away), and culture (no smoking indoors!) conspire to put different people together in the same place for a period of time, in predictably random groupings.

When you look at it this way, you can see that while big changes have big impact, even small changes can make a difference. When it comes to serendipity, all it takes is one little thing to go right, and since every company already has culture, structure, and ritual baked into their everyday activities, it's not hard to change your environment to affect at least one of these three elements. With a little work, they can be tweaked to encourage serendipity. Twitter, Message Bus, and Gangplank did just that.

Twitter: Rearranging the Structure

Dick Costolo, CEO of Twitter, the social information broadcasting phenomenon, has a particularly unique challenge running an organization as unusual as Twitter. As CEO of one of the world's fastest-growing and most successful startups, Costolo has naturally had to develop strategies for coping with the extreme rate of change inside his organization. When it comes to office environments, his approach to creating motion is simple—and relatively easy to achieve—as long as you're willing to move some furniture around: "totally open" space and no private offices.

According to Costolo, the current office space should be made as open as possible—remove as many walls as you can and try to make it so that a person standing on one end of the room can see all the way to the other sides. Any offices that currently exist should be made into rooms with a couple of desks, but don't use those reconfigured spaces as private offices—instead, use them as conference rooms that can also double as a place to take a call, or for any other activity where someone needs some privacy. Costolo believes that this approach to creating motion in your office environment works for three reasons, and those reasons apply to any office, not just an Internet startup like Twitter.

First, he says, "Speed of communication begets speed of execution. News travels a lot faster in a big open room with no walls than it does in an office with corridors and private offices. When everybody is up to speed on what's happening in the company in real time, it's easier for everybody to zig and zag at the same time." In other words, wide-open spaces—instead of private offices, or even cubicles—maximize the opportunity for chance collisions to occur. Fewer barriers between people mean fewer barriers between ideas.

Second, "friction begets friction, transparency begets transparency. One function of an open-space work environment is that you get transparency up and down the organization. When the engineering team can hear the support team constantly fighting the same battles on the phone, they have a better appreciation for the product issues. There were many times when just overhearing a phone call would help countless people in the company correct an issue before it occurred." By contrast, "You don't get that serendipity in a private office environment; you get friction. Friction requires a lot more formal communications processes, and processes in small companies have the potential to create more, not less, friction." A speedy internal flow of information is a competitive advantage, as employees who are exposed to more information are able to make decisions faster than employees organized in a more traditional fashion, where information isn't able to move as quickly.

The third reason for getting out of offices and cubicles, Costolo contends, is simply staying motivated. "The beauty of a big open space is that you're not going to just sit there and dial it in, or at least if you do, everybody will take notice," Costolo argues. "When you see your sales director on the phone with a particularly tough customer and really grinding out a long negotiation, it makes you think that you can't just sit there and suck your thumb. You feel like you have to do your part. You feel more part of a team."

Finally, one other benefit that Costolo points out to this approach is that it also removes the distance caused by traditional organizational hierarchies, a huge boon when it comes to getting ideas to move around faster. "Whether people will admit it or not," he says, "most of the time you end up in an environment with a private office for status reasons." He adds that this isn't necessarily about what works best for the business: "Status has the downside of causing people in the company to work toward status instead of working toward results."

Message Bus: Adapting the Ritual

Perhaps the most commonplace ritual in any group is mealtime. Everyone has to eat, right? In our harried work lives it's increasingly common to grab a sandwich and a diet cola and eat while staring into our computer monitor. Or we hang with our regular "lunch buddies" and talk about the same things we spoke about the last time we had lunch. The predictable recurrence of mealtime, in or around the familiar environment of our office, makes it an ideal ritual for hijacking in the name of motion.

A startup company in Mill Valley, California, called Message Bus does exactly this. Narendra Rocherolle, one of the company's founders, says that all of his best business experiences have been in office environments that encouraged exposure to outside thinking, so when starting his own company he actively invited serendipitous experiences into the Message Bus offices. Rocherolle started with a monthly lunch series—aptly titled "Serendipity Sessions"—where he orders in lunch and asks outside speakers to come address his 15 employees, as well as anybody else in the building (or anywhere else) who wants to attend. The topics discussed, usually though not always technology-based,

range greatly depending on who's speaking and what their current
interests are. The goal, according to Rocherolle, is not to drill specific
information into his employees' heads but simply to help them learn
new things and see if inspiration sparks as a result.

"Anytime I have an opportunity to expose people to outside thinking, I take it," he says. "You can spend time and resources in many ways,
but if you can bring people through and get them engaged in different
types of thinking, it's so much better. If you're in charge of a bunch of
people, the best thing you can do for them is expose them to whatever
outside ideas you can."

What makes this kind of mealtime incursion work so well for a
company with a few dozen employees is that it's so lightweight. It works
within the confines of the existing ritual—people still stop working
at noon, grab some food and give themselves some time to catch
their breath. They're primed for a provocation. Furthermore, it doesn't
require changing the physical space—you can pour an unexpected
element directly into the room as it is, whether that element is a guest
speaker, a group activity, or even a mariachi band. The effect of this
disturbance to ritual, though, is to shake things up between people who
have every reason to settle down.

This approach has been so successful that Rocherolle has gone
looking for other ways to bring new ideas into the building. For example,
he says, "Every Thursday we play a TED talk [an online series of lectures
from smart thinkers from a variety of disciplines] for 20 minutes,
about anything under the sun. Maybe it will produce insight into our
developer's code, or maybe instead someone here will one day go on to
solve one of the world's great challenges, and this will contribute. Who
knows? But we have the opportunity to create an environment where
the potential for something like that to happen exists."

Of course, there are hundreds of rituals that are shared between
people within an organization, from morning coffee breaks to quarterly
sales meetings. To the untrained eye they can look like the enemy of
serendipity, banishing chance and creativity through their very predictability. To us they look like ripe opportunities for an intervention.

Gangplank: Baking It into the Culture

So far, we've seen how big companies like Pixar and Twitter invest in making motion, as well as firms with dozens of employees such as Message Bus. But in some ways it's the smallest organizations that are best positioned to reap the benefits of motion, as they often can make faster decisions than larger, hierarchical organizations. In fact, the most innovative organization we've found that has embraced the possibilities for this kind of serendipity isn't a huge Internet startup or a major corporate chain; it's a company formed of a small group of like-minded individuals in Tempe, Arizona, a suburban community of Phoenix, called Gangplank.

Gangplank is described by its founders as a "collaborative workspace," dedicated to "creating an economy of innovation and creativity" within the local business community in and around Phoenix. Multiple companies of all types and sizes share space inside the Gangplank building, working side by side to foster economic growth along the main drag of this Arizona suburb. To achieve this goal, Gangplank was founded and planned from the beginning to encourage serendipity.

Gangplank began, according to Derek Neighbors, one of the cofounders, out of sheer frustration over how hard it was to find true business opportunities in his community. He says, "Back in 2007, a bunch of us small technology startups in Arizona started to meet together, and we found ourselves in similar boats. As soon as they had the opportunity, people said, they were planning to move their companies or their families out of Arizona. And it was always for one of three reasons: not enough access to capital, not enough access to talented engineers, or not enough access to the right mix of people to make things happen."

Wanting to address these issues without skipping town, they decided the problem was primarily financial. So they agreed to take a significant chunk of their own funds and launch several local startup businesses to see how they would fare. But, he says, even though these businesses were able to grow, the going was slow. "Even when they were successful," he says, "they could only get so far out of orbit. And the reason they could only get so far out of orbit is they didn't have the right connections. We didn't have access to the right network makeup in order to really succeed."

So they went back to the drawing board. If it wasn't just about money, what else was missing? They decided the problem was fundamentally one of culture—their town didn't have the right kind of culture to allow for the kind of businesses they wanted to build. "We just felt like we didn't have the right kind of room in Arizona to make things happen. We needed space and time for our ideas to develop, to blossom from being hunches into something bigger." They decided the best way to do that was to make it easier to share ideas and to build a culture around sharing ideas, in order to maximize their ability to grow. "We figured if you condense people, you condense ideas into a smaller space, you increase the chances that serendipity will happen. You share your ideas with other people, you hear what they think, and your ideas build up over time. You speed up the time it takes for a great idea to develop. That's where real innovation comes from."

The group named their new approach to their work environment, entertainingly, "chaos." From just the right amount of chaos, they believed, would come creativity. "We believe there's a certain amount of chaos that needs to exist in order to allow interactions to happen," says Neighbors. "Artists, business people, technologists, you want to get them in the same space, you want to get them interacting, because that chaos starts to create relationships that work in ways that you could never map out. Ideas flow and bounce off each other. We know you can't necessarily plan for a lucky outcome, but you can increase the chances that something good will happen by creating a plan that allows it to happen. Gangplank was the petri dish we put together so we could try to we model this theory and see if it really works."

The best environment for a startup today, they were saying, wasn't two founders in a garage, but fifty founders in a warehouse.

To achieve this, the Gangplank team looked at all sorts of different aspects of the organization and how to deliberately construct them to maximize motion. First, they knew they needed to make their space as open as possible to allow for collaboration, both expected and unexpected. Like Costolo at Twitter, they decided it was important to make sure that there was no place that was really private. But they took it even further—at Gangplank, you have to share by default because you aren't given any other choice!

According to Neighbors, it's about more than just making sure the space is as open as possible. People who work at Gangplank understand that there is a cultural mandate to share with each other—their ideas and knowledge, their equipment, and even sometimes the space that their own companies occupy. Everything about the way Gangplank is set up practically begs to get repurposed, and that in turn empowers the employees who work there to adapt the entire environment as necessary to suit their needs. At Gangplank, it's not just the people who move—the entire space, right down to the furniture, is constantly in motion as well.

"We're totally open to how the people in the space need to use it," Neighbors says. "In the front we've got a bunch of tables that are movable, and it's not uncommon for us to take all the tables out of here and have a music or an art event, so that someone would think this is a music venue or an art gallery one day, and then the next day they come in and think somebody's pulled a prank on them because the stage is gone and the lights are gone and there's a whole bunch of desks in here. The space is configurable, and people have the permission to configure it as they need."

The Gangplank culture of decision-making is equally driven by a desire to make not just space but also choices configurable. Every decision is what they call the "smallest possible decision." Any chance they have to make a change, they ask, "What's the least that can be done, so that when we learn something new based on what's already been done, we can tweak and adjust?" As an example, according to Neighbors, "When we were trying to answer the question, 'What should this room look like?' instead of developing a master plan for what the room should look like and spending months on it before developing it, we said to ourselves, let's just start using the space, figure out what works and doesn't work, and then adjust on the fly."

The team considers time as well as space an open resource for everyone to use. The entire building frequently gets taken over for any number of different activities. "We have a ton of events," says Neighbors, "but we organize very few events ourselves. Instead, we leave the space open to possibility. You want to have an event here? Great! You don't even have to work in the space. Anybody can use it! We've had a ton of unique events that have happened as a result of this approach."

In its own way, Gangplank's culture is just as intentionally serendipitous as Pixar's, in that it embodies at every level the goal of facilitating unexpectedly valuable interactions. Their approach has been so successful that they now have other underserved local communities around Arizona and elsewhere clamoring for a Gangplank of their own. According to Neighbors, "Now we're in the process of asking how we can replicate our culture in other places. Can we create the same petri dish elsewhere? Can we provide a chaotic environment for smart, vibrant people to get creative, to then share that creativity and those ideas? If we do that, can we start to foster innovation anywhere?"

Risk and Reward

As the first and most basic skill of serendipity, motion can also be the most frightening to adopt. Being open to the unexpected and making room for it on a regular basis can be scary to individuals, but especially to organizations that have historically succeeded by removing risk from their operation through routine and process. When the crew at Gangplank named their approach to serendipity "chaos," they weren't kidding. Introducing motion and serendipity into many organizations might seem like introducing "chaos"—and more than most companies can handle.

No matter how we try to make motion and the chance collisions that come with it normal and part of our routine, the truth is that chance, at base, is all about accepting risk. We create chance opportunities when we're willing to take actions or put ourselves into situations that are new, or uncomfortable, or most importantly might not work out for us. Allowing for the possibility that we might not get what we want, or not find what we're looking for, is the only way to make something new and good happen.

Getting lucky requires recognizing that sometimes we also need to get a little messy. Because it's only in the middle of a little bit of messiness and uncertainty that serendipity has room to take root and unexpected greatness gets the chance to bloom. Or as Neighbors from Gangplank likes to say, "When you put all that—space, openness, opportunity, chaos, possibility—together with fun and an air of excellence, innovation falls out the other side."

3

Skill: Preparation
Anatomy of a Geek Brain

"Imagination is the mother of Truth."
— Sherlock Holmes

The professor pulled a snow white rabbit out of the cage, its pink nose twitching. The six second-year NYU medical students stood eagerly around him as he held it out for them to inspect. Dr. Lewis Thomas, the charming new head of the pathology department, looked back at them through his goofy coke-bottle glasses.

"Last night, I gave this little fellow an injection of papain, an enzyme made from papaya. Let's sit him next to a bunny that hasn't been injected." He took another white rabbit out of an adjacent cage, and sat the two side by side. "What do you see?"

He saw delighted recognition cross their faces. A few of them chuckled. "The ears on the rabbit you injected are floppy!"

It was true. While the normal bunny's ears stood upright, "rabbit-style," the papain bunny's ears had collapsed, hanging limply down the side of its head.

Dr. Thomas had shown off this trick hundreds of times, often to colleagues, just to see their reaction. It always produced this bizarre cosmetic change. The first time he'd seen it was quite by accident, seven years before. He'd been on the trail of a solution to rheumatic fever, testing the effects of various enzymes in rabbits. He tried papain for no other reason than it was available in the lab. Like all the other enzymes, it failed to produce the hoped for results. It was in that moment of despair that he noticed the bunnies' ears had become floppy.

"What causes it?" someone asked.

"That is the mystery. I've been trying to figure that out for years."

He had tried everything but was no closer to understanding it. In fact, the only reason he was showing these students now was because it had become interesting, an unsolved puzzle he couldn't quite shake. He was stuck on his other projects, and this was the unsolved mystery he kept falling back into in times like these.

The next few moments would change everything.

The Case of the Floppy-Eared Rabbits

Our story begins in 1955, the year Thomas first observed the effect of papain on bunnies' ears. At almost exactly the same time, another professor stumbled on the same phenomenon—Dr. Aaron Kellner, who ran pathology at Cornell University.

This was remarkable. Two doctors, working a few hours' drive from each other, had both tripped unexpectedly over the same finding. But there was a very big difference between them: one, Dr. Thomas, was about to put the pieces together to explain the phenomenon, while the other, Dr. Kellner, would miss it altogether.

It was a rare opportunity in the history of science to see something that resembled a control study of serendipity. What were the differences between these two doctors, of equal pedigree and experience, that led one to serendipity gained and the other to serendipity lost? Were they approaching the problem differently, did one have more resources, or was there an institutional bias?

Dr. Thomas explained to his students how he'd approached the problem so far, his students rapt. He'd cut sections of the ear looking for anything unusual. The connective tissue was intact. No inflammation, no tissue damage. He even checked the cartilage, even though it was well known to be a quiet, inactive tissue. It was normal as well.

Sensing an opportunity to present an everyday skill of the pathologist's craft, he made a quick—and as it turned out, fateful—decision.

"Don't take my word for it, though, let's cut the sections together."

He normally examined tissue from the floppy-eared rabbit alone, inspecting it with his own finely-tuned sense of what healthy tissue looked like. This time he wanted his students to understand the basic science. He would have them cut sections from the normal rabbit as well as the affected one.

The group prepared the sections and went to work on examining them. While assisting them in their inspections, something caught Dr. Thomas' eye.

He had his students open up the cartilage sections to see them more clearly. The doctor's eyes darted from one sample to the other. He gasped. In the flicker of a moment he had the answer that had eluded him for so long. It *was* the cartilage.

"Good grief, that's it!" He hadn't found the answer before because he never dissected the ear of an unaffected rabbit alongside the ear of an affected one. He'd never wanted to waste his scarce animals. The matrix of the injected cartilage clearly wasn't as dense when you saw it side-by-side with normal cartilage.

Little did he now it then, but Thomas had stumbled on the root cause of tissue destruction in diseases like rheumatoid arthritis. New treatments for this common ailment were suddenly within reach. He had cracked the code at precisely the moment he wasn't looking for it. To Thomas, the solution seemed painfully obvious after the fact. If it was so obvious, though, why hadn't Kellner solved it too?

What's the Difference?

The first answer that comes to mind is Louis Pasteur's statement, "Chance favors only prepared minds." But Pasteur's statement begs a question: what exactly *is* a prepared mind?

If we had to whittle the definition down to one line, we could say that it is an individual's mental readiness to recognize and create new ideas from disconnected experiences. If the skill of motion exposes us to more creative collisions, the raw material of serendipity, the skill of preparation is what allows us to make the mental leaps required to render those collisions meaningful.

The case of the floppy-eared rabbit suggests that there is more to a prepared mind than we might think. When we look at the story closely, there are three clear behaviors that led Dr. Thomas to his breakthrough. These behaviors hold the secrets of why some people see the patterns that others miss. Together, they unveil the skill of preparation. The behaviors are:

1. *He was driven by pure curiosity*. Thomas couldn't stop thinking about the question of why the bunny's ears flopped over, despite the fact that solving it was not part of his stated research goals. When asked why, he said: "All I could think of was that it was so entertaining." His personal motivation—pure curiosity and a sense of fun—was more important than the formal academic goals that guided him. By contrast, Kellner considered it too banal to study seriously. He was intensely focused on cardiovascular disease. Not only was cardio his specialty, the lab itself and the staff was designed to investigate this one area exclusively. He quickly set aside his floppy-eared rabbit finding to focus on more relevant work.

2. *He was able to "arrest an exception."* When he first injected papain in the bunnies, the comical effect of the bunny's floppy ears immediately caught Thomas' eye, whereas Kellner ran the experiment thirty or forty times before he noticed the changes in the rabbits' ears. Thomas was also immediately struck by the unfailing regularity of this phenomenon, which he knew was rare in scientific research. There must be something powerful behind the change in the bunny's ears, he reasoned. Years of reading medical journals and practicing his specialty led him to believe with confidence that this unfailing regularity—this

novelty—was important. As a result he continued to return to the puzzle again and again over the course of years.

Like Dr. Thomas, most of the great scientific minds throughout history have shown an ability to zero in on the uncommon. Charles Darwin's son, for instance, described his father as having this quality in spades: "There was one quality of mind which seemed to be of special and extreme advantage in leading him to make discoveries. It was the power of never letting exceptions pass unnoticed. Everybody notices a fact as an exception when it is striking or frequent, but he had a special instinct for *arresting an exception*." In other words, he didn't just notice the phenomenon—he grabbed a hold of it.

"Arresting an exception" is an evocative way to describe our ability to zero in on a problem, a unique dilemma, or a phenomenon and hold it captive in our minds. It suggests we have the ability to handcuff the suspect, so to speak, keep it from getting away, and investigate it for as long as it takes.

3. *He forgot what he knew to be true.* When we talk about the prepared mind we are typically referring to the training and practical know-how that people acquire as they make their way in their field. This is certainly part of it, as we've seen. We have no way of seeing the potential in an observation unless we have a thorough understanding of what we're looking at. Yet the doctors' training was also their biggest hurdle in making the investigative leap. Their "know how" was more of a straitjacket than a way forward after the initial discovery.

Both doctors pursued the same standard lines of investigation initially. They each knew the literature, knew that cartilage was almost certainly not the culprit. This assumption blocked even Dr. Thomas from making progress, despite his continued efforts. It must have seemed like his own version of Bill Murray's *Groundhog Day*, with frustratingly similar actions resulting in the same result over and over. Yet as in *Groundhog Day*, the repetition—each time with small changes—eventually led to a breakthrough: his research routine was turned upside down in a single teaching moment. Looked at differently,

Dr. Thomas was able to approach a problem about which he actually had a great deal of experience as if he knew nothing. It was only then, when he saw things through naive eyes, that he found his answer.

We can see that the prepared mind may have as much to do with what drops out of our minds as what we put in. It's one of those pesky paradoxes—we are in a position to see and understand an anomaly because of our training, but we tend to make the critical leap only when we deviate from it. Of course, it's not so easy to forget what we "know" to be true. We paid good money to get it in there, so we're understandably not eager to let it go!

A Mind for Serendipity

What connects these three behaviors is one basic truth: we cannot create new opportunities in the world if we do not first create room for them in our minds. Unfortunately, the social systems we're a part of—our businesses, schools, governments—are designed to fill our minds to overflow. From the way we segment academic subjects in school to the tasks we do in our jobs, we invest heavily in order, organization, and compartmentalization. As a result, there isn't a lot of room left to combine and recombine disparate ideas and experiences, even though that very act is what serendipity is built on. It takes this special skill, preparation, to keep our cognitive space open. It is an essential ingredient for planned serendipity.

A good way to see this skill in action, and to learn how to practice it yourself, is to spend some quality time with a type of person who has mastered the skill of preparation: a geek. It doesn't matter what kind of geek; he or she can be a computer geek, an economics geek, a design geek, a baseball stats geek, or a modern dance geek. Indeed, any two geeks are likely to have very different interests, but if they're deserving of the term they'll share an *obsessive curiosity in an area of knowledge that causes them to forget themselves*. This is what the term means today. It's why so many of our best and brightest claim the label for themselves.

Spend an afternoon talking to the geek of your choice about their work, get them spun up about the problem they're working on, and you'll notice a few things that can teach us a lot about the skill of preparation. It may take a bit of goading to get them to completely open up, but once they do they will talk for hours about their obsession.

Geeks are people that pursue their interests not because it's their job, but because they are compelled by an irresistible force. They simply can't get it out of their minds. As a result they can sometimes seem difficult to their managers. They have such strong intrinsic motivations—aesthetic attraction, sense of justice, emotional connection, neurosis, mischievousness, humor—that traditional work incentives like cash and job title may have little to no effect on their behavior.

You might view geeks as aliens from another planet. Maybe you find them annoying, dropping bizarre references that seem intended to make others feel stupid. Or you may surround yourself with them, finding their relentless interests entertaining and inspiring. Or perhaps you are a geek yourself, in which case you should know exactly what we're talking about.

We use the word "geek" purposefully. It's a word, like its cousin "hacker," that's charged with both positive and negative connotations depending on where you're sitting. Although our companies often highly prize specialists, they also tend to marginalize people who don't line up neatly with expectations or respect the pecking order. As a result, geeks often find themselves as outsiders—and as we'll see, when it comes to being prepared for serendipity, this outsider status is a gift that keeps on giving.

And yet geeks aren't social outcasts. On the contrary, they are the very personalities who are able and willing to challenge the status quo, even if they're not always welcomed into the inner circle. They are passionate, articulate, and smart, often willing to speak the truths that others are unwilling to say.

If you step back from the archetypal geek, you may notice that there's something childlike about them. Listen to a four- or five-year-old babble and you're likely to hear about the child's current obsession—*Star Wars* or butterflies or cars or mommy—and how it relates to everything. They do not see any hard boundaries between what's at the top of their minds and the dizzyingly complex world around them. This curiosity comes naturally to them, just as it once came naturally to us.

We'll be introducing you to many of our favorite geeks throughout this book—from accidental entrepreneurs and corporate rebels, from theme park designers to sports heroes. Some are easy to spot—there are many celebrated geeks in business culture, from Mark Zuckerberg to Martha Stewart—but the vast majority go unnoticed by us. Some geeks hide in plain sight; they may not fit our traditional expectations of what kind of jobs they have, but they have unmistakably geek brains. A case in point: the great professional basketball coach, Phil Jackson.

The Zen Master

Geeks often have a fiery side, driven by a desire to achieve, to break new ground, and to make their mark. This side of them is fearless in the face of risk and can be aggressively competitive. At the same time, their ability to obsessively focus makes them capable of deep reflection in the midst of activity or chaos. These counterbalanced traits—fierce curiosity married to an ability to free the mind from needless distraction—are the basic elements of the skill of preparation.

No one embodies the yin-yang of ferocious drive and the ability to transcend the moment more than Phil Jackson, famous for leading his teams, the Chicago Bulls and the LA Lakers, to a record eleven championships. Standing almost seven feet tall, his one-of-a-kind mind casts an even longer shadow. Jackson is a shining example of the quintessential geek brain.

Basketball is an ideal laboratory for planned serendipity. "It is a sport that involves the subtle interweaving of players at full speed to the point where they are thinking and moving as one," Jackson says. The breakout plays often happen unexpectedly, when the openings present themselves on the court, and the coach's planning and preparation are what sets the stage for this improvisation by the players once they hit the court.

In May 2001, the team Jackson was coaching, the LA Lakers, was heading into the final minutes of the third quarter in their second playoff game against the San Antonio Spurs. Despite the efforts of star players Shaquille O'Neal and Kobe Bryant, the Lakers were down by seven points. It was looking like they might actually lose, putting their seventeen-game streak to an abrupt end. It was then that the normally unflappable Jackson did something completely out of character: he picked a fight with a referee and was slapped with a technical foul.

The referee then commanded Jackson to move off the edge of the court. Instead, Jackson talked back, and the ref responded with a second foul. As Jackson well knew, this meant automatic ejection from the game. He turned and walked off the court.

The players huddled among themselves, suddenly without their coach, and then, amazingly, went on to dominate the Spurs the rest of the game, winning handily. What happened?

"The turning point was when Phil got thrown out of the game," Lakers center Shaquille O'Neal explained afterwards. "I pulled the guys in the huddle and told them, 'Let's go, let's just play loose.' They gave us all they had." The Lakers' last-minute turnaround was led by the legendary Kobe Bryant, but people noticed something different about how he was playing. Normally known for his self-serving heroics, in this game Bryant was sacrificing some of his own glory in favor of plays that allowed the team to rise to the challenge together, players supporting players.

Getting ejected from the game was no accident—it was a classic Jackson strategy. He was known for declining to call timeouts when his team was playing poorly, instead expecting the team to devise their own solutions. He was expert at rewiring the psychology of his players, and seemed to have a limitless toolbox of mind games for nudging his teams to their collective potential. He'd taken the most talented yet impossible-to-manage players in the league, people like Kobe Bryant and Michael Jordan, and built winning teams around them.

Jackson's secret weapon was a geek obsession that framed his entire coaching philosophy: Zen Buddhism, which he had mashed up with a wide range of new age and spiritual ideas. It was the very opposite of the authoritarian whip he'd seen backfire so many times. Jackson followed the mantra "Selflessness is the soul of teamwork." It was a philosophy that ran counter to all the conventions of coaching, and one that could have only come from a coach so invested in mastering his sport that he was willing to take inspiration from any non-traditional source that he felt could up the level of his game. Jackson's approach combined the seemingly contradictory perspectives of eastern philosophy with the strict discipline of the Pentecostal household he was raised in. Mix in a strong personality resistant to traditional social pressures, and you have a classic example of a true sports geek.

Even more impressive, Jackson was able to transmit his passion to his players. To change the way that his team related to one another, Jackson created situations that pulled the players' minds away from the all too familiar gymnasium. He arranged the players into a circle and told parables of the sacred white buffalo of the plains while burning sage. He led them in meditation and trained them to develop an "open focus," where the goal was to banish judgmental thoughts. "Clear the mind," he would tell them. "Listen, observe, notice." These strange rituals were effective, removing the players from their comfort zone and helping them develop the skill of preparation by opening up space in their minds to the possibilities available to them on the court. In a sense, Jackson was creating the conditions for team serendipity—allowing for the unknown and seemingly impossible to happen, again and again—by taking inspired and often utterly surprising actions that awoke his players to the full range of their capabilities.

He explained, "My goal was to find a structure that would empower everybody on the team, not just the stars, and allow the players to grow as individuals as they surrendered themselves to the group effort." Jackson's tactics made his players speak his language, surrender their preconceptions about their abilities, and buy into his belief system. The coach who became known as the Zen Master quite literally transfused his geek brain into theirs. The result was the winningest record in basketball history.

Amplifying the Weird

Dr. Thomas himself had a geek brain, and like Jackson sought out inspiration for his interests from sources outside the range of the familiar. Yes, he was a consummate scientist, but he had another consuming interest that profoundly affected his career. Thomas was a young man in the Jazz Age, drinking at speakeasies and writing humorous prose. He fully embodied the whimsy and irreverence of the period, and he developed a lifelong love of poetry and literature. Alongside practicing his scientific craft, he also became a groundbreaking popular science writer whose books reveal the extent to which he saw the world through a literary lens, even winning a National Book Award for the now-classic *Lives of a Cell*.

This passion allowed him to observe things in his research that others missed. Thomas himself made this connection in 1974, though he cheekily referred to people like himself as mutants. "The real surprises, which set us back on our heels when they occur, will always be the mutants. They have slightly different receptors for the information cascading in from other minds, and slightly different machinery for processing it, so that what comes out to rejoin the flow is novel, and filled with new sorts of meaning... Perhaps there are more of them around than we recognize."

Legendary marketer and bestselling author Seth Godin, writing today, takes this concept even further. He believes that the way to achieve meaningful success in the business world today is to embrace the geek brain, or as he succinctly puts it: "The next breakthroughs in our productivity and growth [are] going to be relentlessly focused on amplifying the weird."

Godin points out that it once took extraordinary effort to feed the geek impulse, as the access to knowledge and expertise was hard to come by, especially for arcane interests. It was also harder to follow those interests to the obscure places where the truly interesting stuff lies. But the Internet has changed all that by allowing individuals access to a broad set of information on any topic under the sun. It's no wonder that geek culture has exploded in response, now that we can all feed even our most peculiar personal interests.

The problem is that it just hasn't yet exploded inside most businesses.

That's because companies—a product of our industrial era, developed alongside the factories they were created to manage—are typically modeled on the logic of the machine, with each person's autonomy constrained by an established role and position in the hierarchy. The organizational chart we all labor underneath is a product of this industrial era process. The true skill of preparation—passionate focus and the ability to draw connections between seemingly unrelated subjects, as typified by the geek mind—gets short shrift in this rigid environment.

We are biased to believe that preparation is simply the ability to think logically. After all, logic is the everyday skill that allows us to solve problems such as "should I see a doctor?" or "are these leftovers safe to eat?" But while a vast number of problems can be managed step by step by following a set of rules, in our increasingly complex world the issues that vex us the most—the ones that are most likely to determine our success or failure—can't always be solved in such straightforward ways. This is true for most of our jobs, whether we're deciding which product features to build, communicating with a market in flux, or troubleshooting complex customer issues.

Hard logic is the basis for so much of our education and business life, but it does nothing to help us to form the new ideas or hypotheses that help us cope with unpredictable change. The pragmatist philosopher Charles Sanders Peirce noticed this problem, observing that new ideas owed their existence to "logical leaps of the mind." Peirce recognized this as a different kind of logic, but one that had never been explicitly acknowledged, so he gave it a name: abductive reasoning. The purpose of abductive reasoning is not observation but wondering. Traditional reasoning helps us decide between options but does nothing to aid us in generating new ones, whereas developing novel hypotheses is the whole point of abduction. It is the only kind of reasoning that is capable of generating new ideas—the only one that requires that we be *creative*.

As usual, Albert Einstein said it best: "Logic will get you from A to B, but imagination will take you everywhere." Yet imagination is not part of the vocabulary within most companies. We get employees to focus with the promise of money and status, and then we don't hesitate to steer them away from their curiosity if it falls outside the job they were hired for. The politics that arise from the race up the organizational chart leave little room for the individual who would rather pursue what appears to others to be a distraction. Worse, there is no advantage available to those who forget the "correct" way to do things inside their business, the way that Dr. Thomas let go of what he "knew" to be true in order to make his breakthrough discovery. Instead, doing so is usually a surefire way to upset the apple cart and get your name first on the list when the layoffs come. Perhaps this is why Michael Bloomberg, mayor of New York City and founder of Bloomberg News, has said, "Big companies don't innovate because they build a bureaucracy that makes a lot of sense."

It's the challenge of our time: the people we need the most in our organizations are the ones we don't know how to make space for. The dreaded double bind looms so completely here we might as well announce in every job description we write:

NOW SEEKING CREATIVE THINKERS WHO MEET OUR WELL-DEFINED EXPECTATIONS. GEEKS NEED NOT APPLY.

Going the Distance

If we're going to learn to practice the skill of preparation reliably, we're going to have to seek out ways to make our organizations more amenable to helping employees find their inner geek. In order to do this, however, we first need to understand what makes the skill of preparation tick; that is, how people attain the mental readiness to recognize and create new ideas from disconnected experiences.

Essential to preparation is the ability to create mental distance from the problems you're trying to solve—to put psychological space between yourself and your current task—in order to be able to observe it in an entirely new way. Dr. Thomas, for example, had the ability to look at the problem of the floppy-eared bunnies with fresh eyes even many years after he had begun to study it, so that when the answer was finally in front of him he could recognize it for what it was.

Time after time we have seen similar situations in which people are better able to make mental leaps when they get some distance from the problem at hand. A recent study conducted at the University of Bloomington in Indiana suggests why this is. In the study, students were asked to write down as many modes of transportation as they could come up with (e.g., motorcycles, roller skates, jetpacks). They were given unlimited time to complete the exercise, told that there were no correct or incorrect answers, and instructed that their ideas could be as ordinary or as fanciful as they wished.

Here's the interesting part: half of the students were told the truth, which was that the study was developed by students in Indiana where the exercises were being conducted. The other half were lied to (lying to test subjects is apparently a key skill for experimental psychologists) and told that it was created by individuals in a study abroad program in Greece.

You wouldn't think such a detail would make a difference, but it does. The participants who believed the study was developed in Greece reliably generated more examples and more original ideas than those who thought it was developed locally. Simply adding the *perception* of distance improved the creative output! Familiarity may or may not breed contempt, but it certainly seems to stifle creativity.

In the follow-up to this experiment, the researchers wanted to confirm that it was indeed spatial distance that was making the difference, not just the suggestion of a foreign country. One group of students was told that the research center where the study was developed was located "two miles away from here," while the other group was told it was located in California, "around 2000 miles from here." A third group, the control group, wasn't told where the research center was located at all.

The students were presented with three "insight problems" and were given two minutes to solve each one. The problems were selected because they were considered solvable by the average person, but it wasn't immediately clear how to go about solving them. This meant a successful solution was likely to produce an "a-ha!" experience. For instance, here was the first question asked:

> *A prisoner was attempting to escape from a tower. He found a rope in his cell that was half as long enough to permit him to reach the ground safely. He divided the rope in half, tied the two parts together, and escaped. How could he have done this?*

The results from this experiment were the same as those from the earlier one: students solved more problems when they thought the study had been developed far away. That one little cue made a big impact.

The study was just the latest to explore an idea in psychology called *construal level theory* (CLT). The premise of the theory is that our minds represent things—objects, events, places, people—differently depending on how psychologically distant we perceive them to be. In the experiment above, when the students imagined modes of transportation in a context that was "near" to them (i.e. created locally) they used a way of thinking that was concrete. When the context was distant, they thought about transportation in a more abstract way. It is this higher-level thinking that opened up their ability to generate new ideas.

CLT demonstrates that we are able to manipulate concepts more freely and better connect unrelated ideas when our minds are operating in this abstract mode. When we're thinking this way we stop seeing all the details that steal our attention when we're in a concrete mode. Without these unnecessary details in our heads, we're better able to focus on the core concepts that matter, which we can then convert into a simplified mental form—a model. It's in this form that we can more easily link the idea to all kinds of other concepts floating around in our minds, allowing us to cast the original idea with new meaning.

Here's an analogy: when you're driving around a city you are bound
to think of your movement in terms of the streets, intersections, parking
lots and buildings that surround you. *Turn on the wrong street and
you'll be late for your next meeting.* But now imagine you're looking
down on a city from an airplane. You see its hills, skyscrapers, and
residential neighborhoods, but also the bay that sits alongside it, as well
as the hills, woods, and freeways that abut and interweave it. The very
way that you perceive the city is fundamentally different seen from the
air—*you never realized how close that chemical plant is to that wildlife
preserve!*—because your perspective on it has widened, and you're able
to grasp it abstractly as a whole instead of just focusing on the next tiny
street-level detail you have to deal with. This captures the difference
between the distant and near modes of thinking.

In the University of Indiana study we can see the effect of spatial
distance on how we perceive things, but temporal distance and social
distance produce similar effects. In other experiments, when subjects
were asked to describe what "studying" meant to them a year from now,
they answered in high-level terms such as "doing well in school." If the
same question was asked about next week, their minds went straight to
the specific, e.g., "reading a textbook." When an activity is going to take
place in the distant future we tend to think in terms of its purpose, or
why we're doing it, whereas when an activity is occurring in the near
term, we focus on the means or *how* we're doing it.

Similarly, we think of social groups that differ from ours as more
homogenous, which means we're able to focus on them as abstract
groupings instead of getting mired in the intricate details of social
interaction that govern our relationships within our own social groups.
Interestingly, this helps explain why the experience many geeks have of
feeling socially outcast actually helps them think more creatively about
social problems. Their distance allows them to approach social questions
more abstractly. In this light, Facebook founder Mark Zuckerberg, a
prototypically marginalized geek, was a good candidate to reinvent
the mainstream social experience since he had some distance from it.
Zuckerberg was certainly a far more likely innovator in this arena than

the Winklevoss twins, the popular, athletic students who claim to have had an idea for a similar web site at the same time as Zuckerberg. Their status and achievements on campus meant they were anything but social outsiders, which may have made it more difficult for them to construct the abstract social model Zuckerberg brought to life with Facebook.

In fact, geek brains like Zuckerberg's have a natural advantage when it comes to creating psychological distance of all kinds. Although you might think their obsessions would lead to tunnel vision, they instead have the opposite effect, allowing geeks to see every piece of information they encounter as a new and amazing discovery. Viewed through the lens of geek passion, everyday experiences are transformed into something less routine or familiar, allowing them to arrest the exceptions and make room for breakthroughs. And geeks in successful leadership roles do this not just for themselves, but also for the people around them. Phil Jackson's obsession with Zen and basketball allowed him to introduce activities that routinely changed his player's perspective on otherwise familiar situations. Jackson's rituals were strange and foreign in the eyes of his teams, and this infused in his players a psychological distance from the all too familiar pro basketball routines. In game after game his players' heightened minds were able to see and connect opportunities that other teams couldn't match.

Every Project Is a Side Project

Construal level theory is a powerful tool for understanding how the skill of preparation connects disparate ideas to harness serendipity and solve problems. It helps us see how we compromise this ability when we are too close to the problem at hand, and demonstrates how very small changes in the way we perceive the world can make a big difference. But how do we begin to create this distance within ourselves on a routine basis?

The main barrier to supporting preparation for most of us is our cultural fear of failure. For many of us, fear of failure or loss is the fastest way to shut us down, and within many organizations the stigma associated with failure is significant and hovers over everything we do.

We are so focused on doing things the "right" way that the mere thought of deviating is frightening. If we don't try to make new connections and find new ways of doing things, then we can't fail. This is why so many organizations are hostile to preparation.

But there's a better way for us to think about failure—a more abstract approach that we can develop in ourselves even if it doesn't come naturally to us. Simply adopting a different attitude towards what we're working on—seeing it as a delight instead of a chore, a side project instead of the main event, a fun diversion instead of a critical component—allows us to begin to build the critical mental distance we need. When we are speculating, or tinkering, or fantasizing, or playing a game, we're implicitly embracing the likelihood of it being incomplete or unsuccessful, but in these situations the possibility of failure doesn't crush our ability to proceed. Psychological distance allows us to accept the likelihood of failure and even take it in stride, since it becomes an abstract, unrelated to hard personal consequences. With a little distance, we just don't take failure so personally, and that gives us the room we need to keep going until we succeed.

Case in point: Paul Erlich, the discoverer of the cure for syphilis, tried 605 different compounds for his cure before hitting on the one that worked. As Dr. James Austin points out, "after anyone makes 605 negative attempts to find something, the odds are almost nil that he will encounter it on the next try. When you're that far removed from the beginning of the quest . . . you don't logically expect a solution."

Talk about losing yourself in your work!

Similarly, Lewis Thomas wasn't trying to make his name by pursuing the floppy-eared bunny problem. Working on this puzzle, Thomas hit his head against disappointment over and over again, but this was never a consideration in whether to try again. Because it wasn't a critical project, he was able to pursue it over the course of years without being distressed by his inability to find a solution. His mantra could have been Thomas Edison's line, "I haven't failed. I've just found 10,000 ways that don't work."

The business we founded, Get Satisfaction, also owes its birth to a side project that started as a mere diversion. The intent at first was not to build a real business but to see how far we could take an absurd but entertaining idea. And yet this putative side project led us, serendipitously, to found a transformational business that foresaw the rise of a major new wave of business thinking ("social business") four years before a term existed to describe it. Here's how it started.

The technology industry, and Silicon Valley startups in particular, are well known for doling out large quantities of promotional "schwag." Attend an industry conference and you're likely to come home with all manner of logo-covered shirts, stickers, press-on tattoos, pens, mugs, and sometimes even something more unusual, like a fortune cookie or a condom. Back in 2005, there was as much an explosion in the quality of schwag as there was in the quantity of social networks. There was a new sense of play and attention to detail that made the cheap branded giveaways of previous eras seem grotesque. New Web 2.0 companies like Slide, Odeo, and Dogster, were outdoing each other to create shirts that people would actually want to wear.

There were so many of these free giveaways around, and so many people that wanted to get their hands on them, that Thor and his partners at the consulting business he was running at the time decided to create a "schwag-of-the-month club" called Valleyschwag. For only $14.95 a month, they declared, subscribers would get a care package from "the heart of Silicon Valley," each containing a handful of pieces of coveted startup schwag. It was a ridiculous concept, taking free corporate giveaways and repackaging them up as a subscription product—a bit like bottling tap water for premium resale, another surprisingly successful idea—but they did it precisely because it made them laugh. When anybody asked, Thor didn't claim they were doing it to make money—instead, it was an experiment in "e-commerce as performance art."

Thor's team built the Web site in a day, driven by curiosity and a bit of mischief. Initially launched to the amusement of industry insiders, the site's appearance was also perfectly timed for a public surge of interest in this new wave of Internet startups. Thanks to a cascade of gushing blog posts from the likes of *TechCrunch's* Michael Arrington and *BusinessWeek*, within eight weeks Valleyschwag had attracted over two thousand subscribers from all over the world. Suddenly $40,000 was appearing in the bank account every thirty days like magic.

The success took everyone completely by surprise, and with it came challenges. It's one thing to repackage free t-shirts and stickers to send to a couple of friends on a lark and quite another thing to do it for two thousand people. The team had to frantically work to put together the machinery to support the masses of unexpected customers. Their work week quickly shifted from the usual consulting tasks to locating schwag, wrapping schwag, and shipping schwag.

A bunch of software developers suddenly in charge of a surprisingly successful commerce site, the team found itself dealing with all sorts of activities previously unfamiliar to them: product sourcing, fulfillment, and most of all customer service. Each day they were more overwhelmed than the last by the crushing river of e-mail from customers who had questions and problems: "Where's my order?" "My t-shirt is the wrong size," "Do you ship to my area?" Team members answered each e-mail personally, and whenever possible within minutes of receiving the e-mail. Every day they had to figure out something new.

Thor's team had never felt so ignorant about their own business, but at the same time they were completely energized by the new challenges. Without intending to, they were operating an e-commerce business with the qualities of a social network, years before the rest of the world had discovered the potent power of that combination.

It was this collision that struck us like a herd of buffalo. We knew a lot about social networks but almost nothing about e-commerce. The result was a cascade of insights that would shape the direction of the next five years of our lives.

First, the nature of the business was very personal. The team's attitude towards customers was a personal reflection of what they thought of them, which led the team to take customer e-mail responses very seriously. Team members attached their real names to every interaction, and sometimes one of them would even send a handwritten note. This evoked a rapturous reaction from customers. Second, the team had a blog for Valleyschwag where they would post updates about the latest edition, ask for customer input, and discuss future plans. The comments section of the blog quickly became a lively forum for engaging discussion about the business, and, intriguingly, customers were asking many of the same questions in the comments area that they were e-mailing in via the contact form on the site. In fact, whenever the team responded publicly on the blog, they could see that they were answering many customers at once, and the amount of customer support e-mail they received dropped because the customers had already gotten their answer. Public conversation with customers was leading to better customer service and stronger customer relationships.

The combined effect of these experiences led Thor to have a flash of insight about the future of the relationship between companies and their customers:

- The Internet had given individuals the ability to communicate about companies on their own terms, and they were taking full advantage of it.
- A public blog was a legitimate and highly effective new tool for customer service.
- Talking publicly with customers required a human, conversational tone that most businesses would need to learn to adopt.

This new way of doing business would turn employees inside the company into peers with their customers, and Thor knew instantly that it was revolutionary. The public customer conversations that the Valleyschwag team was engaging in every day represented the future of customer service. Even better, this new approach brought value to both customers and companies: it made a single employee response usable by countless other customers, instead of being locked up in an e-mail message that only one person would ever see, and it even allowed customers to solve their problems together without ever getting an employee involved. It was by connecting these disparate ideas that Get Satisfaction was born.

We could never have predicted that Valleyschwag, a fun little side project, would have taken us in this direction. If we had intentionally set out to build Valleyschwag into a huge business, odds are good that we would have been so focused on the daily grind of making that happen that we would never have been able to put the pieces together and see the bigger picture that was Get Satisfaction. Our willingness to treat Valleyschwag as nothing more than an enjoyable side project gave us just enough psychological distance from the endeavor that, even when the money started rolling in, allowed us to focus on locating the kernels of insight that we could use to actually build a world-changing company.

Fast forward half a decade, and the future Thor envisioned is firmly here. The product we built around these ideas has touched millions of people and companies of all sizes use tools like Get Satisfaction, as well as Twitter and Facebook, to publicly communicate with their customers on a daily basis. And all because people love to get schwag in the mail.

Of course, as with all things serendipitous, it's never quite as simple as it looks after the fact. Back in 2007 it wasn't clear to anyone except us that public conversations represented the future of customer service. When we were pitching venture capitalists, most of them thought we were smoking crack when we explained our ideas. They knew all the reasons it wouldn't fly. No company wants to air its dirty laundry in public. Online customer communities only work for the world's largest and most popular brands, and they'd never buy from a small startup like ours. Customer service was a mature category, resistant to change. It would be impossible to reach large numbers of small companies affordably. Over and over again, those who "knew better" had good reasons to tell us we were wrong.

Still, we stuck it out, partly because we believed we were right but mostly because we didn't know any better. Microsoft's founder, Bill Gates, once said, "You need to understand things in order to invent beyond them." But this is not quite true. Sometimes *not* understanding frees us to make the connections that the experts say are impossible. Sometimes we can only arrest an exception when we're the outsiders experiencing a phenomenon for the first time.

Strength in Numbers

Preparation is an individual skill, but get enough of the right kind of people together and this personal skill—or the lack of it—becomes a collective phenomenon. As we saw with Coach Jackson, a talented individual can transmit his geeky skill of preparation into the people around him through structured activities. These activities allow others to get the right amount of distance away from an idea or a situation, in order to truly see it clearly. Similarly, office environments and activities can be structured to create—or more commonly smother, unfortunately—the mental distance that allows insight to happen.

Back in 1997, Thor found himself consulting at one of the world's largest computer chip manufacturers. Like many before him, he experienced one of the great frustrations of corporate life—meeting hell. It wasn't that the meetings were innately bad, or the people were ill-intentioned; in fact, these meetings should have been opportunities to bring the best ideas and contributions together for this project. But *every single time* the team members would try to share their ideas it ended in an argument. Usually a big one.

The dysfunction occurred no matter the subject of the discussion. In one incident, a seven-member team of designers, marketers, and product managers met to exchange ideas to launch a new product that had been in the pipeline for eighteen months. To everyone's credit, people came in prepared. Notebooks were filled with ideas and data from previous launches. A carefully organized agenda was sent out beforehand with a rallying cry: "Let's rock this!"

The meeting started off enthusiastically. One participant, Derek, cleared his throat and began describing his idea to partner with a Hollywood movie studio during the release of an upcoming summer blockbuster. Derek put his heart and soul into his well thought-out pitch.

Midway through his explanation the marketing director interrupted. "I don't see how the logistics work on our timeline." Derek started to respond, but before five words had left his mouth, Rob, the VP, piled on: "Have they done this kind of deal before? I know how these media companies are, and I'd be very surprised if they'd throw any real weight behind it."

Derek groped for a suitable response, but the conversation had drifted away from him. Somebody else, one of the designers, was suggesting an alternative idea, which was met with a similar barrage of doubts and interrogations. If you'd been a fly on the wall, you would have seen each person's defenses flare up in the form of crossed arms, pursed lips, and avoidance of eye contact.

The exchanges continued for another half hour, getting more and more painful. For Thor, it was the same scene he'd seen again and again at this company ever since starting his contract. Despite being the one outsider in the room, he decided to take a risk.

"I have a suggestion," he offered. "For the next half hour, why don't we limit all conversation to sharing the ideas in our notebooks? No finding flaw, no analysis, no support, no criticism. Just pure ideation. We can discuss their merits or flaws later."

Silence. Nobody seemed to know how to respond.

"What do you say?" he coaxed.

Finally, the VP shrugged. "Sure. Let's try it."

Thor got up out of his chair, grabbed a marker from the whiteboard, and wrote down the ideas on the wall that had been offered up so far. Slowly, people began to offer more ideas from their notebooks, each of which was added to the growing list. At a certain point, one of the designers made a bad pun combining two of the ideas. This was met with a groan, then laughter, followed by a spontaneous cascade of new ideas from the group. Many of them were combinations or novel variations on other ideas.

The team went on to successfully launch the product to millions of users based on a combination of the ideas that came out of this ideation session (and yes, it did involve partnering with the movie studio).

It's easy to make bold pronouncements about why meetings fail. Jason Fried, founder of 37Signals and creator of the popular Basecamp project management software, thinks meetings are the enemy of real work: "The real problems are the 'm & ms'—the managers and the meetings. Managers' real jobs are to interrupt people ... and managers most of all call meetings, and meetings are just toxic; they're just terrible poisonous things during the day at work."

We have a different interpretation. As we've seen in Thor's example, a well-designed meeting can do wonders for group creativity. So if your meetings suck, you're doing it wrong. Fried is aiming his ire at the symptoms, not the root problems.

What makes meetings go bad? Until its rescue, the meeting described above had fallen prey to hostility and wariness. Team members came in prepared to share their ideas but then shut themselves down when put on the defensive. It wasn't criticism and debate that was smothering creativity, but each participant's lack of trust that they were being heard. This made it very difficult to think abstractly.

Idea-sharing meetings can be ground zero for a business looking to harness serendipity, but only if the meeting is structured in a way that facilitates psychological distance from the subject under discussion. As Thor found in his group encounter, placing the idea exploration activity before criticism allowed for an explosion of connections to occur, and the abstract mode was sustained well into the debate period. Once people are given the cognitive distance to imagine—once they have the appropriate preparation—groups begin to see serendipity in their midst.

In Practice

Contrary to popular belief, geeks are made, not born. You too can nurture the skill of preparation in order to create the conditions for serendipity to strike, as well as to create those conditions in others. Like cooking a turkey, it's all about proper seasoning (or brining) and plenty of time in the oven. It's about giving yourself the space to indulge in an obsession. But remember, it's not the obsession itself that contributes to preparation. Rather, it's the way that immersing yourself in it changes the way you think. Here are some practical tips.

Find Your Obsession

What are you deeply interested in? What are your passions? By this we mean the pursuits that invigorate you and positively affect how you see the world. By identifying your passions and bringing them into your daily life, you can attain the psychological distance to see familiar things with fresh eyes.

When you love something it doesn't feel like work, but it might be work to find the thing you love. It takes effort to identify that thing (or things) that you connect with. Here are some activities that will help you get going:

- Make a list of activities that are their own reward for you, and that you would do even if you couldn't make money doing them. The more specific the better. If there's something unusual or arcane in your background, pay special attention (that's often where the magic happens). You're looking for narrow interests that light you up, even ostensibly weird interests like "collecting toy guillotines," "curing your own meat," or "dinosaur hunting." Do not list goals or your job function with activities: "winning," "making money," "self-improvement," or "programming" don't count for this exercise.
- Identify the subjects that capture your imagination. What do you like to read about? Is there an area of knowledge that you're constantly surprised that other people don't share with you? What did you want to study more of in college, but were afraid would be a waste of time?

Start a Side Project

Maybe your response to this is to say, "I have interests, but no passions." That's all right. You can use this as a starting point. For many people, the deep love of something grows out of being intimate with it, not the other way around. Young piano students often fall in love with piano music as they develop the skills to actually play it.

Find a small project to do in an area where there's the potential for more interest—doing some in-depth research to understand it better, writing a series of blog posts to explore the subject further, or maybe taking a class or two on the subject to get a wider perspective. Side projects give you the ability to explore interests that may blossom into passions. There are lots of reasons to pursue side projects, including regularly updating your personal job skills, but mostly it's about following your curiosity to see if anything lies beyond it.

Find Your Tribe

Once you've uncovered your passion, connecting with others who share it is the best way to develop it into a healthy obsession. Thanks to the Internet, it's never been easier to find others who share an interest, no matter how arcane. They may be scattered across the continents, but they're there. Become an active member of a community that's not part of your normal social sphere. Find someone to collaborate with on a project, whether in person or online.

Finding your tribe will help you sustain your interest by getting constant feedback and support from peers. But more importantly, it exposes you to a broader range of relevant ideas, and allows you to follow the example of others who connect their obsessions in their everyday lives.

Create Sacred Time and Space

Do not assume you'll fit all of this—finding your obsessions, starting side projects, connecting with your tribe—into your busy life. Acquiring the skill of preparation, along with the psychological distance that preparation needs to thrive, requires setting aside time and space to do the work and indulge the obsession. But time and space are hard to come by in this fast-paced world, so if you're like most of us, you probably need a few social hacks to pull it off.

First of all, carve out some regular time for this indulgence. Put a recurring event in your calendar that you consider fixed and stick to it.

Consider adding a self-imposed penalty every time you break the date in order to maintain some discipline.

Second, stick it out. This might sound obvious, but at the end of the day it's probably also the hardest thing to do. We are surrounded by a thousand and one distractions, so it can be easy to spend all our time in "the shallows," that realm that includes celebrity gossip, Farmville, talk radio, Facebook status updates, and discount shopping. Even those of us who have lifelong obsessions find it easy to forget them amidst the immediacy of these trifles. But that just means it's all the more critical to make time and space in your mind for the things that matter to you.

Finding and sticking to our obsessions in a world where it's easy to get driven to distraction is the proven way to open up our minds to all the serendipitous connections available to us. Distance, focus, and a little bit of obsession around the subjects that matter allow us to see the world anew every day, and that gives us the ability to see the full range of what's available to us in the world. This kind of obsession requires commitment. It's worth it, though, because you can't plan for serendipity to strike if you haven't learned to see it when it's right in front of you.

4

Skill: Divergence
The Garden of Forking Paths

"We don't make mistakes. We do variations."
— A Sign at The Oslo Opera House

Greg Perry and Dino Pierone are the founders of Real Door, a thriving custom woodworking business in downtown Los Angeles. For years they've built a reputation with some of the most exclusive home builders for their one-of-a-kind doors and window frames using extremely high-quality, exotic woods. Their innovation is a woodworking process they invented called "Neverwood," which creates a unique laminate with intricate waving patterns. It's stunningly beautiful.

That beauty came with a cost, though. One of their biggest challenges early on with the business was that every order they filled produced its own weight in waste. At any given time they were sitting on a mountain of hardwood scraps—expensive woods like teak, mahogany, cherry, wenge, bubinga, and walnut. It physically pained them to see such quality materials go to waste.

In 2008, as Pierone's daughter's eleventh birthday approached, she told her dad she wanted a new skateboard. In particular, she pined for a longboard, the larger, more cruise-worthy cousin of a traditional skateboard that was exploding in popularity at that time. The request gave Pierone an idea. He realized he had everything he needed to build a longboard for his daughter that would be unlike any other. Using the Neverwood technique, the left-over scraps from his door business, and premium skate trucks from Randal, he had soon fashioned a heartbreakingly gorgeous longboard.

But forget how it looked—how did it ride? One of Pierone's neighbors was an avid skateboarder, so it was easy to find out. Peirone let him take it out for a test drive, and he came back with jaw agape. The quality of the wood added significantly to the experience of skating. "That is one amazing ride," he told him. Others wanted one for themselves. "You could sell a ton of these if you wanted to," they urged, and after spending some time riding it herself, Pierone's daughter agreed.

Pierone and his partner Perry, like true small business entrepreneurs everywhere, devoted a significant amount of their time to running their business. Despite the positive feedback the longboard had garnered, there were only so many hours in the day, most of which were already consumed keeping up with the orders they had coming in for Real Door. They had every reason to dismiss this unexpected distraction—this serendipitous discovery—and remain focused on their core business.

Instead, Perry and Pierone recognized an opportunity to explore a fresh path. They kept their Real Door business on its plan, but also formed a new brand, Loyal Dean, dedicated to the long boards. Working out of the same shop, and finally putting to good use the wasted wood from their original business, they had spun up a whole new world of opportunity. In fact, it was a viable business only because of the path they took: they were able to experiment, and offer affordable prices for their early longboards made out of artisanal hardwood only because they already had a profitable business that was generating excess hardwood as waste. Had they bought the wood specifically for the purposes of constructing longboards, it would have driven the retail cost of the boards well out of the reach of most recreational skateboarders.

It's still early days for Perry, Pierone, and Loyal Dean, and many things could yet happen at this young business. They could spin up additional product lines in much the same way, streamline their operations around a smaller number of products, or even eventually find it actually makes more sense to phase out one of their businesses entirely. Serendipity will surely play its part in determining which of these win out. What we can say for sure, however, is that the reason Perry and Pierone will be ideally positioned to take advantage of new opportunities when serendipity strikes is because they have mastered the elusive skill of divergence.

Straying the Course

In most organizations, our ability to take new directions is shut down by the most basic of psychological hurdles. We want ourselves and our leaders to be decisive, clear-headed, and fully committed, and we hold a collective belief that single-mindedness in the pursuit of a goal is the most effective way to get results. Openness to experimentation and the willingness to change course can seem to run counter to this belief.

Examples of this bias towards decisiveness and steadiness are everywhere. When politicians change direction we call them flip-floppers. When business leaders do it the market punishes them for being indecisive. When scientists do it they're labeled untrustworthy. And nowhere is our need for firm direction truer than in the presence of uncertainty. As President Bill Clinton once explained, "when people are insecure, they'd rather have someone who is strong and wrong than someone who's weak and right."

Let's be clear: commitment is an important trait, and one we'll address in detail in the next chapter. But a willingness to change, and to know when and how much to change, is every bit as important a skill as commitment. People tend to use the word "changeable" as a criticism, to suggest that someone is unsteady, impulsive, and without core beliefs, but sometimes changeability is a feature, not a bug. Most of us who work in companies know that the biggest problem is not that we take too many chances by going in new directions, but that we take too few. Think of it as change-"ability," or as we like to call it: "creative divergence."

Creative divergence is the ability to explore, and sometimes take, alternative paths spurred by chance encounters, many of which challenge our current thinking. Divergence is all about how we get from here to *over there*—the place on the horizon where our sights are set. There are lots of business books that describe how to manage change, of course, but what we're talking about is something else. Divergence is how lucky accidents, great and small, create the possibility for a new route to our destination—a direction we didn't expect and couldn't have predicted when we originally set out. If the skill of preparation gives us the ability to recognize a chance opportunity—to arrest the exception and connect the possibilities in front of our eyes—then the skill of divergence determines whether or not something actually comes from it.

It's relatively easy for a single person, or even a partnership like Loyal Dean, to respond to serendipity if they're primed for it—to diverge when a new path presents itself. An individual can change course as quickly as her mind can make the connection, if she's willing. For example, a professional chef we know accidentally prepared margaritas in a pitcher that still had some cucumber water in it. The result was a tasty cucumber margarita that she now serves on all her menus (try it—it's good!). The chef was always on the lookout for new and interesting recipes, and was therefore primed to appreciate and take advantage of this lucky accident when it happened—not just recognizing its potential, but seamlessly adding it into her daily routine.

When we get together in larger groups, however, divergence becomes a hard skill to master. We struggle in the best of times to change course when there are so many people to coordinate, and when they're all invested in the status quo, but it's especially difficult when circumstances (market conditions, staff turnover) conspire to make us uncertain about the path we're already on. When we feel threatened or insecure, such as during hard economic times or under threat of competitive pressure, creative divergence may be the most important skill to have, because it shows us how to steer ourselves towards a brighter future. Yet our insecurity can make it harder to abandon the comfortable, well-worn route we already know, especially when we've seen so many other roads lead nowhere at all.

Given the risk of dead ends and wasted time, it's not surprising that organizations almost unfailingly err on the side of "staying the course." But that doesn't mean it's always the right thing to do. Divergence is the business skill that allows us to determine whether or not the second condition of serendipity, creativity, can help us find our way to a better path—to "stray the course"—instead.

A Low Tolerance for Creativity

Talk to any seasoned entrepreneur, like Perry and Pierone from Loyal Dean, and they'll tell you that it's second nature for them to spin on a dime when new opportunities arise. Practiced entrepreneurs don't expect every new direction to work out, but that rarely stops them. In fact, it's often this relentless hunt for new approaches to try that exhilarates entrepreneurs and drives them to do what they do.

If that thought instead fills you with dread, don't panic. Most entrepreneurs are borderline psychotic in this regard. There's a good reason that most of us find it hard to take new directions much of the time: human beings have an allergic reaction to uncertainty. To avoid it, we tell ourselves stories that reinforce the status quo—all the reasons that change can't happen, why the alternatives are worse.

Moreover, in the organizations we inhabit, we often find ourselves in situations where our ability to successfully diverge is hampered by a pernicious case of the double bind. In 2010 a trio of researchers at Cornell University, Jennifer Mueller, Shimul Melwani and Jack Goncalo, published a paper called *The Bias Against Creativity: Why People Desire But Reject Creative Ideas*. In two separate studies involving hundreds of participants, they showed that people exhibit a bias against creativity when they're feeling uncertain. More surprising, this bias made it harder for people to even recognize a creative idea.

In the first experiment, subjects were divided into two randomly selected groups: the *baseline* and the *uncertainty* group. Both groups were asked the same series of questions that measured their bias towards the creative and the practical, but those in the uncertainty group were told they would have the chance to earn money after they answered the questions based on a random lottery. People in the baseline group showed a bias *towards* creativity, while those who had been exposed to a degree of uncertainty by the additional presence of the lottery demonstrated a strong implicit bias *against* creativity. The addition of this one little bit of background insecurity—the lottery—noticeably downgraded people's opinion of new ideas, even though there was no explicit connection made between the questions being asked and the existence of the lottery.

From the perspective of trying to understand how it is that organizations squelch creativity, their second experiment was even more compelling. The research team took three groups of people and asked the participants in two of these groups to write an essay. One of these groups was asked to write their essay in support of the statement "for every problem there is *more than one* correct solution." The second group was asked to write in support of the statement "for every problem there is *only one* correct solution." The third group got off without having to write anything at all.

After the first two groups completed their essays, all three groups were asked to rate various ideas for their perceived creativity on a scale of 1 to 7, including one far-out idea, "a running shoe with nanotechnology that adjusted fabric thickness to cool the foot and reduce blisters." The people who had been asked to argue in favor of the idea that there is only one solution to any problem rated the running shoe idea as less creative than the other two groups had, both of which rated it as very creative. Having previously been asked to defend a belief that options didn't exist, these test subjects had become implicitly biased against creativity when it was presented to them.

These results show how easy it is to create environments hostile to divergence. Divergence is fundamentally a creative activity. Taking the uncharted path always requires using imagination to picture how it might work out. But the Cornell study above shows prizing creativity as a quality within an organization isn't enough. Even the people who are most inclined to support creative acts find themselves unable to appropriately value it when a situation or an institution generates a hidden bias against creativity. In these cases it can be almost impossible to effectively practice the skill of divergence.

Now consider the daily practice of most businesses. Fostering a creative environment is not top of mind for most companies, compared to the constant daily effort required to manage human resources, coordinate supply chains, or make the quarterly numbers. Worse, in order to make sure that they do hit those numbers in a predictable fashion, these businesses create systems that reward consistency and punish deviation—exactly the environment that this research suggests erodes the ability to "recognize and accept creativity."

When we are asked to be creative inside our organizations—asked to look for newer, better ways to improve on what has come before—we are too often locked into a routine that implicitly inhibits our creativity and thus our ability to imagine and move in new directions. What we are asked to do and what we are allowed to do are two different things: a classic double-bind scenario.

A Show of Confidence

The silver lining of the Cornell study was that it showed that creativity generally blossoms where people are more confident and secure. We see evidence of this finding in business as well: Pierone and Perry of Loyal Dean had already experienced some initial success before they spun out their longboard business, and the self-assurance it gave them allowed them to grab hold of the new opportunity. So if past success and the confidence it brings are key to the creative process, it stands to reason that large, thriving businesses should be ideally suited to practicing the skill of divergence. Certainly we see examples of this: some of the most innovative work is often produced by hugely successful companies like

Apple, Pixar, Steelcase, Google, and Facebook. Yet confidence alone doesn't explain why these companies are able to take new paths that lead to further success, because plenty of industry leaders become laggards. Why isn't every market leader a master of divergence?

In 1997, Harvard business professor Clayton Christensen introduced the "innovator's dilemma," a concept that describes the trap that high-tech companies find themselves in once they've achieved success. High-tech companies typically invest in "disruptive innovation" to become dominant. After all, few companies ever displace an incumbent by doing more of the same; it takes a product that can define a new market in some way to make this kind of shift. But then success turns these disrupters into the incumbents, and like clockwork they move their focus—and more importantly, their resources—to incremental improvements, or what Christensen calls "sustaining innovation," in order to preserve their success. They *seem* to be doing everything right: staying close to their customers, responding to their needs, and positioning against other big competitors. To the incumbent it appears that they're still innovating as they always have, while all around them upstarts are approaching the problem in new ways. The result is that the displacer becomes the displaced. Waves of new companies repeat this pattern each generation, fueling cycle after cycle of innovation and extinction.

Simply stated: when our businesses are in their early stages, fixated on disrupting a new market, we might be short of cash but we're primed to explore new paths. But when we're all grown up, though we have plenty of resources, our ability to implement change is actually shackled by the success those resources represent—by the need to make our pesky quarterly numbers. In the name of reliable returns, we choke the life out of our ability to diverge.

It's not just technology companies, either. Hollywood, epicenter of the entertainment industry, is a classic example of this phenomenon. What was a barren western outpost a hundred years ago today bills itself as the Creative Capital of the World. It brags that one in six residents works in a creative field, whether motion pictures, broadcast television, commercial photography, video games, or one of many others. By any measure, Hollywood seems to be the world's most vibrant creative ecosystem.

Except for one thing: despite this dizzying concentration of artistic skill and a long history rich with invention, Hollywood is a surprisingly difficult environment for people with original ideas.

Michael Lambie, Sr. Television Research Director at Nielsen, explains why this is the case in the television industry. A pilot episode for a potential new show costs anywhere from $3 million to $10 million to produce, making it a very high stakes endeavor for television studios. In fact, studios are merciless in their willingness to shelve risky shows. Studios produce "pilot" episodes of potential new shows—a single episode of the show created to help the studio determine whether or not the show concept has merit—but for every ten television pilots made, no more than a few get "green-lighted" to become a full series. Lambie's job is to conduct audience tests for these pilots and then produce detailed reports that tell the studios which kinds of people liked it (if indeed anybody did). Studios then use the audience information he provides to help them decide which shows to green-light or make changes to.

"Networks say they want fresh ideas and really distinctive new shows," according to Lambie, "but in the end, they almost always want something that looks familiar. They don't really want to take a risk when this kind of money is on the line."

Think of Hollywood entertainment as falling along a continuum. At one end is *con*vention and at the other is *in*vention. Every piece of work that comes out of its well-oiled machines falls somewhere bet-ween these two ends. Generic sitcoms, police procedurals, and reality shows tend to lean heavily on convention (you always know what's going to happen next, more or less), while great shows like *Twin Peaks*, *The Sopranos*, and *The Wire* push the boundaries of their art by challenging audiences with new ideas and storytelling devices. The rule of thumb in the industry is that any story that is too conventional will bore audiences, while too much invention just confuses them. As a result the industry is always in search of a "Goldilocks formula"—looking for the "just right" place along that continuum.

One way to find the sweet spot has been to find novelty by combining well-known hit show concepts: "It's *How I Met Your Mother* meets *Law and Order!*" What better way to take the risk out of originality than to cross-breed things you know have worked? This approach has become so commonplace in Hollywood it's almost a running joke, even as it has become standard procedure in many other industries as well—including Silicon Valley, where it's not uncommon to hear startup pitches go the same way ("It's Farmville meets TurboTax!"). CBS, for instance, commits almost 50 percent of its primetime schedule to variations on crime dramas, including three separate CSI shows and two versions of NCIS. Given the choice between the tried-and-true versus the new and untested, studios usually bet on the former.

But not always. Occasionally, belief in a new, unproven creative path wins out over confidence in what is already working and successful. In 2009, the FOX network considered airing a pilot for a new show by *Nip/Tuck* creator Ryan Murphy. It was a daring concept—a musical comedy with hard-edged irony and high-school characters that could be as hard to like as they were hilarious. The question that loomed large was whether a prime-time audience would want to watch this hip musical comedy with main characters described by *Variety* as "over-the-top buffoons." It seemed the kind of show that would turn off more viewers than it attracted.

Beyond the unconventional concept, the network and show producers also knew that every other series that had attempted musical comedy, forgotten shows like *Cop Rock* and *Viva Laughlin*, had massively bombed. This new series seemed likely to sink under the weight of its own ambitions, as it didn't fit comfortably into any categories. The audacious goal was to create a true ensemble production, a non-stop stream of guest stars and spectacle. The high cost and difficulty of licensing and recording songs week after week made failure an expensive prospect.

In light of these unmistakable risks, FOX's entertainment president Kevin Reilly would have been prudent, in Hollywood terms, to steer clear of the show. Yet Reilly bought the show anyway and debuted the pilot immediately after one of the network's biggest audiences of the year, the season finale of *American Idol*. Most shocking of all was that he launched it *four full months before the regular season started!* Reilly was risking everything on a strategy of finding early fans and letting them spread the word. His marketing team would fan the flames through the summer up to its Fall premier.

FOX was coming off a good year. Its track record of succeeding with category-busting shows gave it the confidence to see this risky gamble as a creative opportunity. They figured that people would fall in love with it if given the chance, even if they didn't get it at first. They also knew that if they got it right it would be much more than a hit show. A success with this idea meant recorded music, live performances, merchandise. A monster franchise.

The bet paid off. The show, of course, was *Glee*, one of television's biggest hits in the 2009 and 2010 seasons. And the multimedia empire expanded like a soufflé, right according to plan. While at the time of this writing there is some question about the show's staying power, it stands as a counter-example to the risk aversion that famously plagues Hollywood.

The skill of divergence requires the willingness to make challenging but necessary choices in order to take advantage of serendipitous options when they appear in front of us. Yet our ability to grab hold of the opportunities presented in these situations is frequently quashed as a result of the fragile nature of the creative process, which can be easily overrun by institutional forces that value consistency over creativity. What the story of FOX and *Glee* reminds us of, though, is that companies of any size—and the individuals who inhabit those companies—are much better able to diverge from the status quo when their organization is suffused with confidence and, equally importantly, signals to every employee a willingness to express it. Whether or not a company is able to successfully practice the skill of divergence, it turns out, is entirely in its own hands.

But given that most of us, individually and organizationally, are more often allergic to uncertainty, the next logical question to ask is, what kinds of divergence are we actually capable of pursuing in our business, and how can we do it as effectively as possible?

Branching Out

We all like to think we'd jump at a brilliant idea—like say, producing a show like *Glee* or creating an awesome longboard from leftover materials in our shop—if it smacked us in the head, but few of us or our companies ever do. This, more than anything, is why people like to say that ideas are cheap. In truth, great ideas are priceless, but we only know *which* ideas are great with the benefit of hindsight, after the daring path has successfully been taken—and we're rarely privy to the other ideas and choices that might have been tried and discarded along the way. It's hard if not impossible to know which directions will bear fruit, so without an organizational mindset to try out divergent paths, uncertainty and inertia conspire to keep us ignorant.

Few organizations ever develop such a mindset. Instead, most companies follow the common refrain to "put all the wood behind one arrow"—that is, to focus all resources on one goal or priority. The problem with this setup is that it's inherently limiting. To expand the metaphor: the arrow must be aimed perfectly, to penetrate its target in just the right spot. Everything relies on the skill of the archer: her ability to select the right target, assess the wind and environmental conditions correctly, and perfectly execute the angle and force of the shot. That's a lot of pressure to put on one arrow—or one business.

In the modern company, of course, our activities are so multifaceted and our economic circumstances so complex it bears no resemblance to stalking prey. In a marketplace as unruly as the one we have to contend with, accuracy and precision are fleeting if they appear at all, which explains why two of the most challenged big tech companies of the last decade, Sun Microsystems and Microsoft, both used this phrase to describe strategies that ultimately failed them.

The monolithic bookstore chain Borders is a tragic example of a wood-behind-the-arrow approach to running a business. Since its founding in 1971, Borders grew from an independent bookstore in Ann Arbor, Michigan, to over 500 stores in the U.S. by 2010, employing almost 20,000 people. They expanded beyond books to become a multimedia retail giant selling massive numbers of books, CDs, and DVDs, channeling their leadership position to cement their competitive advantage by building a sophisticated merchandising system that could optimize and predict purchasing behavior in real-time.

In the late '90s, online e-commerce was just hitting the mainstream, infusing a great deal of uncertainty into the book and media industries. Borders, facing this tidal wave of uncertainty, decided to put all of its wood behind the arrow that had brought it so much success to date. Rather than get distracted by the shiny new world of Web-based commerce and probe for new ways to pursue its mission on this new medium, the company doubled down on its physical stores, spending billions to refurbish them and increasing the prominence of CD and DVD merchandising. Instead of putting a similar effort into bolstering their Web presence, they outsourced the operations of their online store to an upstart competitor, Amazon.com.

Borders had recoiled to what they thought of as their core strengths, in-store retail sales, perhaps expecting that others would get waylaid in the quicksand of new technologies. In other words, Borders made a big bet on the status quo, took aim with their arrow, and missed their target by a mile. Unfortunately for them, shoppers did not buy more as a result of their store remodelings, and they didn't buy more CDs and DVDs, either. Instead, they shifted to buying online and downloading music and movies digitally, and as a result Borders ended up strengthening the hands of Barnes & Noble and Amazon.com, their rivals. As Borders' business quickly disintegrated, the company found itself out of time and money to pursue new paths.

The cautionary tale of Borders reminds us that the modern organization is in a perpetual state of finding its path in the world. The business environment is constantly in flux, and this has never been more true than in today's hyperconnected world. The only way a company can survive over the long term is by finding or creating new niches while simultaneously inhabiting present ones, a tricky balance to maintain. Divergence—the ability to explore different paths—determines whether companies are able to adapt to new conditions as they emerge.

The problem with the arrow is that it's dead wood. It can't grow or change; it has been fashioned for one purpose, to eject from a bow in only one direction. When we talk of engaging with a world of many serendipitous opportunities, it's living wood that provides a better metaphor. For this we turn to the world of plants, for which divergence is as critical a skill as it is for businesses.

Here's how plants do divergence: in a word, they *branch*. Branching is how plants spread their tendrils, splay their leaves, and concoct their blooms. Some branches thrive, giving rise to new shoots, while others become dead ends as they reach the plant's outer limits. Branches help plants spread their seeds to new parts of the garden, where some take root and others do not. Branching is fundamental to the life of nearly every plant, because it's how they grow, change, and spread.

As a metaphor, branching works well because it comes naturally to people as well as plants. Branching is an everyday tool for exploring new paths that might lead to serendipitous collisions, and as individuals we're intimately familiar with it in our daily lives. How many times in the course of a project do we have the opportunity to do something differently than planned or respond to some new learning? Every time we ask ourselves whether we should stick with the approach we've laid out or take the fork in the road suddenly ahead of us, we have reached a branching opportunity.

But when we get together in groups, we don't always practice branching as successfully as we might were it just up to us. Alone, curiosity is enough reason to zig when others are zagging. Together, there's incredible pressure for us to be sensitive to the negative consequences of change on our teammates. We get frustrated by the ensuing inertia rather than working to understand and stretch the constraints placed upon us and our organization.

The most basic constraint we struggle with in a group setting is this: we can only branch from a previous branch. If we're a large book retailer like Borders we can't suddenly and without warning become a consumer electronics company. It takes time and effort to diverge in a new direction, and like plants, we can only branch on top of what has come before.

This is our *branching range*, the spectrum of viable paths available to our business at a given time based on our current position—not only the products we make, but the beliefs we keep and the relationships we form. All of which affect our ability to take action on the serendipitous opportunities available to us.

We can see that Borders was trapped within a very limited branching range just as change accelerated around it. By choosing to do more of the same—selling books, CDs, DVDs in their stores—and explicitly not branch outwards to the world of online bookselling, Borders reinforced their limited scope of options as circumstances shifted. If a staff member had a breakthrough idea for electronic book delivery there was no viable path for Borders to get from their current business to commercializing the innovation in a reasonable time.

Meanwhile, their main brick-and-mortar competitor Barnes & Noble invested in branching: during this same period, they aggressively created and marketed their own online store, which eventually led them to develop an e-reader, the Nook, to compete with Amazon's version, the Kindle. Each branch Barnes & Noble pursued opened up new possibilities for further branching. Though the transition from a traditional retailer hasn't been easy, Barnes & Noble is still very much in the game, unlike the bankrupt Borders. The reason is that they've continually expanded their branching range. They are a book retailer that *did* become a consumer electronics company over time, through its Nook product, by employing a successful branching strategy.

One way to develop the skill of divergence, then, is to do as Barnes & Noble did: *to actively and consistently expand your branching range.*

Growth Strategies

What can we do to make sure we're more like Barnes & Noble and less like Borders? How can we make certain that our organization is capable of expanding our branching range for maximum divergence?

The short answer is that we need to make branching a planned and routine part of our business operations.

This can seem contradictory, as divergence by definition means actively moving *into* the unknown, which sounds like the opposite of planning. Moreover, the uncertainty associated with new directions makes them psychologically less attractive to us, especially inside organizations. The trick, then, is to turn branching itself into something familiar and known by operationalizing it and making it an everyday, expected occurrence.

Formalizing our branching strategy has two huge benefits. First, it allows us to jump on serendipitous opportunities as they arise, like Perry and Pierone did so easily when they stumbled on their amazing longboard, regardless of the size of our organization. Second, it allows us to continually expand our branching range for its own sake, as Barnes & Noble was able to do. The act of continually extending our branching range means we expose ourselves to successively greater and greater opportunities, many of which would never have been accessible to us without the branches that came previously.

We can see this play out spectacularly by continuing to examine the way the retail book business has played out over the last decade.

There's no question about what Barnes & Noble's core business is—it's retailing books. Their investments, organizational structure, and product line are all aligned around this single billion dollar business. If Barnes & Noble were a tree, selling books would be its trunk.

Yet as we've seen with their foray into the digital world, Barnes & Noble has branched off this trunk in measured, coordinated ways as necessary to keep their business healthy. They've done it for years, even before they went online—from launching their own publishing imprint for public domain titles (publishing the works of William Shakespeare, Sigmund Freud, and F. Scott Fitzgerald), to building their own infrastructure for online retail, to starting a successful brand-partnership with Starbucks to encourage in-store activity, to early and rigorous investment in their own Nook e-reader once digital books became inevitable.

For years, Barnes & Noble has pursued branches around their trunk. They didn't know what the landscape around them would look like in one year or ten, but they knew that people would still read books. They extended themselves, branch by branch, to meet the changing habits of the book buyer. Because they knew their business was books— because they were confident in their trunk—they were able to monitor their environment and branch appropriately. They weren't afraid to diverge, but by design the new approaches those divergences represented always had a clear and meaningful connection to the core strategy of their business.

What's notable about their branching strategy is not just that it has allowed them to navigate a very treacherous market (though it has), but that it has done so in support of this very straight and fixed trunk. The scale and strength Barnes & Noble has achieved in its category has given it a broad market presence, increasing the odds that any one of its branches will thrive. Barnes & Noble is the quintessential example of a trunk-and-branch style of divergence.

There are some challenges to this approach. While the branches might be strong, a thick trunk is immobile and doesn't bend easily. If market conditions change in a direction that falls outside a company's view of the market—its branching range—a trunk-and-branch-style company might not have the latitude to adapt. It's urgent to grow this range before it's too late.

Amazon.com, on the other hand, has a branching style that could never be confused for tree-like, despite the fact that it is ostensibly in the same business as Barnes & Noble. No, as time goes by Amazon's shape has far more in common with diversified conglomerates like 3M or General Electric. Companies like these have dozens or hundreds of business units, sometimes only remotely connected to one another. They are more bushy than tree-like, shapeless masses sprawling in every direction.

In its infancy Amazon billed itself as the "world's largest bookstore," but today it sells products in dozens of product categories, everything from homeware to apparel. Along the way, Amazon realized that it had super powers in e-commerce fulfillment and merchandising, so it branched a new business unit that operated the online stores for companies like Borders and Toys-R-Us. A failed auction site (designed to compete with eBay) later branched into Amazon Marketplace, which blossomed to allow third-party companies to sell used merchandise right alongside the products Amazon itself sells. Over the past few years, Amazon's bushy-ness has only accelerated, as it has branched into media streaming, film production, original book publishing, and its extraordinarily successful Kindle device and marketplace.

Unlike Barnes & Noble, with its single trunk of a business and many subordinate branches, each business unit in a company like Amazon is more like a separate stem, operating individually but always connected up at the base of the plant by a common root system. In Amazon's case, the root system is their technology infrastructure that allows them to slice and dice their e-commerce services in dozens of different ways, combined with a business culture that leads it to constantly strive to be "the world's most consumer-centric company."

Today, Amazon's many individual stems are as critical to its structure as the single trunk is to Barnes & Noble's. The benefits of this branching strategy are obvious: its divisional structure affords far more opportunities to try (and sometimes fail) with new flavors of business. This allows Amazon a promiscuous branching range, supported by their core platform. Talk about making branching part of the plan— they have literally machine-enabled the activity.

On the flip side, sprawling businesses like Amazon require substantial and unabated resources to fuel their mass, plus the right people and systems to keep the parts working together as part of a whole. Remove one or both of these ingredients and the entire collection of business units can collapse like a house of cards, no matter how diverse or strong each business is individually. The Sunbeam Corporation, which made a variety of enduring outdoor and household products including Coleman barbecues and Osterizer kitchen blenders, experienced just such a collapse in 1997. That was the year its CEO, Albert Dunlap, was discovered to be using the sprawl of the business to obscure a massive accounting sham, in which $60 million of profits proved to be fraudulent. The scandal and his mismanagement sent the company into bankruptcy and almost killed it.

To the credit of Sunbeam's product lines, however, the company is doing well again after being acquired by the Jarden Corporation in 2004. Resilience is a do-or-die skill when doing business as a bush.

Divirtuoso

Divergence is *the* critical organizational skill in the practice of planned serendipity. We can put people in the path of serendipity by getting in motion, and we can see the possibilities serendipity presents to us by developing the skill of preparation, but without the ability to take divergent action, serendipity will never stick. Divergence is how we exercise and recognize our creativity in the presence of chance, and the way we take advantage of all the work we've done to get to this point.

When we do it right, the results can be stunning. Occasionally, a company will make a move so seemingly improbable that it's hard to imagine how it could possibly lie within their branching range. The divergent path that this company takes is so bold and unexpected that it appears to casual observers to be completely disconnected from anything that came before in the company's main business even though the truth is it's a natural result of consistent divergent practices. This amazing feat doesn't require suspending the laws of divergence; it's merely the next step in making divergence a core activity in the business. By continually stretching their branching range, sometimes in unconventional directions, these companies find themselves in a position to act on possibilities than no one else can even fathom.

Amazon.com is such a company, and its CEO, Jeff Bezos, is a maestro of divergence. Amazon surprised its entire industry in 2004 when it launched a revolutionary new product called Amazon Web Services (AWS), and the story of how AWS came to be is instructive. As we've seen, Amazon had become masterful at investing in many simultaneous branches. Yet each of these business groups had its own technology that had to work with the centrally managed systems that all the business groups used. The significant coordination overhead created by all these different technologies was sucking up a huge amount of time and slowing things down across every business unit. In response, Bezos issued an edict that would in very short order transform the company.

Here's what it said: all teams in the company from that point forward must create software that could talk to other software inside Amazon. This alone was a big deal, forcing every developer to write their applications in a way that would allow others to access it over the network with no additional coordination. This solved the initial problem that Amazon was struggling with, because now every service and piece of software could interact seamlessly. But Bezos' edict also required something else, which would turn out to be an even bigger deal. It required that every single one of those applications be written in a way that would allow software developers from *outside* the company to access it.

What this meant, in layman's terms, was that every part of Amazon's expertly managed infrastructure—from its computers that process mountains of data, to its infinitely scalable hard drive storage, to its streamlined payment systems—could now be offered as services to the outside world. It would take the next several years, but one by one Bezos began offering these services to third-party software developers for a fee.

AWS was completely unlike any product Amazon had ever offered before—instead of an e-commerce offering, or a service designed to facilitate online sales for other businesses, AWS was a pure technology offering aimed at companies building services on the Internet. Further-more, it was a product unlike anything the market had ever seen before. Previous to AWS, when a company wanted to launch a Web business, it had to invest significant amounts of money into putting together the technology platform to support it—buying or renting servers, hosting them in a dedicated location, and paying the high bandwidth costs associated with running a commercial site online. Amazon now pro-vided these components as a utility service—pay for what you use, and scale up or down your usage at any time. To top it off, AWS was offered at a lower price point than anything else on the market. Amazon was able to do this because of the economies of scale it had incurred building up its own infrastructure, as well as smart technical decisions it had made as it grew, that now allowed it to sell that infrastructure to anybody.

But a student of planned serendipity can see that there was much more to it than that.

Bezos had stumbled onto a problem—the massive difficulty of providing technology services for all Amazon's different business lines—and made a creative leap that allowed him to envision a completely new path where he offered these services to any company on the planet. And not just any path, but one that challenged the way an entire industry thought about how to sell technology services.

From an outsider's perspective, this new business line had nothing to do with what seemed to be Amazon's core business of selling products via e-commerce, but Bezos had a different understanding of what his core business was (and the geek brain to help him maintain enough psychological distance to keep that understanding intact). He knew that the amazing platform his team had built could be good for so much more than it was currently being used for, and it was that knowledge, combined with his certainty about the possibility this new direction represented, that allowed him to branch so significantly.

Most companies haven't evolved a comparable ability. These non-linear moves require a boldness and willingness to imagine possibilities that have no current comparable. They tend to face "triple-headed" uncertainties: market (will customers want this?), technology (will it work?), and timing (is the market ready for this?). If one dollop of uncertainty is a de-motivator, a triple dose can be absolutely suffocating.

But done right, as Bezos did, the results can be transformative. This discontinuous leap has allowed Amazon to position itself in a new category—cloud computing—within the information technology market that it wasn't even in previously. The results have been remarkable: by 2010, it was estimated that Amazon had close to 75 percent market share (or $700 million) in this new category, which wasn't a blip on the radar five years before.

Bezos's breakthrough idea of offering his platform as a service to other companies was indeed a huge organizational divergence, but it was one that his company was well prepared for. He had been expanding its range, branch by branch, year after year.

That's the ultimate lesson we can learn from Amazon. Divergence is not about being at the right place at the right time. It's not ultimately about having a genius at the helm (although that often helps). If we want to reliably make the leaps that serendipity presents, we just have to plan to diverge from the plan. And we have to practice this divergence regularly, growing our range of potential paths as thoughtfully as we grow our revenues. Our future depends on it.

5

Skill: Commitment
Burning the Ships

"In the beginner's mind there are many possibilities. In the expert's mind there are few."
— SHUNRYU SUZUKI-ROSHI

In 1971, Colombia was much like other South American countries: politically unstable, mosquito-infested, scarred by civil war, and overwhelmingly poor. Despite these challenges—or perhaps because of them—an exciting and intense intellectual movement had emerged to reform the country, with a generation of activists and thinkers willing to tackle the biggest issues facing the developing world.

One of these was Paolo Lugari, an obsessive visionary who noticed that the solutions to basic infrastructure—electricity, water, sanitation—coming out of Europe and the U.S. were not being widely adopted in Latin America. He devised an innovative project: a permanent research station in the arid, almost uninhabitable desert area of Colombia, *Los llanos,* that would be committed to developing technologies well suited to the unique needs of these challenging economies. He called it Gaviotas, named for the river gulls that populated the area.

"Think of it," Lugari told Jorge Zapp, an engineering professor at the University of the Andes he was recruiting, "Gaviotas could be a living laboratory, a chance to plan our own tropical civilization from the ground up." Zapp's imagination was set ablaze, and he in turn invited his star students to join him, explaining that their goal would be to "figure out how to build the future of civilization from grass, sun, and water."

Lugari and a few dozen initial scientists and their families headed out to the practically treeless plains. It was the very image of no man's land. "They always put social experiments in the easiest, most fertile places," Lugari explained. "We wanted the hardest place. We figured if we could do it here, we could do it anywhere."

The station ultimately grew to hundreds of researchers and their families, who worked together to create a truly amazing array of technologies that captured the imagination of the public. In addition to a multitude of solar inventions designed for the area's unique climate, they developed a see-saw that pumped water from deep underground when children played on it, a sunflower-inspired windmill, and sawdust-based hydroponic vegetable gardens. Their innovations were cheap and easy to construct from often-recycled materials available anywhere on the continent. Every invention reflected the ideals of the lab's founders. And unsurprisingly, these new tools were more often than not the result of harnessing chance discoveries made possible by the open, serendipity-friendly environment of Gaviotas.

Despite these successes and the adoration of many Colombians, twenty years later the game seemed to be up. By the early '90s, a disintegrating political situation in Colombia combined with a global preference for cheap petroleum over solar power meant Gaviotas had lost its funding. Many of the engineers and their families had left for lucrative opportunities elsewhere. It was obvious to Lugari that he would have to focus on newer, more profitable activities, and fast.

With their brain trust and track record of innovation, the team at Gaviotas had many ways to potentially market themselves—as solar panel manufacturers, an engineering services firm, a patent portfolio, or even a designer of amusement parks. But to the team, these weren't options at all in light of their original commitment to building a better, more sustainable future. So when a colleague suggested they advertise their services as a consultancy, Lugari was immovable.

"We're a foundation, not a corporation," he replied. "We'd lose our non-profit designation—but much worse, we'd lose our credibility. People would think Gaviotas technology was just one more consumer product, instead of a truly different way of living."

While pondering what to do, Lugari chanced upon an article in the newspaper one day about a convulsive shortage of the raw material for resin, called natural gum colophony. The high costs of labor and the availability of petroleum-based alternatives had led to decreased production of natural gum colophony in Western countries, but now demand was exploding for it as resin was being used in all kinds of products, including paint, glue, and medicine.

Eureka! In a flash, Lugari knew what to do: For two decades, his station had been perfecting the cultivation of a type of hardy tree, the Caribbean pine, both for shade and to prove they could green the hostile environment of Los llanos. But the pines were also a natural source of resin. Could it be the trees had another, more practical, use? He rushed to his team and set them to work.

Within weeks they had proven not only that they could tap their trees as a *renewable* source of resin, but that these trees actually grew 20 percent faster in Los llanos than in traditional climates. Lugari was ecstatic. "Gaviotas will still be in the solar energy business," he announced. "Whether we do it with solar collectors or with trees, our future is to transform sunlight into energy." The multi-million dollar Colombian market for imported resin was theirs for the taking.

The rescue of Gaviotas seemed almost miraculous. But the real miracle, it turned out, was what their quickly growing pine forest was doing to the environment at Los llanos. Rather than follow routine forestry practices of clearing underbrush and using herbicides to remove competing plants, the team left them alone out of curiosity and cost-consciousness. As a result, a full-blown tropical forest was emerging spontaneously around the trees. Where before there had only been a few native grasses in Los llanos, now there was a wide range of species—plants like jacarandas, fig vines, crimson-flowered shrubs, *tuno blancos,* as well as animals like deer, anteaters, and eagles. Whether it was the result of dormant seeds under the soil or of birds carrying them from other areas was never clear, but the natural inter-play between these returned species was restoring the landscape to what many believed to be its primeval state—an extension of the Amazon forest.

"This is a gift we can give the world that's just as important as our sleeve pumps and solar water purifiers." Lugari says. "Everywhere else they're tearing down rain forests. We're showing how to put them back."

No Turning Back

We know that the willingness to follow unplanned paths is essen-tial if we're going to take action when serendipity beckons. We also know that there's a very real danger in spreading ourselves too thin by pursuing too many paths at once. More than a few companies have lost their way—and the goodwill of their customers—by chasing short-term opportunities that contradicted everything they had previ-ously built their businesses upon. What the story of Lugari and Gaviotas teaches us is that we can generate and select from serendipitous pos-sibilities most effectively when we have *committed* to the path we have chosen. This commitment gives us the strong roots from which everything about our business grows.

Commitment, an essential skill of planned serendipity, involves organizing ourselves around an overriding purpose. Commitment means having a point of view that's so strong and expressed so pow-erfully that it actually transforms the environment around us. In turn, our commitment stirs up latent desires and intentions in those who work with us, inspiring in them the conviction they need to act on those intentions in situations where they otherwise might not have. When we are fully committed we serendipitously run into things already on our path and recognize opportunities uniquely suited to us, even as others miss these opportunities completely.

Gaviotas is the ultimate story of how commitment within an organization keeps it true to its convictions even when times are hardest. It also shows us how the most powerful kinds of serendipity—happy accidents that fall in line with our purpose—can be exposed by that very commitment.

Lugari and his team planned for serendipity in every aspect of the design of Gaviotas, and practiced all of the skills we've covered so far. Lugari recruited the most passionate geeks he could find and actively encouraged motion in the work environment. He built a physical infrastructure and a social context that gave the team freedom to experiment and play, which allowed their ideas and prototypes to collide with each other and with reality just to see what might happen. But it was their singular commitment to their founding vision that determined their ultimate success, by showing them where to seek inspiration and by making them more sensitive to seeing what was the next best thing to do. Their commitment to their purpose affected who Gaviotas hired, the language they used, and even the external recognition they received, since it made it easier for others to understand and invest in their story. All of this came together to massively reinforce everything they had originally set out to do.

The story could have ended on this note. Things were working well, so they did more of what was working. Except for one thing: when things fell apart, Gaviotas refused to veer from its path.

What would have happened had they taken one of the numerous other more expedient options available to them—if they had become a manufacturer or a services firm? We'll never know for sure, but we can safely say they would have been preoccupied on something other than discovering the miraculous pine forest and its value to both the station and the environment. The dramatic turn of events for them was literally made possible by their commitment to their higher purpose. Serendipity was directly unlocked through the act of *rejecting* a wide range of options.

Even though organizations have a much harder time taking divergent paths than staying the course, this doesn't mean that commitment is the enemy of serendipity. Quite the contrary. Being rooted to purpose is often the only meaningful way we to decide which of our many paths to take. It is the difference between flailing about opportunistically every time chance presents itself, and making the choices that are completely aligned with why we do what we do.

Legend has it that when the Spanish conquistador Hernando Cortés landed in Mexico he burned his ships behind him to keep his eight hundred men from retreating during his conquest of the Aztec Empire. (In fact, he scuttled the ships, but the effect is the same, and fire sounds more exciting.) Hundreds of years later Cortés' dauntless action continues to make its point with utter clarity: he would make no allowance for retreat, once the direction was set. He and his men would move forward, always forward, to meet their glory or their deaths. Cortés had engineered a situation where he and his men would *have* to remain firm in their direction because no other option remained. Anything that happened from that point on would be a result of this commitment to their path. In a sense, Cortés primed his men to see and grab hold of serendipity, because chance was the only thing they had left.

Commitment requires us to ask ourselves whether we're ready and willing to burn our own ships.

Serendipity Suppressed

Before you torch anything, let's explore why commitment is so important. It has to do with an unintended consequence of getting good at the skill of divergence. The better we become at divergence, at taking alternative paths, the more paths will unfold before us, like an entrepreneur with a thousand new ideas. The bad news is that *too* many options can paralyze us into inaction, or force us to be arbitrary in our branching. Serendipity is the likely casualty.

As anybody who has ever planned the details of a big party or filled out a wedding gift registry knows, by the end of a long period of decision making we're ready to say yes to almost anything just to get it over with—or we just shut down and refuse to make any more decisions at all. Studies show that we do not have an inexhaustible supply of mental energy to make decisions. In fact, it's incredibly easy to deplete our decision-making energy, to potentially disastrous effects.

John Tierney, co-author of the book *Willpower: Rediscovering the Greatest Human Strength*, described the symptoms of this decision fatigue:

> *The more choices you make throughout the day, the harder each one becomes for your brain, and eventually it looks for shortcuts, usually in either of two very different ways. One shortcut is to become reckless: to act impulsively instead of expending the energy to first think through the consequences . . . The other shortcut is the ultimate energy saver: do nothing.*

In a typical workday we are faced with an incalculable number of decisions, many of them made under duress in meetings that go on and on and on. This is a classic example of a situation that leads to this kind of fatigue.

"Big decisions, small decisions, they all add up," Tierney continues. "Choosing what to have for breakfast, where to go on vacation, whom to hire, how much to spend—these all deplete willpower, and there's no telltale symptom of when that willpower is low." Our decision-making ability deteriorates the more we use it, and we don't even have a good way to know it!

So here is our dilemma: by embracing planned serendipity, and specifically the skill of divergence, we dramatically increase the number of new choices in front of us, but at the same time the more choices we have, the more it becomes increasingly hard to take advantage of any of them.

Commitment is the remedy to the indigestion of so many alternatives, for a very simple reason: it slashes the number of acceptable choices in front of us, leaving the ones most attuned to our truest aspirations. If Lugari had pivoted Gaviotas to market it as an engineering consulting company, it would have become just another engineering firm. By remaining true to its purpose and ruling out options that didn't directly support it, Lugari instead stumbled on a new path that Gaviotas was uniquely suited for. His commitment was what both narrowed the range of available options, and also guaranteed that what was left would be the right path to follow.

Commitment Issues

Though we talk about it as a single skill, commitment depends on two distinct qualities. First, commitment is nothing unless it's in the service of a *meaningful purpose.* Driving relentlessly towards a goal that is changeable or fails to inspire will only erode commitment and the appearance of serendipity itself, as we'll soon see. Purpose is the reason our companies exist, as well as a big part of what makes for a healthy, serendipity-friendly culture and activities.

The other key factor in commitment is *stick-to-itness*, the steadfast determination to stay true to your purpose. As Lugari demonstrated when Gaviotas' situation was at its most dire, real stick-to-itness is maintaining your resolve precisely when it is hardest, when others think you're crazy for not relenting to convenience. Developing the skill of commitment means turning stick-to-itness into a habitual response that consistently reduces the volume of decisions to make, without creating decision fatigue. Stick-to-itness is the attitude that says *the ships have been burned, there's no turning back.*

These are the two sides of the commitment coin: stick-to-itness and a meaningful purpose. One without the other is simply insufficient—a conviction easily forgotten is as worthless as firmness in the pursuit of vanity. Still it's easy to pick a starting point: everything important about commitment radiates from purpose.

Purpose

In Chapter 3 we learned that for individuals, an obsessive curiosity in an area of interest is a basic ingredient to being prepared for serendipity. Purpose is the organizational equivalent of this trait. The French have a pithy phrase for it, *raison d'être,* by which they mean the ultimate reason for something's existence. Anything we create has a raison d'être, even if we don't name it or even give it any thought. Though some would say that every business's raison d'être is to provide shareholder returns, this is a sad and unsatisfying answer. It's like saying that the reason for living is to replicate—it may be a biological imperative, but most would agree it's not what stirs humans to seize the day. Our businesses are vehicles for us to engage with the world in a particular way. They take on the shape of our desires, be they deep or superficial.

Of course, what this purpose is can be murky. The unfortunate fact is that many of our companies have proclaimed this purpose for us by plastering a mission statement around the office, yet we're still struck dumb when asked what our company is really about. When we do respond we're likely to answer by describing what it is our company makes—its products or services—or even less accurately our aspirations for dominating one market or another. None of these answers are the same thing as purpose. The products that our companies make can change. Market leadership comes and goes. If our business is the result of a series of blind pivots towards the most lucrative short-term opportunities, chances are we've lost sight of our purpose or were never fully able to articulate it in the first place.

A real, honest-to-goodness purpose is a core conviction that remains true no matter the external changes to technologies, tastes, or stock prices. It's *meaningful* because it reflects the unique perspective of the firm and its members. The content is not what matters here—what does is the power our purpose has to move us to act.

A well-articulated purpose is one that provides an enduring sense of overall direction that can also be translated into action on a daily basis. It shouldn't be something as vague as "make the world a better place," because almost any action can arguably fit into a statement like this. There's nothing about that statement that narrows options—it just coats them all in a meaningless wash of good feeling. In addition, for a purpose to persuade and inspire inside an organization, it must be easy for anyone in the organization to explain it to the outside world.

From the standpoint of planned serendipity, nothing is more important than people understanding and believing the organization's purpose. When it is poorly conceived or badly articulated, getting purpose wrong can be hazardous to a company's health. Borders, as we saw in the last chapter, was forced into liquidation through its inability to take new paths in the face of changing customer preferences. At first glance it would seem as if the company had a clear mission—to provide the best physical retail experience for books and media of all kinds. It's certainly actionable, as it drove them to invest in more and better stores, bigger inventory and smarter merchandising systems, and it might be meaningful to people who care passionately about books. But the problem with Borders' purpose as articulated here is that it focuses on the means—physical bookstores—rather than the underlying need, which we could describe as "enjoying books and media." Their purpose fails the endurance test—it stopped making sense as technology and tastes evolved. Barnes & Noble, as evidenced by its actions, had a more durable sense of purpose: it fundamentally cared less about what kind of store it was selling from, as long as it was able to facilitate a meaningful book buying experience. As a result, it was more readily able to adapt to the new ways that readers wanted to buy and consume books on the Web and on e-readers.

Borders' poorly articulated purpose directly affected their adaptability as change whipped through their industry—it led them to hire managers from traditional big box retailers, to confuse their focus on means (physical stores) for real customer desires, and ultimately to have too narrow a view for them to harness any serendipitous opportunities that might have saved them. A meaningful purpose, by contrast, makes it far more likely we'll run into unplanned opportunities that are aligned with our deepest desires. Paolo Lugari could not have planned the harvesting of organic resin from those trees or the regeneration of the ancient tropical forest in the Colombian desert, but it proved to be the fullest realization of his vision. The discovery was only reached after saying "no" to the expedient but ill-fitting choices. In contrast to the skill of motion, which expands the raw quantity of chance collisions, commitment actually increases the *quality* of serendipity.

We can see the serendipity-enriching effect of purpose at a company that once considered growth and profitability as its only reason for existence. Upon starting his carpet manufacturing company, Interface, in 1973, Ray Anderson was an unapologetic industrialist, inventing the first free-lay carpet tiles and growing his business into a major force in the carpeting industry. Carpeting has historically been a petroleum- and waste-heavy business, but this was never a consideration for Anderson one way or another—it was just how the textile business worked. That is until one day, twenty years into the business, when one of his employees asked what his company's environmental philosophy was during a weekly staff meeting. Struck dumb by the question, Anderson realized they didn't have one.

Anderson's lack of a meaningful response ended up simmering in the back of his brain, until a book by Paul Hawken landed on his desk a few weeks later, "as if by pure serendipity," Anderson recounted. Called *The Ecology of Commerce*, it challenged businesses to rethink their relationship with the environment; according to Hawken, a business could be a good steward of precious natural resources and by doing so, actually create a more modern, competitive business. These turned out to be ideas perfectly tuned for Anderson's now-prepared mind.

In one of the most celebrated conversion experiences in this epoch of green business, Anderson announced to his company, his investors, and the market that Interface's days of exploiting natural resources for financial gain were over. While the world bickered about how many businesses any new environmental regulations would kill, he proudly and loudly announced that Interface would show big business what real commitment looked like. By acting unilaterally and publicly he was following in the footsteps of Cortés, as his excoriating words about the destructiveness of business as usual had eliminated the possibility of retreat.

Anderson articulated a purpose that was unambiguous and so bold that people inside and outside the company couldn't help but repeat it, even if just to declare him a lunatic. It was as meaningful a purpose as you can get: Interface was to lead the business world into its sustainable future by example. They would show that it was possible do right by the environment *and* still be one of the most profitable carpet manufacturers in the world. He would turn what others assumed was folly into the ultimate competitive advantage.

In addition to being meaningful, the purpose was also actionable. Anderson declared an audacious goal: the entire company would aim to get to zero negative impact on the environment by 2020. Zero, zilch, nada. It would take a focused, determined, company-wide effort to embody the total commitment they had made.

Fast-forward to today, and Interface has cut its greenhouse gasses almost in half and its landfill waste by 77 percent. It has cemented its position as the undisputed global leader in modular flooring, one of the fastest growing categories of carpeting, and has become the first name in sustainability, which has become a key criteria for buyers around the world since Anderson made his declaration.

It was an amazing transformation, and one made possible only because of Anderson's bold declaration. When he made it, Anderson had no precise idea about how to make his company that audaciously sustainable. But he knew that if he didn't commit to his vision, and if he wasn't able to transmit this commitment to his entire team, Interface would never develop the ability to see the possibilities for developing radically sustainable practices that up to that point they had missed.

One of the most striking examples of the effect of this new vision was in the development of a new line of modular carpet tiles. With Anderson's directive firmly in mind, the product design team, led by David Oakey, set out to conduct primary research into what the experience of natural, organic design should be like. They ventured into the woods, expecting "to come back with designs of flowers and leaves." What they stumbled on, however, was a far more profound observation. They were struck by the way that leaves on the forest floor, or rocks on a riverbed, were randomly scattered by the trees but still lay all together. When you stood back and looked at the whole scene, it gave the impression of a seamless pattern even though none of the leaves had been placed intentionally, and none of them were perfectly arranged. This was their eureka moment: it wasn't the beauty of the natural objects that inspired them as they'd expected, but instead the way that the disorder of the leaves and rocks gathering at random actually created a feeling of order and cohesiveness.

This got them thinking, what if the carpeting industry's focus on cookie-cutter sameness was all wrong? What if instead of perfect regularity, every carpet tile was different? What advantages would this deliver?

As the team continued their research they realized they'd hit the jackpot. By designing in infinite variability they had found a way to eliminate virtually all the waste in the manufacture of the carpet tiles. They could use exclusively recycled material—since no two tiles would ever be entirely alike design defects would be a non-issue. Also, there were huge benefits for home builders, who could lay the tiles down randomly, which would reduce time for installation and also allow people to replace individual tiles at any time. Moreover, like fall leaves on a forest floor, they were beautiful.

Customers agreed: within eighteen months of launching the new line, which they branded Entropy, it had become their fastest-selling product in the history of the company. Anderson's bold purpose had sent the design team looking for one thing, but more importantly it had given them the eyes they needed to see in something unexpected the thing that was most meaningful to their cause. Commitment had set the stage for serendipity.

Stick-to-Itness

Over and over again we find that the luckiest organizations are not the most opportunistic, but those, like Gaviotas and Interface, that have taken a stand. Each action taken in pursuit of our commitment becomes a reflection of our purpose and as a result winds up changing what others believe is possible. In this way, our purpose becomes a self-fulfilling prophecy.

But this can't happen unless we act on our commitment, day after day, come hell or high water. Like Gaviotas and Interface and every other successful company in this book, our companies need the fierce resolve to push our purpose to the limit. That's where stick-to-itness—the relentless follow-through in pursuit of our purpose—comes in.

In 1991, the man who would become one of the most revered chefs in the world had a culinary experience that would inspire him for decades to come. Thomas Keller was already a star, having founded the Napa-based The French Laundry, which famous food writer Anthony Bourdain once called the "best restaurant in the world, period." Keller's friend had dragged him to this place in Southern California to experience what some argue is now the region's most legendary dish.

The delicacy: a cheeseburger. Not just any burger, though; it was an In-N-Out Burger, washed down with a bottle of Ridge Lytton Springs Zinfandel they'd brought along. To Keller, this burger was a revelation. He realized that he'd found in a fast-food chain the essence of what he practiced in his own Michelin starred restaurant: "If you think about cooking," he explains, "you'll find at In-N-Out or French Laundry, it's about product and execution that's consistent."

On the surface, this seems a simplistic explanation, for in the years since Keller's visit In-N-Out has become an epic phenomenon. "Quality and consistency" doesn't seem sufficient to explain why the opening of each new store is a major event for the area it's in, complete with local news coverage and lines around the block; or why a rumor about an opening in a new city can send people into a tizzy; or why people make pilgrimages from many miles away to fetch themselves a $2.75 burger; or why the In-N-Out concession truck is featured every year at Vanity Fair's ballyhooed Oscars party as if it itself was a celebrity guest.

But this explanation is all we need. Keller was describing the recipe for commitment. Quality + consistency = purpose + stick-to-itness.

In-N-Out Burger's rise is serendipity writ large. They started out aiming to be one thing, just a local burger stand committed to high quality in the face of a food industry more than willing to compromise on it. Instead, they achieved cult-status as one of America's most pure-at-heart eateries. In-N-Out did this with an excess of stick-to-itness and a purpose that seems so simple it's hard to believe it explains anything.

In-N-Out was founded by Harry Snyder, a painter's son who was eking out a living delivering boxes of sandwiches to soldiers, and his wife Esther. In 1948 they decided to start a drive-thru hamburger stand in Southern California, the epicenter for the new car culture that was transforming post-war America.

From the beginning, the Snyders were focused on what they knew to be their purpose: quality. They had an obsession with quality and used it as the basis for virtually every decision they made. "Quality" didn't just mean sourcing the best beef or making fries from freshly cut potatoes. No, quality meant a good life (and high relative wages) for employees, service with a smile at every location, and unflappable management. It meant complete and unerring consistency. For Harry and the generations that would follow, this translated into the habits that made sticking to quality the only acceptable option. Time after time they refused to budge.

In-N-Out is a perfect showcase for the power of unshakable resolve. Many companies claim to value "quality" but few have transformed it into a remarkable, decades-long track record like In-N-Out has done. In contrast to many of the stories in this book that focus on companies that have seen dramatic changes, In-N-Out Burger is a business whose adaptability is actually measured in how *little* it seems to have changed. Indeed, the real innovation of the business is in how it has maintained its purity in a world and at a scale that looks nothing like it did in 1948.

Serendipity has consistently struck as a result of this committed focus on quality and the stick-to-itness it represents:

- The Snyders did not initially intend to expand the business beyond its initial location—it took three years before they opened their second drive-through. In fact, the Snyders were initially resistant to growing because they feared they would lose control of the level of quality they prized. The expansion from one restaurant to several was not driven by revenue growth but by the unexpected desire of the employees to continue working with the company.

They had assumed that employees would work for a year or two, develop some skills, and then go off to start their own businesses. Instead, they were surprised to find that staff had no desire to depart. Because of the Snyders' belief in treating them like family, they agreed to launch new restaurants as a reward for the dedicated staff that made quality possible in the first place. An unexpected need, combined with the Snyders' refusal to budge when it came to quality of life for employees, led to a very purposeful divergence.

- Once established, the In-N-Out growth strategy had always been to purchase the land where their drive-thrus would be located in order to avoid landlord disputes that would undermine quality of service. In addition to putting a natural restraint on the company's growth, purchasing their own land also meant that their locations tended to be in suburban and outlying neighborhoods. Instead of damping consumer desire, they found that people would drive well out of their way to buy their burgers, but the bigger surprise was that by making it harder to buy their food they were actually *stimulating* demand. By making In-N-Out burgers harder to get than the average fast-food burger they actually managed to quite unexpectedly enhance the allure of their brand. It would have been easy to chase hot new locations opportunistically, but by holding fast to their purpose they were able to find the right path to serendipity.

- The Snyders eventually became sensitive to the inconvenience this distance was causing loyal customers, because of driving times, long lines, and the cold fries that could result. Only then did they put together a plan to expand into dense urban and tourist areas, and to increase the overall number of drive-thrus. Many on the management team were concerned that this would have a negative impact on the mystique they'd stumbled on with their harder-to-reach locales. After much debate, In-N-Out moved forward with the plan and was surprised to find that per-location sales actually *increased* after the expansion. Their reputation had become so great over the years that it had created a multiplying effect by the time they had decided to pursue faster growth. In-N-Out could never have planned this result—it followed from their refusal to deviate from their commitment to quality.

We can compare this result to what happened to Krispy Kreme Doughnuts when they pursued their rapid expansion campaign in the last decade. Krispy Kreme is a firm whose ethos and allure was comparable to In-N-Out Burger prior to its 2000 initial public offering. People went crazy for Krispy Kreme's doughnuts, with a taste and a store aesthetic that seemed straight out of the glory days of the 1950s. But following their IPO they decided to explode their growth into hundreds of new locations, executing aggressively on a plan that they believed would make them an international food staple. Though they had built their business carefully over the course of decades previously, Krispy Kreme gave up any semblance of stick-to-itness in order to pursue a pell-mell growth strategy. Within six years they were on the verge of collapse, with stores under-performing and franchisees filing for bankruptcy, a situation from which they are only now recovering.

As their business took off, the Snyders could have easily embraced the profit-generating practices of the rest of the fast-food industry—franchising, mass-produced patties, lower wages, and a constant stream of new menu items. But as with Gaviotas, In-N-Out's unwavering ability to stick to its self-determined cause rendered most of the "obvious" choices unthinkable, and the result of this stick-to-itness has been a set of organizational habits that generated breathtaking success through opportunities that others never even saw.

Habits Born of Commitment

Commitment is most effective when it helps us create habits that reduce the constant barrage of choices within an organization. Habits take the guesswork out of staying true to purpose. Lugari declared that Gaviotas "will reject any option that turns our technology into just another consumer product"; In-N-Out flatly refused to reduce worker salaries in light of much lower industry standard wages; Interface's policy condemned any manufacturing methods that added to waste.

In each of these cases, these determinations formed the basis for organizational habits that make stick-to-itness a no brainer.

Roy Baumeister, the pioneering researcher of decision fatigue, explains why habits make all the difference: "Studies show that people with the best self-control are the ones who structure their lives so as to conserve willpower .... They establish habits that eliminate the mental effort of making choices."

Habits convert many everyday decisions or questions into automatic behaviors. Even better, they stoke the appearance of serendipity that aligns with purpose, and consistently steer our attention away from the many paths that don't. Here are three habits we see over and over again when it comes to commitment.

Saying "No"

The number one habit of committed organizations is the willingness to turn away good opportunities that aren't in sync with their purposes. For behaviors to become automatic they need to be based on a clear mandate. A company might even maintain a list somewhere that itemizes all the things that the company will not do. In-N-Out, for instance, has made it clear they won't be expanding the menu anytime soon. "It's hard enough to sell burgers, fries, and drinks right," Harry Snyder's son, Rich, has said. "And when you start adding things it gets worse." As a result the company has left their five-item menu virtually untouched for over sixty years, at prices that seem from another era ($2.99 for a Double Double burger at this writing). No Happy Meals, no fancy wraps, no breakfast menu. It's not that they're unimaginative or closed to change—it's that they have principles of the business that are sacred, and the menu is an expression of these principles.

This habit should flow effortlessly if we're in touch with our purpose. Once we know what we stand for, it is self-evident what we stand against.

Patience

Patient companies have developed the habit of waiting for results. While certain kinds of short-term metrics are essential to guiding any business (cash flow, if nothing else), commitment balances the short-term view with long-term aspirations. Ray Anderson knew it would take Interface decades to re-engineer its business for zero environmental impact. In fact, their total emissions actually *rose* for several years after Anderson's declaration before finally falling sharply ten years in. To realize their purpose they had to be willing to de-emphasize near-term metrics, and to instead be patient and focus on the activities that would eventually have the desired impact.

A different case is In-N-Out Burger, which opted for a completely different measurement of success than the rest of its industry. Its primary measures revolve around quality, rather than financial or market growth, and this has allowed them to be patient about how they expand their market. Today In-N-Out has a mere 258 locations, compared with more than 33,000 for McDonald's. Its molasses slow growth in the face of massive expansion of this new industry was neither originally planned nor a problem for the business. Whether or not to grow faster was simply never the right question—instead, whether or not the level of quality was consistently high was. Their ability to be patient was a result of giving precedence to qualitative measures over the quantitative.

Controlling the Controllables

It's common for the skill of commitment to be accompanied by a strong urge to exert control, but committed companies also understand that not everything *can* be controlled. These companies learn to focus on only those areas where control is possible. This habit drives companies to stop trying to control major areas of the business more open to the intervention of serendipity. In-N-Out realized they could and should control the training of their staff in such activities as the use of the potato fryer, but they also knew they could never control the people themselves—their thoughts, actions, or beliefs. In response, they created In-N-Out University to make sure every employee understood the company's purpose and approach, and importantly part of this approach was that employees were encouraged to use their own judgment to make decisions of all kinds.

These are broad outlines of three common habits, but every company has the chance to custom design habits that reinforce its goals. Each time we take the guesswork out of the skill of commitment for our companies and our employees, we connect high-level purpose to everyday action and make stick-to-itness a fait accompli.

How Does Your Garden Grow?

We end the chapter where we began, amongst the trees.

Finding your way to San Francisco's most celebrated garden store is a bit of a trick. It is not located in the posh Pacific Heights district, fashionable Hayes Valley, the hipster-friendly Mission, or the gay epicenter of the Castro. No, you'll have to make your way to the most dangerous and least trafficked part of the City, the Bayview. Along with Hunters Point, this part of town single-handedly doubles the murder rate of San Francisco. It's an area that most residents like to pretend isn't within the city limits.

Yet in the midst of this ghetto is one of the most successful small businesses in the city, one that has reinvented the modern garden store and thrust its founder, Flora Grubb, into the national spotlight.

Flora Grubb grew up dirty in Austin, Texas. And by dirty we mean she spent her days creating gardens in the midst of the city's simmering heat. While other girls her age were mastering Ms. Pac-Man, she was learning the how to transplant a Sabal palm tree. Though she never took any formal education in botany, she learned by experience the finer points of nurturing immature succulents, of biodynamics, and of working with semi-literate migrant laborers. Most of all she developed an eye for what worked to make a stunning garden. It certainly wasn't a common hobby, but it was the most natural thing in the world for her. It was simply her favorite thing, and she received nothing but encouragement from her counter-cultural parents.

It was this confidence in her abilities and beliefs that stayed with her as she grew up, eventually moved to San Francisco, and started her own landscape installation company after a brief detour at a dot com startup. Flora was relentlessly driven to share her gift of a green thumb, and people of all walks of life responded to it. Driven by this conviction she found herself talking about her ultimate ambition every chance she got: to open a garden store her own way. Within a year she'd inadvertently exposed this vision to a client, Saul Nadler, who happened to be looking for a new business to invest in. As soon as he heard her talk about it, he knew he wanted in on the opportunity.

Meeting the man who would become her business partner in this accidental way (via her big mouth) was just the first of a cascading sequence of serendipities resulting from her relentless pursuit of her purpose. Flora and Saul opened their first store, which turned heads with its unusual selection of mostly flowerless plants, as Flora preferred these drought resistant plant varieties she knew so well from her hometown. Her unique approach led to an unexpected invitation to deliver her first ever public speech at an industry event where she made a deep impression on the editor of *Home & Garden Magazine,* who was in attendance. In a high honor ordinarily reserved for very established designers, he named her a "tastemaker," giving her a national reputation overnight.

Attracted by the purpose she'd exuded, the owners of a remarkable piece of land in the Bayview reached out to her and asked her to move in. They'd always dreamed of a garden store on their property. It was one serendipitous event after another!

The result was one of the most unforgettable retail experiences in a city rich with head-turning stores. Sitting on three acres in an otherwise sketchy part of town, Flora Grubb Gardens is like walking into a veritable garden of Eden, albeit one with more than its share of succulents, a rusty old '50s car transformed into a planter, and a gorgeous solar paneled modern structure at its center. According to Flora, it's beyond what she ever could have imagined.

And here's where the story gets interesting. Over the years Flora also became expert at the skill of divergence. She ended up with a garden installation service, an in-store café, an events business, a radio show, and an online store, all built around her passion and her specialties. Beyond what she's already accomplished she had many other ideas for things like books, branded garden products, and an educational series. Everything she did seemed to work, and it all connected back to everything else. Without any organized effort, the press lavished attention on her, giving her store's luscious garden full-color, multi-page spreads and even promoting specific products. Visions of a diversified garden empire danced in her head.

Then one day she realized something just felt *off*.

The business was going gangbusters—Flora was amazed every day by how financially well the company was doing. Yet she was tired all the time, and there never seemed enough hours in the day to get her minimum tasks completed. This made her feel anxious when she would try to spend time with her husband and baby. Her staff seemed to struggle to master the basics of the business—what was simple and obvious to her was a constant struggle for them. She began to have a tougher time making decisions.

Flora started talking it over with her mentors, and one of them recommended she bring in an independent consultant to help her get some perspective on her angst. Suppressing a natural urge to object, she took her friend's advice.

The consultant started to show up once a week at the store, and Flora gave herself over to what turned out to be an enlightening conversation. It was like talking to a shrink, except one who could also talk cash flow and marketing spend. The experience was a far cry from the jargon-drenched management training she had feared—mostly, the consultant asked questions about who she was, why she'd started the business in the first place, and where she wanted to go in the future. As simple as the questions were, they prompted Flora to dig in and locate the root of her problems:

> *"It hit me. Like so many entrepreneurs I like starting new things more than I like running old things. I fall in love with my ideas, and I can't let them go. I came to the realization that constantly sending my organization in new directions was destabilizing the business."*

"In the beginning, nothing was stable. Everything was new. The top line goes up and you say, 'Woohoo! We can sell more, and more.' If you tried to build a business that was stable from the beginning you wouldn't get anywhere, because the magic and the willingness to do anything is what makes it work. But at a certain point you need to stabilize and build a machine that works, but many entrepreneurs don't want to do that. Because it's boring. It requires a bunch of skills we don't have. But what does that do to the people who are here in my care? It means that they never get great at what they're doing, because I'm constantly asking them to do something else, or add fifty new things to their task list. Or to figure out how to do something really, really hard instead of mastering what should be increasingly easy."

Flora began making lists of all the different business activities and ideas that occupied her and her team. Once they were all out she realized that they naturally fit into three distinct groups. In fact, many of them made more sense together in these groups than apart. One direction was centered around cultivating remarkable in-store experiences. Another focused on e-commerce and online activities. And a third was media-centric, involving books, radio and ultimately television. She showed these lists to her mentors and they all agreed: these were three very different directions, all of them interesting and viable given the platform she already had created.

Flora had to choose. She knew it. It would give her business the clarity, the *purpose*, that would allow her to resolve the tension she'd been struggling with. She studied each group carefully, feeling like she was being forced to choose between three children she loved. *Pick*, she told herself, *just pick*. It was a very uncomfortable place. With such rich choices it should have felt like the world was her oyster, but instead she felt as if she was being robbed.

She realized she had to anticipate. What would she be doing if she picked one purpose over another? If she went long on e-commerce, she'd be spending much of her time in warehouses, dwelling on logistics and search engine marketing campaigns. If she went down the media path, the inevitable outcome was that she'd be living a life like Martha Stewart's, running from photo shoot to editorial review on impossibly tight schedules. Framed this way, both outcomes sounded awful to her.

Finally, after talking with people who knew her best, Flora found peace with where her heart really lay—a one-page vision for her business's future, on the meaningful purpose that she could stick to. It was decided: she would put her remarkable store at the center of her business, because her purpose was to open people's eyes and hearts to the visceral beauty of botany. The store had already become a destination, and she knew that she'd just gotten started. There was so much more to do.

Of course, just because it's about the store doesn't mean Flora was closing off the possibility of new directions—she'll still host events at the space, and invest in things like the café, which enhance the appeal of the store as a destination. Most importantly, she would still embrace the creative wellspring of serendipity, just not if it diffused her energy, distracted her thoughts, or drove her employees to distraction. She still relies on surprise and accident to find new possibilities around her—after all, every gardener knows that even though we can prepare the soil for our gardens, we can plant seedlings, and we can design for color and maintainability, nature still always has a will of its own. What her newfound commitment instead gives her is a way to finally develop that all-important habit of saying "no" to the greater plentitude of possibilities that just aren't right for what she knows she is supposed to do.

For most of us, the issue isn't that our businesses are divorced from purpose. Our initial motivations are usually rooted in something deeper than pure profiteering—even taking a money-centric job in sales often involves an appreciation for developing relationships with people alongside the pure joy of the hunt. It's just that the structure of our business life and the creeping demands and expectations it insists upon systematically alienate us from the things that truly matter to us. It's entirely common to lose sight of our purpose, as Flora did as she experienced the first waves of big-time success. The question is whether we have the grit to find our way back to it.

Or as Flora would put it, "Pick. Just pick."

6

Skill: Activation
Church vs. Stadium

"I wouldn't have seen it if I hadn't believed it."
— MARSHALL McLUHAN

Imagine you're at the mall, riding an escalator up to the second floor. As you step off, a charity worker for a local organization approaches you. What do you do? Do you pull out your wallet and drop five bucks in her can? Or do you avert your eyes and walk on by? To decide what to do, you might carefully consider what other charitable giving you've done lately, how much money you have in your bank account, and whether you agree with the goals of the charity this person represents. Perhaps you have a policy to never give money without first consulting with your spouse. Whatever you choose to do, you'll do it based on a rational decision, right?

Wrong. Or at least not exactly right. In a set of studies completed in 2010, hundreds of people were tracked through four activities designed to pressure test a very bizarre finding: people are, on average, more than twice as likely to give money to a charity worker at the top of the escalator (16 percent) than when they rode an escalator to the bottom (7 percent). This was a big difference, and one that held up with similar experiments that added the unexpected variable of height to tests of generosity, including placing people on stages and showing them videos of flying in the clouds. The researchers saw the same results in every subsequent experiment: People are willing to give more money if they are exposed to some element of height.

It's remarkable. You're going about your day, moving from one place to another in full possession of your wits. Suddenly you're confronted with a decision that seems entirely in your hands—except you are nudged by an invisible force to be more generous. Your charitable side has been activated and you don't even realize it. What's going on?

Lawrence Sanna, the psychologist at the University of North Carolina at Chapel Hill who conducted this experiment, has a theory: when people gain altitude, their minds make subconscious associations with height. Metaphors like "moral high ground" and "higher purpose" are common turns of phrase, and as a result we associate "up" with "good." Going up, or even imagining ourselves moving upwards, appears to trigger our brains to view situations through this associative lens.

Sanna's theory jibes with what neuroscience says about how we make decisions. A well-tested phenomenon called "readiness potential," a measurable electrical change in the brain that precedes a conscious action and is believed to indicate that the brain has made the decision to act, has shown that our unconscious mind experiences events far more quickly than our conscious mind does. In 1977, the psychologist Benjamin Libet measured the difference between this "readiness potential" and the moment when his subjects *reported* they made their decision to act. The results sent shockwaves through the world of neuropsychology: subjects were making decisions a full half-second before they were aware that a decision had been made.

The "readiness potential" phenomenon suggests that by the time you get off the escalator and register that charity worker, your subconscious has already done a whole lot of work: it has noticed that she's asking for money, processed this fact, and decided whether to donate money or not. Only then does your conscious mind consciously weigh alternatives and make its final determination.

As a result, simple things like escalator rides, which don't necessarily seem like they would affect our decision-making capabilities, end up having noticeable effects on how we think, feel, and act. Our subconscious factors the positive mental associations caused by the elevator ride into our decision before our conscious brain has even begun to process the situation.

We operate under the assumption that reason alone is enough to ensure things run according to our best-laid (business) plans. In this light, the evidence that our subconscious has far more control than we realize should be sobering.

The role of the subconscious is just as central in planned serendipity. Countless cues in our environment strongly influence whether we are observant, open-minded, and adaptable rather than fearful in the face of change. Factors we downplay, like the quality of natural light, the dress code, and the presence of laughter, may in fact make all the difference.

Welcome to the skill of activation.

Activation by Design

Broadly speaking, activation means designing experiences that trigger openness, engagement, and creativity, prompting people to respond to the world differently than they ordinarily would have. It means knowing (or guessing) the right buttons to push in people to get their impulses firing in a desired direction. Activation is how we reset our social norms in order to make people conducive to adopting serendipity-friendly social interactions and states of mind—like the other skills we've discussed in the previous chapters: motion, preparation, divergence, and commitment.

Anybody who's visited an old church can see that activation has been practiced for hundreds if not thousands of years. Take a gothic cathedral: the entire building is designed to exert a visceral response from us, from the imposing entry which marks a transition from the worldly into the spiritual realm; to the resplendent nave facing an elevated pulpit that reinforces the protective relationship between the minister and his flock; to the stained glass windows that mark the clerestory above, a symbol of enlightenment from on high. It's not just the physical structure that invites a response from us, either—it's also the reverberant acoustics, the chill coming off the stone walls and floor, the somber half-light, and countless other experiential cues large and small. Everything about the space moves us to reverence and respect, and, depending on our background, the palpable sense of being in the presence of the sacred.

Like a cathedral, a professional sports stadium is designed to gather large numbers of people at one time for an event. Yet what different experiences these two structures elicit! Instead of solemnity, hushed voices, and a hyper-sensitivity to social graces, the stadium is a giant playpen. It not only allows rowdiness, it encourages it, with concessions barkers shouting ("Pizza! Peanuts! Beer!"), crowd-baiting songs ("We will, we will rock you!"), and information overload on screens at every sightline. The quiet reflection of a church is replaced by an in-your-face partisanship. And it's all by design.

No less than the architects of churches and stadiums, we can regularly craft experiences that shape the ways people behave, feel, engage, respond, decide, and express themselves. Too often, however, when it comes to our work environments we focus overwhelmingly on managing by objectives. We talk of hard work, discipline, and financial incentives. If we care about cultivating serendipity and the innovation that goes along with it, though, we also need to activate deeper instincts that make the skills of motion, preparation, divergence, and commitment feel like second nature.

One way to think about activation is as the ability to identify human blind spots and compensate for them through clever tricks—a kind of mind-hacking. Or we could say that it is knowing our strengths and finding ways to amplify them through design. Either way, employing activation means having a strong sense for the kinds of responses we hope to elicit from people, and a willingness to redesign everyday experiences to achieve these responses.

The human mind is prone to idiosyncrasies that can be activated to drive serendipity—almost too many idiosyncrasies to count, the "escalator effect" being just one. Some are mild in their influence, while others can make a huge impact on a person's behavior; a great many are subject to an individual's cultural associations or personal experiences. Some of these triggers are documented with empirical psychological research, like the "escalator effect." For example, did you know that physically leaning to the left makes things appear to be smaller? It's true! Some of them are more controversial, like the idea that certain colors of light prevent suicides (train stations in Scotland and Japan installed blue lights and reported that suicides dropped by as much as 9 percent, though no studies have confirmed this).

To create the mental and emotional conditions for serendipity to occur more frequently, we must be willing to exploit idiosyncrasies like these in ways that lead to more and better creative collisions, employing this mental trickery to help us better generate, notice, and respond to serendipitous occurrences. In this chapter, we're particularly interested in activating four distinct shifts in our experience that create opportune conditions for serendipity.

- *The ambient shift* creates environments that allow us to notice peripheral events.
- *The temporal shift* allows us to connect ideas that unfold out of sequence.
- *The social shift* frees us to be personally expressive in distinct ways around peers and strangers.
- *The emotional shift* allows us to be receptive to others' feelings and ideas.

Activation may seem like mere psychological manipulation, but it isn't any more manipulative than giving employees praise for a job well done or defining clear boundaries around project responsibilities with coworkers. What we're advocating is being more deliberate in how we craft our environments and routines to achieve luckier results. The skill of activation allows us to offset the rote organizational behaviors that conspire time and again to kill spontaneity and chance. Activating these four distinct shifts gives us the power to change our daily behaviors in ways that open our senses to serendipity.

The Ambient Shift

As we've learned, serendipity depends on being able to take notice of unusual occurrences—to "arrest the exceptions" when they happen, instead of letting them sail right by unnoticed. Our environments—the flow of physical movement, sight lines, acoustic dynamics, the appearance of light, aesthetics, ergonomics, and all the other components that make up our real-world experience—have a huge impact on what we are able to attune to. The ambient shift influences what and where we invest our attention.

A few years ago the *Washington Post* constructed an experiment that dramatically showed how reliant we are on our physical environment for cues to determine where we place our attention. It demonstrated how easy it is for us to miss the most remarkable occurrences even when they're literally right in front of us.

Oblivious

To commuters passing through the L'Enfant Plaza metro station in Washington, DC, one Friday in 2007, it seemed like just another typical weekday. Passengers fresh off the latest train from the suburbs whisked this way and that amidst the shoeshine stand and the magazine kiosk, government workers, parents taking kids to school, waiters at nearby restaurants, postal workers—everyone making their way from point A to point B along their routine path. Even those who may have been unfamiliar with that particular station, the tourists and visitors in town on business, knew the way that subway stations work: keep on moving, and whatever you do, don't hold up the person behind you.

Just before 8 A.M. on this particular day a tall, boyishly handsome figure pulled out a violin from a case. The man placed the violin under his neck, positioned his bow and began playing a Bach piece called Chaconne, one of the most difficult violin solos in any violinist's repertoire, and one of the most revered. The acoustics of the station picked up the notes and amplified them throughout the arcade. It wasn't just the music that was remarkable, however, for this was not just any violinist—this was Joshua Bell, ranked by many as the top classical musician in the world. Bell is an idol who fills the greatest music halls in the world, a figure whose image decorates posters on billboards, concert halls, and yes, subway walls. And Bell wasn't playing just any violin. He had in his hands a Stradivarius masterwork, a 300 year-old instrument considered one of the finest violins in the word, last sold for $3.5 million.

It was the kind of performance that was impossible to miss. And yet, almost everybody did.

For the 43 minutes Bell played in the station, the commuters methodically tuned him out as if he were just another cup-wielding vagrant. This was true for people of all ages and backgrounds. Of the 1,097 people who walked by during his ad hoc performance, a mere seven stopped for at least a minute to hear him play. Twenty-seven of them dropped money into his open violin case, a few giving only pennies, for a total of $32.17. Only one very lucky (i.e., observant) person recognized the celebrity; she was one of the few to stand and listen to the world renowned violin player perform entirely for free for more than just a brief moment.

The author of the *Washington Post* article on the experiment, Gene Weingarten, describes his experience of watching the scene unfold in a video recording of the experiment:

> *Try speeding [the recording] up, and it becomes one of those herky-jerky World War I–era silent newsreels. The people scurry by . . . . [But] the fiddler's movements remain fluid and graceful; he seems so apart from his audience . . . you find yourself thinking that he's not really there. A ghost.*

It's not really a mystery why these oblivious passengers ignored this famous violinist performing in a subway; most of us have been in the shoes of these commuters before. On our way into our workday, we don't have time for diversions, and anyway, if the musician is really so good why would he be playing in a subway? Our own biases hurry us by the performer—the forward momentum of our lives carrying us past the things that are unusual and toward the familiar, the routine, and the comfortable. The environment plays its part, as well: the entire physical space of the station is sensibly designed for flow, to keep us moving so that the people behind us can get through. As a side effect of this design, the station exerts a subtle social pressure to avoid stopping and paying attention to "street artists" or anything else out of the ordinary that might intervene on our commute.

We can compare the subway station to the concert hall and point out all the ways that the latter lavishes our attention on a famous performer in a way that the station does not. By activating the ambient shift, though, we can enliven our senses to stop and notice chance events in precisely those places where we don't expect them—like when we're passing by a virtuoso who happens to be performing in a subway station.

A Light at the End of the Tunnel

Joshua Bell's subway performance clearly demonstrates how our environments make it difficult to arrest the exceptions that lead to serendipity. At least one other subway system has attempted to address this problem. New York's Metropolitan Transit Authority takes a proactive approach to activating the ambient shift. Recognizing the high caliber of talent willing to perform in the city's subways, in 1985 its Arts for Transit office established a program called Music Under New York (MUNY). Since then, each year Arts for Transit auditions hundreds of performers, accepting around 10 percent of the most highly regarded acts. Today there are over 100 musicians that receive permits to perform across 25 locations throughout the subway network, divvied up on a schedule.

Many performers have benefited from this program, including musical saw artist Natalia Paruz, who also writes a blog covering the colorful subway music scene. She is joined underground by artists like the Colombian dancer Julio Cesar Diaz. He has no Stradivarius, just a life-sized doll, a dancing partner made from old plastic packaging, broomsticks, inner tubes from bicycles, and mattress foam he found in the street. But in contrast to Joshua Bell in the Washington, DC, station, Paruz, Diaz, and the other artists often attract significant crowds when they perform in the underground stations.

How? MUNY has activated the ambient shift: The activation—a largely subconscious signal—is physically embodied in a banner each performer hangs on the wall behind their performance areas, which, generally, are the choice spots in station mezzanines, right in the flow of foot traffic. The banner is a small thing, but it validates the performers—it tells the crowd, "Hey, I'm here legitimately"—with the effect of nudging the attention of passersby, making a second glance or a quick stop in the middle of a busy commute more likely.

"The banner gives musicians a back," Natalia says. "It makes them feel like they are supposed to be there, and it eases their initial anxiety of connecting with the audience. It also tells the audience that this musician has passed a rigorous audition, meaning that their musical level is high."

By granting the performers the spotlight in this way, MUNY affirms them as worthy of notice by commuters. Furthermore, the Transit Authority is actively casting the stations as performance venues, albeit secondary ones. The combination of these signals grants commuters the permission they subconsciously need in order to stop and give some attention to performers in an environment originally built for something else.

The life of the street performer is not an easy one. Most subway riders will continue to hurry through the station and miss the experience of hearing a talented artist on their way to wherever they are going. But MUNY creates an ambient shift in how New York subway riders perceive street performers. They make it harder for riders to treat the performers like ghosts, which means more people get a chance to hear the music.

As in the subway, the most innovative office design in the world won't foster serendipity if people are motivated to stay out of each other's way. Our desire to squeeze high performance from our teams by keeping them "on task" focuses their attention entirely on their work and intentionally invites a near total loss of peripheral awareness. Achievement cultures are so execution-oriented that they suppress the out-of-sequence or seemingly random occurrences that we are drawn to when we follow our own curiosity.

Many work environments have found ways to avoid this trap. On a recent visit to CNN headquarters in Atlanta we noticed the pervasiveness of newsfeeds throughout the building. Whether you are in a corridor or an open work room, the background stream of breaking news—the IV drip of *what's happening now*—is impossible to miss. It is designed to activate the peripheral awareness of the raw materials of newsmaking. (Though as effective as it may be for the typical CNN employee, it may also be a dangerous environment for sufferers of attention deficit disorder.)

Similarly, you can't miss how e-commerce juggernaut Zappos activates the ambient shift when you walk through its Las Vegas headquarters. Famous for its emphasis on "creating fun and a little weirdness," Zappos empowers every business group—from the various merchandising teams to the finance department to the numerous customer service teams—to form a literal "tribe." Each tribe is given a budget and internal support to decorate its workspaces and conference room in a way that promotes its area of focus. Every tribe develops its own colorful decorative theme for its section of the office (our favorite is the jungle safari), and a tribal gesture such as shaking party rattles or turning on flashing lights during a moment of celebration or to grab the attention of passers-by.

The explicit goal of this zany approach to team building is to foster a sense of collective belonging for employees within the larger Zappos culture, and to grant them a sense of participation and ownership over their environment and their role in promoting the Zappos experience. At a deeper level, the office's deviation from the usual drab cubicles changes the way that the staff experiences the environment. Their senses become alert to difference, to the colorful and out-of-place, encouraged by the entire company culture to stop and notice whatever catches their eye.

The value of activating the ambient shift in our organizations is to heighten others' attention to peripheral events—some of which may be the catalyst for serendipitous breakthroughs or get us to probe new paths. This activation prompts us to *notice* what we are otherwise conditioned to ignore.

The Temporal Shift

We not only need to activate our spaces for serendipity, we need to activate our time for it as well—to give ourselves the opportunity to make connections between events that don't happen in sequence. This might seem like a stretch in a work environment where every minute is already accounted for, but time, it turns out, is more malleable than we might expect.

Society has historically allowed for a more nuanced view of time than the one we now have. Even before the Ancient Greeks, people recognized that what we now consider the conventional notion of time—sequential, where events unfold one after the other in a linear fashion, the tick-tock time you can set your watch to—is only one of the ways in which time operates.

Furthermore, this perspective on the temporal actually lasted a lot longer than you might realize. It wasn't until factories and railroad timetables became ubiquitous in the nineteenth century that our sense of time became standardized and reliable the way we all take for granted today. The era of industrialization, with all the machine-like punctuality it required of workers, insisted that we sync up our watches with each other in a way that hadn't previously been the case. Suddenly, clocks across the country started to run on the same schedule. We're now so intimately tied to this view of time it can be hard to imagine anything else, but there was a time when it was something entirely new.

Ethnographer Edward Hall calls this *monochronic time*, the linear experience of time necessitated by railroads and factory life, and embraced as an organizing principle by modern economies. No time to lose! As we've all experienced, monochronic time leads inexorably to a rigorously scheduled life, where value is placed on completing tasks according to plan, and time is considered a precious resource. People worry about using it up and wasting it, like sands in the hourglass.

The counterpart to monochronic time is polychronic time, or P-time, a fluid, multitask-oriented approach that emphasizes flexibility over schedule. To a practitioner of monochronic time, P-time appears as a blatant disregard for sequence and punctuality, an excuse for not minding the clock. An American visitor to Jamaica attending a reggae concert advertised to begin at 8 P.M. is surprised to find that this isn't to be taken literally, that the show will "begin when it begins," and that the rest of the crowd accepts this as perfectly normal! The Jamaican audience lounges in front of the stage, happy to while away the hours in conversation and relaxation until the band is ready to start. In P-time, people don't do one thing at a time according to a schedule; they do many things at once. Tight scheduling is out of the question—the goal is looseness, agility, connection, the opportunity for multiple activities to overlap and influence each other in new and fluid ways.

We don't have to travel that far to encounter P-time, either. While in general, American and European societies have engineered themselves around monochronic time, operating "like clockwork," our culture also allows certain roles to observe polychronic time. Artists, for example, are often granted a degree of "flakiness" because, we rationalize, their creative temperament makes it difficult to mold them into mainstream expectations, including keeping a "normal" schedule or being punctual. "Mad scientists" are also left alone to tinker in their labs, and thus benefit from this long temporal leash.

In a side-by-side comparison of monochronic and polychronic time a few contrasts really jump out:

Monochronic Time

- Interpersonal relationships are de-emphasized for the sake of a rigid schedule.
- There is a sharp division between work and personal lives.
- One task is tackled at a time.

Polychronic Time

- Interpersonal relationships are prioritized, hence appointment times are flexible.
- There is little division between work and personal lives.
- Multiple tasks are tackled simultaneously.

Despite our overall adherence to monochronic time in the business world, polychronic time has its place too, particularly for entrepreneurs. Entrepreneurs know so little about their emerging business in the early stages that they are constantly juggling many tasks and relationships, with the effect of completely blurring their personal and professional lives. To an entrepreneur, a discrete task such as conducting a customer survey is indistinguishable from the larger company-building goal of releasing a new product; where one begins and the other ends is not always clear to them. It's no surprise that many entrepreneurs report being chronically late to meetings—in an entrepreneurial setting, the many tasks at hand often win out over the scheduled tasks ahead. An entrepreneur's well-developed skill of divergence, the desire and the ability to explore alternative paths, makes P-time a natural fit.

P-time is on the march in other parts of our lives, too. The rise of social media—and social business in general—applies pressure on all of us, not just entrepreneurs, to embrace P-time. Increasingly, people carry on a multitude of simultaneous conversations on social networks and mobile devices. The ubiquity of this always-on, real-time interaction is conditioning people to multitask, leading to a compulsive involvement in each others' lives, albeit virtually. What was once considered anti-social behavior—tapping out a message on a phone in the middle of a dinner party—is increasingly socially acceptable, and now that people can text each other if they're running late, many find themselves less concerned with strict punctuality.

From the standpoint of serendipity, the benefits of P-time are compelling. It offers those who embrace it time to think outside of the scheduled box and makes it socially acceptable to participate in many conversations at once. This affords both the possibility of exposure to more serendipitous activity as well as the room needed to act on it. As a more fluid approach, P-time moves people in and around each other in unpredictable ways. Freed from a rigid schedule, they can easily respond to unexpected events and let curiosity and chance be their guide.

Still, despite the benefits of P-time, activating this temporal shift is not easy. One of the things that the ethnographer Hall makes clear in his research is how difficult it is for the two approaches, monochronic and polychronic time, to work together. They seem mutually exclusive, and it's not hard to imagine how they create irreconcilable differences in work styles and bureaucracies. If we prize punctuality and schedules in our organizations, we can't very well collaborate with those who refuse to show up on time to meetings!

Of course, there's nothing wrong with schedules, deadlines, or monochronic time in general. They are essential ingredients of modern life and necessary to run a successful business. But these two approaches to time are increasingly colliding, given the significant changes to our culture and technology created by both the advent of social media and an explosion in entrepreneurialism. Figuring out how to make these two temporal modes play together nicely is becoming an ever more critical business (as well as serendipity) skill.

Fortunately, there are paths available to businesses that want to activate P-time right alongside its more rigid counterpart. Perhaps the best example of temporal activation has been a quiet revolution occurring in the world of software development over the past decade.

Historically, building software has been done according to a pre-defined specification, a fixed schedule, and a hard budget. The only thing reliable about this rigid process of software development is how unreliable the results are, particularly when it comes to the ship date of the software product. The problem is that programmers rarely know exactly how they are going to solve a problem until they actually start coding it. Planning a big software project—and establishing a schedule for its release—involves estimating, ahead of time, the effort and time it will take to solve the hundreds or thousands of problems expected to arise, most of which are unknown and unpredictable at the outset. So it's no surprise that this method leads to inaccurate ship dates: like most estimates made in ignorance, they turn out to be dead wrong.

In the 2000s, a revolutionary new approach to software development called agile programming changed the way that many companies build software—and it did so by embracing P-time. Here's the Agile Manifesto in its own words:

> *We are uncovering better ways of developing software by doing it and helping others do it. Through this work we have come to value:*
>
> - *Individuals and interactions over processes and tools*
> - *Working software over comprehensive documentation*
> - *Customer collaboration over contract negotiation*
> - *Responding to change over following a plan*
>
> *That is, while there is value in the items on the right, we value the items on the left more.*

Today, companies that have embraced agile programming, or simply "agile" as it's known in the world of programmers, include many of the largest and most successful firms in the world, from Google to Verizon Wireless. You might not expect this from such titans of business, but, when it comes to software projects at least, their sense of time has fundamentally shifted. By taking up agile, the programmers that work at these companies are essentially declaring independence from the fixed schedules that have failed them so many times before. Instead, they offer a rational alternative—one that focuses on constant communication ("here's what we're working on right now"), collaboration ("let's talk about what we really need now that we know more"), improvisation ("hey, that random idea could really work!"), and adaptability to changes great and small.

Agile provides a version of P-time that works well within monochronic environments. It works because it provides measurable improvements over the old, conventional model, and it does so with a set of simple practices that can flourish practically anywhere. Agile is a prime example of the way companies can change their process to activate the temporal shift.

Walk into a company that practices agile software development and you're likely to see something different than the usual dark room with banks of solitary programmers tapping away on their own keyboards. Instead, you'll see a hive of bustling activity, people in twos and threes in conversation with one another. Some are typing code, while others sit beside them, offering advice as they program. There's so much conversation taking place—it's noticeably *social.*

Rather than setting quarterly goals knowing exactly what tasks they'll tackle, in exactly which order, agile teams often meet weekly to discuss how they'll organize their time for that week, then tackle a list of "stories" that describe the upcoming problems they need to solve. Whenever possible, these problems are supplied by a non-engineer: a customer describes a need, a customer service agent reports a bug, or a product manager defines a new feature. The list of stories is organized in a particular order, but it's fluid; the team can reshuffle the list or add new stories to it as frequently as necessary based on the emerging needs of users, product managers, and so on. Programmers are constantly in touch with the people who made the request, showing them work-in-progress and exchanging feedback on it.

The truly amazing thing is that while agile vigorously rejects the assembly-line manner and rigid scheduling of traditional project management, it's actually far *more* reliable at shipping features: the team releases working code to the world regularly (e.g., weekly) no matter how small the functional changes that have been made—quite a contrast to the traditional approach, where a software project can take months or even years to see the light of day, if it even makes it out at all.

This unconventional programming approach often freaks out seasoned business types. "Why are these programmers talking all the time?" they ask. "Where's the commitment to hit a hard date?" After a short time with it, however, they realize that when working in agile, the ability to deliver within a specific time frame doesn't get lost. What *is* lost is the illusion that programmers know *exactly* what they'll deliver by that deadline. What is gained is a robust view into the development process that's actually far more valuable than having a ship date no one actually believes in. Agile is a relentlessly honest process.

Agile shows us that it's possible to activate a fluid approach to time that can work for just about any company, no matter how conventional its scheduling habits are. This software development method is relationship-centric, replacing heavy process with constant communication and trust, so it is better suited for uncertainty. By offering an alternative to linear processes, agile makes more room for serendipity. Agile process lets new knowledge and events flow in as necessary and connect on a regular and recurring basis in a way that a regimented, top-down approach never allows.

The temporal shift means we adapt agile's lessons to other parts of the business—to look for places where we can build process not around sequence, but around flow.

The Social Shift

We now turn to the organizational challenge of activating the social shift, which means making room for self-expression in environments that might otherwise dampen it. The *social shift* frees us to express ourselves within inter-personal relationships. On any given day, our social interactions—online, around the water cooler, on a train—can introduce us to unexpected ideas that just happen to perfectly relate to what we're working on (it certainly occurred constantly in the writing of this book). The more open we are with others about the ideas and experiences that move us—and the more others reciprocate—the more access we have to this rich source of serendipity.

Yet the full potential of the social shift is not always available to us. Sure, we talk a lot about being "social" these days, but our willingness to express ourselves in a way that others can hear varies greatly depending on the circumstances. We might be shy as mice in one environment and as gregarious as puppies in another. What pushes us in one direction or the other? Answering this question is the first step in designing experiences that encourage us to be more social in a wider range of situations.

One highly intuitive explanation is that we are profoundly influenced by the social norms telegraphed by the behavior of those around us. Václav Havel, the former President of the Czech Republic who presided over his country's transition from Soviet satellite to fledgling democracy, took power after decades of rule by controlling Communist bureaucrats. To communicate the positive change that his presidency represented, and to encourage those around him to free themselves from the mental prison of the previous decades, Havel took to roller skating around the palace from meeting to meeting. The sight of the president of the country enjoying himself in such a lighthearted, joyous manner demonstrated to the workers inside the palace as well as the country at large that they, too, had permission to open up and express feelings and attitudes they had previously repressed.

Similarly, the best example we've ever seen of a meeting that activated a social shift in its participants had the audacious title "The Most Interesting Meeting in the World." It was the brainchild of Keith Messick, Get Satisfaction's former Vice President of Marketing, who wanted to "shake up a roomful of attendees like a snow globe and watch the creative brilliance fall like snowflakes." He placed a red velvet rope in front of the door as a sign of exclusivity to the invite-only affair. The meeting started with a sing-a-long of the Backstreet Boys' "I Want It That Way." What followed was modeled on a high-paced pitch meeting, more like TV writers brainstorming than high-tech marketing planning. Keith brought sound effects—sad trombones, laugh tracks, and applause that he would trigger throughout the meeting—to emphasize others' contributions. The meeting was raucous fun, but more importantly, it silenced everyone's inner critics and got people to open up and share their ideas.

Technology can also play a significant role in getting us to shift socially. It opens up new channels for people to direct their self-expression. This was our main goal when we set out to create a new kind of online customer community with Get Satisfaction, one designed for everyone and anyone to express themselves. The steps we took, and the process we used, are a quick study in how to activate the social shift.

Customer communities have existed for many years, mostly by way of forums set up by a company or brand, or independently by users of its products. Many technology companies—Microsoft, Apple, Adobe—have had thriving communities since the dawn of the commercial Web in the mid-1990s. But it wasn't just technology companies who drew communities of customers; we also saw the rise of forums for autos (e.g., Volkswagen, Harley-Davidson), toys and games (e.g., Lego, Sony PlayStation), and virtually any product that attracted the hobbyist or hacker culture. Yet these early forums fell short in two major ways: they weren't attracting mainstream users and they didn't make sense to most of the business world. They were an anomaly suitable only for early adopters, hobbyists, and the brands they cared about.

It was easy to write forums like these off, because they seemed like a fringe activity. "Only forum-dwellers use forums," people would say. It was a self-reinforcing truth: forum users often developed an insular way of talking to each other that led to an elite attitude. This made newcomers to the forum or chance passers-by feel unwelcome, as if they were strangers at a party where everybody else has known each other for years.

"Search before you post!" they would scream in ALL CAPS at a fellow customer who'd dropped in to ask a question that, unbeknown to them, had already been answered. And this was when they were being nice! Or they would unleash an acronym-encoded profanity like "WTF? RTFM, noob!," which managed to be both insulting *and* incomprehensible to the innocent visitor.

Beyond being socially exclusive, old-school forums had other problems. They were (and still are) organized around arcane categories, which meant you needed to know exactly where other people would categorize a given message to find it—not exactly a simple task. Locating an answer through their built-in search function was equally difficult, as the search technology for forums tends to be crude. The design of the old-school forum rewarded the hardcore forum dweller and scared away the vast majority of casual customers.

At the same time, while forums had their flaws, their advantages were hard to ignore: They allowed people to help each other by publicly posting information that anybody else could stumble on whenever they liked. The information-rich forum conversations could be ideal material for serendipitous discovery—particularly those that Google was able to index and make searchable. There was a lot of value to work with there, so with Get Satisfaction we decided to see what we could do to improve upon it.

We started by studying the kinds of conversations that were taking place on these traditional forums. What did they say about people's basic needs? After combing through postings on dozens of communities—including forums for John Deere tractors, Mini Cooper cars, and a scrapbooking supply company—we discovered a handful of patterns that repeated themselves across every customer community that we looked at. First, we found that most people weren't interested in just shooting the breeze; they were looking for a specific outcome. The outcomes they were after ranged from answers to questions (many of which were impossible for the company itself to answer, since they related to particular uses of the product beyond what the business had intended), to resolutions to problems with the product, to feedback and suggestions for product improvements. Second, it became clear that these communities were born and sustained by people's desire to form relationships with brands and fellow customers. Even if they didn't get the exact outcome they were after, customers wanted to feel heard.

This was the secret to creating customer communities: help people reach outcomes and allow them to feel heard.

Our activation challenge followed from this. How could we get mainstream customers of everyday products and services to express themselves, and to reach out to others with questions about a product or to resolve a problem in a public, Web-based environment, when they had never done something like this before? The solution was to avoid re-creating the alienating experience that traditional forums delivered to all but the most dedicated forum-dweller without losing their serendipity-friendly qualities.

We weren't the only ones experimenting with this kind of activation. Twitter and Facebook were working on building their own all-purpose social networks at the same time, both of which were quickly adopted by brands that wanted more interaction with their customers. These three services got companies and their customers talking to each other on the Web in a new, more casual, more social way, but each approached the problem of how to draw people out and get them to express themselves quite differently.

Despite the top-level similarities between the three services, their distinct approaches elicit wildly different responses from people. Each service activates the social shift in a unique way, touching on idiosyncrasies in our personalities that drive us to express varying aspects of ourselves online.

- *Twitter.* Twitter's approach is defined by several distinct features. First, by limiting posts—or as they call them, tweets—to 140 characters, people are freed from having to write much at all, especially compared to the daunting task of writing a full-length blog post. A simple one-line thought is enough for a tweet. This takes all the social pressure away from having to come up with justification, evidence, or depth for whatever you post.

Regular users post more frequently on Twitter than on other social systems, often dozens of times per day. The impulsive nature of the service often makes it the best way to express immediacy, passing thoughts, or real-time updates from an event. The brevity it enforces also makes Twitter an ideal place to share interesting links or content, rather than e-mailing them, because the limit of 140 characters requires little or no additional explanation.

Twitter's users view it not only as a means of public expression but also as a way of communicating directly with anybody else on the system, including any brand on the network. People casually and frequently broadcast their opinions, secure in the knowledge that their intended audience will receive them. This makes Twitter a phenomenally open and accessible environment that collapses the distance between individuals and the people and companies that matter to them.

The combination of all these features activates an uninhibited, performative instinct in Twitter users, making Twitter an ideal tool for serendipitous discovery between large groups of people. It's easy to scan hundreds of tweets for something that catches your eye—something unexpectedly valuable that somebody just tossed out that inadvertently changes the course of your own work. What any given tweet lacks in depth, it makes up for by being easy to read at a glance, and further exploration on the subject is just a link or Google search away. Twitter is an unending stream of raw material for serendipity.

- *Facebook.* By contrast, Facebook requires every user to use their real identity; the company is known for summarily closing an account if they discover that a person isn't using her real name. The strong bonds that Facebook has been able to build between groups of people who've known each other their entire lives is a direct result of this commitment to enforcing real identity.

Facebook allows childhood friends to find each other and business colleagues to stay in touch. This desire to connect with old friends and new creates a motivation for individuals to add personal details to their Facebook profiles, sharing information about themselves like relationship status, job history, and college affiliation to make themselves easier to discover. "Friending" other people generally requires their explicit permission, which creates a much stronger and reciprocal set of relationships than is the norm on a service like Twitter.

The experience of using Facebook revolves around the news feed. This is a stream of content shared by the people that you have friended, but instead of an unedited feed of everything that others post, Facebook uses a complex algorithm to determine what content to show you. People generally post less often to Facebook, since they aren't limited to 140 characters length and it's considered bad form to dominate the news feed. But those items that do get posted are usually more personal in nature and result in more robust conversations, since more closely connected people end up reading and reacting to the same items.

Facebook does have some of the same lightweight, serendipitous benefits as Twitter, especially with the advent of their ticker feature, which is a scrolling feed of all your friends' activity down the side of the user interface. But at its core, Facebook activates intimacy, even among mere acquaintances, and this intimacy allows for a more interactive kind of serendipitous discovery, granting us the ability to see and make connections between the things and people that matter to us most. If the broadcast nature of Twitter provides more raw material for serendipity, the intimacy of Facebook allows us to mine for the gold.

- *Get Satisfaction.* When we started Get Satisfaction we knew that almost anybody was willing to send an e-mail to a company if they were motivated by curiosity or frustration about a product. Yet even though sending the e-mail was easy, getting a useful response—or sometimes even an acknowledgement—wasn't. So we set out to make posting to a public community feel as simple as sending an e-mail.

We did this by creating widgets that could be easily embedded into a company's "Contact Us" page, intercepting the traditional "send us an e-mail" request common on these pages with a newer, more public approach. Our widgets not only collected feedback and problems from customers but also displayed them right there on the page, showing at any given moment both the latest customer concerns as well as the most common ones—a far cry from the opaque e-mail queue that customer feedback had previously been condemned to.

By making the experience of posting a public message feel second-nature, we activated people's willingness to express and share a wider range of feedback and ideas on products and services than e-mail alone was able to. Knowing that other people as well as company employees were going to see and respond publicly changed the nature and the quality of the feedback customers shared.

On Get Satisfaction people don't friend or follow each other, but they do share a common goal of getting the most out of the products and services they've purchased. Customers come together when they have similar issues with a product, and often help each other or collaborate with company employees.

Every message that a customer posts to a company's Get Satisfaction site is associated with a desired activity—a question, problem, idea, or praise. Each of these is associated with a specific outcome—once a question is answered, a problem solved, or an idea implemented by the company it is publicly declared "completed." This focus on outcomes, as opposed to open-ended discussion as was the case on traditional customer forums, activates a collaborative attitude on the part of the people using the site. It makes not only a more positive experience for everybody involved, but also encourages other employees and even other customers to get involved in reaching a resolution. In fact, the best and most relevant answers are often those that come from other customers—makes sense when you think about it, since they're the ones who use the products the most!

People are often driven by emotion when they reach out about a product or service, and far from suppressing it, Get Satisfaction actively encourages this emotional response in a way that's positive and outcome-oriented instead of angry and undirected. We created what we call the "Satisfactometer"—a kind of emoticon widget that gives people the means to express their raw emotion in pictures and words. It lets customers blow off steam, add some levity, or express joy alongside their regular comment.

What we discovered after we implemented the Satisfactometer is that irrespective of the outcome of their post, using it made customers feel heard about how they *felt*. At the same time, it made customer feedback more likely to be seen and digested by a company. By adding this emotional component, something traditional customer service tools lack, we'd increased the serendipitous potential of the voice of the customer within the business.

Each of these three online social services enables communication between customers and companies, but by adopting specific design features like limiting posts to 140 characters (Twitter) or requiring every post to be categorized as a question, problem, idea, or praise (Get Satisfaction), each activates slightly different social triggers in their users. Creating the conditions for serendipity isn't just about opening up information flows and tearing down conventions—rather, the social shift happens when we design "just-right" limitations that free us to be more of ourselves.

The Emotional Shift

To foster the conditions for serendipity, we're called on not just to express ourselves but to become more receptive to each other's contributions. It's not enough to encounter a serendipitous occurrence; we must also be primed to receive and act on it. Fortunately, we can activate a collective ability to hear and respond to each other by making an emotional shift in our environment.

The basic mechanism for receptivity is the feedback loop: if one person is expressing, others need to be hearing and responding. Twitter, Facebook, and Get Satisfaction all bake feedback loops into the way they work in order to keep the flow of conversation moving along. Twitter allows people to support others by "following" their tweets; Facebook lets users click a "Like" button to show approval of each others' postings; Get Satisfaction provides a button for customers to indicate "I Have This Question, Too" in order to increase its visibility to the company and the rest of the community. Each of these services provides a way for its users to validate fellow users and make them *feel* good and confident by telling them *"Nice job—what you said had value."* It is this emotional response to feedback that completes the loop and motivates the participants to continue their participation instead of shutting down.

One increasingly popular method of activating receptivity in groups is improvisational theater. The core mantra of improv is *"yes, and ...."* In order for an improvised scene to work, the suggestions made by others in the moment must be accepted and built upon without fail, never rejected. No matter how bizarre or unrealistic the last person's statement was, all the other participants in a particular improv scene are tasked with finding a way to make it work inside the situation they're acting out. Every scene requires that participants practice receiving and extending others' ideas.

This basic rule—build on what others provide—constantly moves the scene forward, creating confidence in the participants and moving them together towards a positive conclusion. "Yes, and ..." is a simple structure that shifts the player's emotional response to what's happening around them—and could double as the mantra for serendipity, since it's about following chance without judgment.

One firm that has embraced this approach as a business practice is the design firm Forty Agency, which has made improv a key part of how it cultivates openness to new ideas in their work.

The company is a small development firm based out of Scottsdale, Arizona, that finds creative ways to bring brands to the Web. They've been around awhile, but when they hired David Cosand a few years ago, things changed fast. The company brought him on for his creative strategy skills, but they had no idea of his secret plan to turn them into an improv theater troupe. David explains how the idea germinated in his head:

> *"I saw my first improv show in high school, and was immediately drawn to the spontaneity and cleverness of it. I took some work-shops, and auditioned for a semi-professional group. The work I was doing focused more on relationships between the participants, with narrative that unfolds on the spot."*
>
> *"It changed my life. Something inside just clicked. It allowed me to understand meaning and my role in a group. Even after the practice it allowed me to be much more connected in my daily*

life, both in work and personal relationships. It allowed me to
communicate better, understand and listen better, and empathize
better, because in improv you always have to be listening for the
scene to go anywhere."

Within weeks of starting his new job at Forty, David realized that
this was a company that might be willing to explore improv as "part
of their fabric." He worked with them to establish the basics: listening
skills ("fully absorb what the others are saying"), acceptance ("embrace
the awkward"), and support ("you look good if you make others
look good").

David began gradually introducing improvisational exercises at the
beginning of each day, gathering the team in a circle. It's a habit
they've had ever since, and one that has impacted nearly every part
of their work, from daily collaboration to client interaction to creative
brainstorming. "Now, when we miss our morning improv warm-ups,
there's a grogginess that's hard to shake the entire day," his colleague,
Amy, explains.

The exercises they use—almost thirty of them now—range from
simple physical interplay to the full-fledged dramatic improvisation
that many of us think of when we hear the term "improv." More than
anything the notion of "Yes, and ..." provides a way to reinforce the
need to be receptive. It made the team aware of how sensitive they were
to feedback from others—recognizing that when they felt secure that
their input would be accepted, they were more willing to roll with the
twists and turns of daily business life. Improv helped them see that as
soon as insecurity set in, they became resistant to change, unable to
branch in new directions. David explained:

"Sometimes we wrestle with pushing back with our client, if we
think we have the answer and they're not hearing it. When they
tell us which creative direction they think we should be heading,
we need to acknowledge that the client is part of this scene.

When we look at it through an improv lens, we can't just say the client is wrong, we're going to go do our own thing. To be a good 'performer' in this scene we have to support them, even if it's not the brilliant idea we had in our mind. 'Supporting' in this case means allowing ourselves to move in an unexpected direction. It's being willing to let go of our brilliant ideas and trust that the group together, including the client, is going to find the right solution. We are merely players."

When it all comes together, "Yes, and ..." leads to something known as "group mind," the holy grail of improv. Group mind is when all pieces of a team are working together in perfect harmony, listening, knowing when it's their turn to contribute, back off, or shake things up.

"You know when you have group mind and when you don't," David says. "It's the same for many other art forms. You can sense when you're firing on all cylinders and everybody's working together. Improv helps us practice pursuing that."

Whether or not we're prepared to adopt improv theater into our own business, we can see how simple exercises like these can condition us to be more receptive to each other, and how they can activate our sensitivities to others' basic need to feel supported. We can think of them as kick-starting productive feedback loops, and once started, they have the tendency to perpetuate themselves. Starting is often the hardest part.

Embracing Our Limitations

Professors Rob Austin and Lee Devin have spent years investigating how artistic practices can be an effective model for product development. Austin, a business professor at Harvard University, and Devin, a professor of theater at Swarthmore College, are an odd couple by any definition. Yet their book *Artful Making: What Managers Need to Know About How Artists Work*, makes their collaboration seem inevitable. Austin and Devin have studied the practices of artists in numerous fields—theater, painting, dance, sculpture—to see how they produce work of such quality in conditions that often seem chaotic to traditional business people.

What they found is that successful artists incorporate chance as a key ingredient in their creative and production process. "If what you're making is something new, something never seen before, your process must be an improvisation," they write. At the same time it is the structures placed around artistic creation—the constraints of stage, of an audience's attention, of a rehearsal schedule, of canvas, of the properties of clay—that activate the artist's full potential. Austin and Devin point out that while a theater company starts the rehearsal process without a sure idea of how they'll stage the production, the overarching framework provided by the schedule makes certain that they'll launch the show on opening night with something (usually) quite entertaining. An artist's openness to the unknown—to serendipity—is made productive by the *designed limitations* of the environments in which they work.

In each of the shifts we've discussed—ambient, temporal, social, and emotional—we've seen how we can use new constraints to activate more serendipity-friendly impulses: the curation of a New York street performer program, the release of working code every week, the 140 characters of a Twitter message, or improv's "yes, and . . ." mantra. This isn't to say that all constraints are helpful, but if we do the work to determine the *right* constraints, we can unlock the potential for entirely new ways of seeing and acting. Constraints allow us to see what we couldn't see, do what we couldn't do, and feel what we couldn't feel before—exactly the kinds of behaviors and responses we need to get lucky.

7

Skill: Connection
Needle in a Haystack

"I am a part of all that I have met."
— ALFRED TENNYSON

How hard is it *really* to find a needle in a haystack?

One way to find out is to sort the hay one piece of straw at a time, examining it for the glint of metal. We may get lucky and find the needle early on in our sorting process, or, just as likely, it may be among the final pieces we examine. Whether we find it first thing, dead last, or somewhere between these two is entirely random. We just can't know which it will be. What we can do, however, is calculate the difference between the shortest and the longest period of time it could take to complete our task. If it requires a half second per piece of straw and there are 5 million pieces in the entire haystack, it will take us between a half second and 28.9 days, assuming we don't stop for meals, bathroom breaks, or naps along the way. Quite a commitment, and not exactly the kind we like.

Okay, but that's a terrible way of going about it, you're thinking. We have machines now—we should be able to automate the process! The popular show *Mythbusters* took this very approach in an episode that aired in 2004. The hosts, Adam Savage and Jamie Hyneman, set out to see if it's still really that hard to find needles in haystacks once we apply modern engineering know-how. They each formed a team and then competed to see who could find the needles first. Each team created a machine with a different ingenious method of sorting through ten bales of hay to find four needles hidden among them. To make things more challenging, the needles were not all the same: three were varying sizes of steel, and one was made of bone (sneaky!).

Savage's machine was the Needlefinder 2000, designed to rapidly push masses of hay through a water filter. Savage's team's theory was that the needles would sink while the hay would float. Hyneman and his team took a different approach. Their machine was called the Earth, Wind and Fire, and it was designed to burn all the hay, leaving only ash and needles behind.

The contest proceeded with both groups moving at top speed to process their hay through their machines. After a vigorous effort—a full day of pumping hay through water and fire, which makes for surprisingly good TV—Savage's Needlefinder found the fourth needle and won the competition. But just barely. Both machines were far more efficient than the manual process of separating hay from needles—one day instead of almost a month—but a day of effort is still a pretty long time. Their conclusion? The adage about finding a needle in a haystack still holds true: we might be able to do it, but it takes a gargantuan effort.

Needle-in-haystack problems are common in our personal and professional lives. They surface whenever we need something—a business partner, a solution to an arcane computer problem, a memorable anecdote for a book we're writing—but we're not sure how to find it. What we're looking for could be just about anywhere in our complex, information-saturated world. And if we have to search for it one piece of hay at a time, even if we mechanize the process like the *Mythbusters* guys, then we're in for a long wait. As they showed us, that process is exhausting, resource draining, and waste generating. We know the needle (or idea, or introduction, or explanation) we want is in there somewhere, but the energy and time required to find it may make it not worth the effort in the first place.

The Network to the Rescue

Luckily, there's a better way to find what we're looking for. The network age presents us with limitless opportunities to connect with the world at large in serendipitous ways. A good thing, too, because when it comes to solving needle-in-haystack problems, isolation is the enemy. Consequently, optimizing the quality of our connections with other people and organizations is one of the most important skills of planned serendipity.

This skill has been essential since the dawn of human history. Over thousands of years we've created innumerable ways to connect with each other: through our local communities, professional associations, churches, political parties, school groups, charity organizations. Consistently increasing our connections to each other—from small tribes, to fiefdoms, kingdoms, nations, and international organizations—has made advanced civilization possible. Connecting to others is what we *do* as a social species. It's how we create shared meaning.

The Internet is only the latest, though perhaps greatest, mechanism humanity has developed to increase the quantity of connections available to us. There's no shortage of social networks or instant messaging tools we can use to link us with somebody else. Sometimes it feels like a new tool to do just this emerges every couple of weeks! At any time of day or night, from anywhere we happen to be, we can reach out to friends, relatives, or people who share our passions and interests to discuss serious matters or just bounce off them whatever loose thought happens to be floating around in our heads.

In fact, we have so many opportunities to connect with others that there are those who say we've actually become *too* connected. Well-known pundits and authors have voiced the fear that the Internet is making us shallower and less likely to make time for personal reflection or consume long-form content (i.e., "serious work"). According to them, we would do better to develop the skill of *dis*connecting. Technology journalist William Powers, for example, believes that we just need to unplug regularly to reclaim time for ourselves. He argues for a "disconnectopia," a weekend respite from online connectedness. No doubt this seems like a reasonable suggestion, but one that is ultimately beside the point. If history is any guide, feeling overwhelmed by the higher rate of connectedness in our lives is just evidence of transitional growing pains that will pass with time.

So if we live in a world of ever-increasing connectivity—and most of us are affected by it on a day-by-day, even minute-by-minute basis—doesn't that mean we're already pretty good at the skill of connection?

Not exactly. Our network- and networking-obsessed world has placed huge emphasis on the *number* of people we're connected to, but the skill of connection isn't about trying to gain as many friends or followers on whatever system we're currently using will allow. The skill is more challenging, more personal, and ultimately much more valuable. It's about allowing ourselves to actively engage with each other in ways that broaden each other's reach—like linking arms. Connection means being accessible to those we don't yet know and willing to reach out to others on their behalf, always in the meaningful context of the networks we're operating within. With connection, we never know who will reach out to us with a serendipitous idea or overture, but it always makes retrospective sense when they do.

4.74 Degrees of Separation

People with a passing knowledge of network theory tend to talk about the six degrees of separation—six being the average number of people separating any two people on the planet. But as of November 2011 there's a new number: 4.74. Facebook and researchers at the University of Milan working together crunched the data and found that the number of connections required to get from any one person to any other is shrinking as social networks increase in global popularity.

Whether or not we take this particular number seriously, the idea of radical connectedness has become a permanent fixture in our popular imagination. Thanks to professional networking sites like LinkedIn, which actually shows us how many connections away we are from the people outside our own network, we have even begun to think of traversing these connections as if they were literal paths.

Many of the relationships in this 4.74 degrees of separation are what social scientists call "weak ties"—those arms-length acquaintanceships that proliferate every time we go to a networking event. Contrary to popular belief, however, these are far from unimportant. They are often the critical connection points to people or groups we have no direct association with, but which often lead to the serendipity we seek.

Weak ties are key to extending the quantity of our connections by providing the all-important bridge to other communities of interest or social groups. But even more important for our purposes, they're also likely to increase the quality of our connections, because they can guide us straight to the people and ideas that are most relevant to what we're working on.

Even for a reclusive landscape photographer in a rural, upstate New York.

For the past thirty years Robert J. Henry has been exploring the wilderness around Lake Ontario, "the most eastern of the Great Lakes," capturing the great vistas and hidden beauties with his camera. His love of nature photography has intersected with an obsessive curiosity about every detail of this landscape. "I always look for something I don't understand," he says. Henry is definitely a nature geek.

Many years ago, he had noticed something unusual along the lakeside beach in early Spring: when the afternoon sun would hit the ground after a freeze, the clay-sand earth would start oozing. "It would flow off the bank like the tape from an old cash register," he explained. It was just the kind of mystery he liked. After considering it for a while he determined this was probably how the Iroquois collected clay back when they inhabited these lands.

One day in late March 2008, with the ground still covered in three feet of frost, Henry stumbled on something that would capture his imagination. Searching for migratory birds to photograph, he found his way to an isolated marshland.

"I started by photographing the landscape with a wide angle, then I stopped and said, wait, what have I missed? I stood there, took a couple breaths, looked down at my feet, and did a 360. I'm frequently surprised that it is the things I've inadvertently walked on or near that will be my best image."

This was one of those times. Growing out of the side of a bank was the strangest thing—an elaborate, petaled flower made entirely of the clay-sand, formed by natural processes. Imagine one of those ornate flowers made of icing on a wedding cake and you'll have some idea. It was marvelous and eye-catching, easily making for the best photos of the day. A name for the phenomenon flashed into his head: "a sand flower."

When he got home, Henry didn't know what he had for sure. He realized it was unique. Perhaps he was the first person to ever see this phenomenon along the Great Lakes—he had certainly never seen it in thirty years of looking. "Most people (if they noticed it at all) would pause for a moment and go on, never thinking of it again," explained his wife, Jacquie, on her blog. "Not my hubby."

Henry had a partial sense for the physical process that was creating the sand flower, because he had seen the clay-sand ooze many times before, but he wasn't sure what was causing the flower shape to form. It seemed that water in the earth was pushing sand out the side of the bank, as if the earth itself was reaching forward; as the mud descended it would form a petal shape, and then it would freeze at night. The next day the process would repeat itself. Over the period of five or six days the layered petals of sand formed. But why this sand, and why this place?

Henry had arrested an exception, but he lacked the geology background to make sense of it. There was only one thing someone with his obsessive curiosity could do: he had to find people who could explain to him what was going on.

Henry e-mailed the University of Buffalo geology department—a nearby university and one with which he was familiar—with a description of the phenomenon and detailed information including topography, weather, and the angle of the sun. A professor in the geology department immediately responded to this detailed and intriguing query, and they began a back-and-forth correspondence, during which Henry sent the professor his beautiful photographs.

The professor's curiosity had been piqued. He explained to Henry, "This is an absolutely fascinating find. I've never seen anything like it, but I know just the man who can tell us what it is." The professor reached out to a geologist specializing in volcanic flows, who had years of experience in the field, pulling him into the conversation.

After some careful study the geologist determined that it was a rare and unusual result of freezing and thawing of the earth's surface; the geologic force at work was a movement of volcanic debris called a pyroclastic sediment gravity flow. Together, the three of them had solved the mystery. The pyroclastic flows were causing the earth to shift and develop into different shapes. But no one had ever seen forms quite like this before, a product of the unique topology and environment where Henry had discovered the sand flower.

Henry had indeed stumbled on a remarkable phenomenon, but it was only thanks to a small but ideal set of surprisingly accessible connections that his finding was made useful. It wasn't a special connection that led Henry to finally solve the mystery of the sand flower, but rather it was a "weak tie"—a cursory familiarity with the local university.

Henry gave permission for the professor and the geologist to use the photo for research and teaching, and provided location information for the university to follow up on the discovery. He included the revelation of the sand flower as a caption for his photograph, which he has sold, along with other work, at local galleries. His wife, Jacquie, also benefitted by blogging the experience, which incidentally, is how we discovered the story. The value of the connections accrued not just to Henry but to every participant, and reverberates still, beyond just the original set of players, creating an ongoing cascade of serendipitous possibility.

Working on a Chain Gang

What makes Henry's story so interesting is that it challenges our assumptions about what makes for good connections. Henry lives in a remote rural village in upstate New York. He is a nature photographer who doesn't spend his time at networking events, or use either Facebook or Twitter. We wouldn't expect him to be able to access a world of connections at the drop of a hat, particularly in a field so far away from his own. Yet none of that mattered.

One thing that did matter was the Internet. "Yes, this *could* have happened prior to the Internet," his wife Jacquie explained, "but this kind of serendipity was just not as likely pre-Internet. Scholars were more isolated. People were more isolated. The Internet has opened the world for both the scholar and the passionate amateur. This free exchange of information helps everyone."

In network terms, we can think of each of these people—the photographer, the professor, and the geologist—as a node. We might at first picture them as three individual spots, linked by lines indicating their connection. Yet this simple image is incorrect; it ignores the massive web of connections all around that they're collectively a part of. A more accurate image would be a dense galaxy of spots surrounded by a thick mesh of lines connecting them every which way, some in clusters and others floating between clusters, some with many connections and others with few.

Looked at like this, the specific outcome of Henry's outreach was incredibly improbable. Henry had no relationship to the two academics that would prove critical to understanding the phenomena when he started reaching out; he had to first find and forge a connection to the professor, who could only then link him to the geologist. For Henry to have found the right geologist on his own would have been like searching for a needle in a haystack. In the universe of all possible geologists, it took the professor's special knowledge to know exactly which one had the kind of expertise to allow him to grasp this particular phenomenon. Henry was able to leverage that first, single connection into the ultimate needle-finding machine.

But this needle-finding machine wouldn't have worked without what we call a "serendipity chain": the initiator, the router, and the receiver. Each link in the chain serves an essential role in radiating serendipity across a network; none could do it without the others. Part of developing the skill of connection is learning how we can inhabit each of these three roles at different times.

The Initiator

Our photographer is the initiator in this story, having stumbled on something he wasn't looking for, and then taking action to solve his mystery. The initiator gets things in motion on our serendipity chain. Henry exhibited many of the skills of planned serendipity (particularly motion and preparation), which directly led to his irrepressible need to share his discovery with others. By reaching out to the professor who might be able to help him, he triggered an unpredictable but highly valuable cascade of connections. It was impossible to know where the connections would lead once he started the process, but the important part is that he started. Serendipity, as always, favors the motivated and the curious.

Initiators are driven by their own interests or the pressing need to solve a particular problem. To do so, they reach out to existing connections or forge new ones, as Henry did, with the goal of finding the exact right person or information they need, even if they don't know where that information will come from or what form it will take. We are all initiators at one time or another.

Henry's chain begins with his moment of serendipity, finding something he wasn't seeking: the sand flower. Like Spence Silver, the 3M scientist who had discovered a remarkable adhesive and then gave lectures for the next several years in pursuit of a connection, the next step in Henry's chain was to connect his discovery with people on the outside who could make sense of it. In the process of reaching outward, Henry was becoming the medium of serendipity for others.

Notably, Henry didn't need a large personal network to find his answer. Though being connected to a lot of people might have sped up the process of finding the right geologist to solve the mystery of the sand flower a bit, being highly connected isn't necessary to be part of a serendipity chain. In this chain, Henry benefitted from targeting a single professor at a university near him, in the department related to his query.

Henry had just enough information and knowledge to know how to connect. He only needed the willingness to get started.

The Router

The professor in our story serves a critical role—to receive Henry's inquiry, decide whether to take action, and then make the critical connection to the one person who is best equipped to help him. This is what routers do; they connect initiators and receivers. They are the glue that holds the serendipity chain together.

It's important to note that the professor in this case is a specialist himself, not a generalist. He wasn't forced to comb through a vast number of relationships in order to make the critical introduction. Instead, he was personally acquainted with many of the top geologists in the country, as well as everyone in the science department at his university. The likelihood of the professor knowing a good match was quite high. Also, he was accessible to Henry. Precisely because of his narrow specialty and limited influence, he was open to being approached and was appropriately thoughtful when he received the request. He was the right person to act as the router because he had a limited but critical amount of knowledge to share.

Yet he was no more connected than any other average professor of his field and tenure. In his book, *The Tipping Point*, Malcolm Gladwell introduced the idea of the "connector" to millions of readers. Connectors are "the kinds of people who know everyone." According to Gladwell they have a gift for developing trusted acquaintanceships across a wide variety of social and professional spheres, and ultimately have a massive influence on the spread of ideas and trends. Gladwell's conclusion is that some people matter more than others, at least when it comes to influence.

In the years since the book's release the idea of the connector has become widely embraced, and nowhere more so than in the field of marketing, where campaigns that target these connectors as "influentials" are one of the fastest growing areas of promotion and advertising. We might be tempted to say that "influentials" are better at the skill of connection.

As intuitive as the idea seems, however, newer research by social scientists like Duncan Watts suggest that this is the wrong conclusion. Working as the principal research scientist at Yahoo! Research, Watts develops computer simulations and real-world tests that show that these influential connectors do not wield the power we think they do. In test after test, he found that people of average connectedness are more likely to kick start the spread of a new idea or trend than people who are super-connected. The reason is simple and straightforward: "If society is ready to embrace a trend, almost anyone can start one—and if it isn't, then almost no one can," Duncan says. There are many more people on the planet than even the most adept of connectors can be connected to. Consequently, it's more or less random who gets to start any given trend. Watts calls the people who do "accidental influentials."

Watts's research suggests that a good router in our serendipity chain is not necessarily the most connected person. In fact, a large number of connections can actually be a disadvantage if it comes at the cost of depth. Routers may be more effective at making introductions when they have more intimate contacts. This intimacy makes the likelihood much higher that receivers—the next link in the serendipity chain—will respond to the introduction. The professor, for example, was able to get the geologist to pay attention to Henry's query precisely because the geologist knew the professor well enough to know that any query coming from him was worth paying attention to.

The Receiver

Getting to a geologist who could answer his question was, of course, Henry's ultimate goal. The serendipity chain is only complete when the receiver is reached. Of course, neither Henry nor the geologist knew, until the connection was made and the problem solved, that this match was the correct one—it was but one more piece of hay until it revealed itself to be a needle.

To the receiver this is a relatively passive—indeed, seren-dipitous!—experience: The opportunity comes to him from a trusted source (the professor), and is already vetted as relevant to his specialty. He just needs to accept or reject the challenge, or alternatively, pass it on to someone else—in which case he becomes another router in the serendipity chain.

The professor had effectively used a "rifle-shot" approach to identify the most likely receiver, since he knew exactly which geologist to ask. But there's another way, the "shotgun" or "scattershot" approach: the professor, as router, could have reached out to a professional network of expert geologists, perhaps on a mailing list, blog, or professional network, described the problem, and let the geologists raise their hands to self-identify as being the right fit.

If the professor had identified a receiver via any of these other approaches, serendipity was just as likely to benefit that receiver as it benefited the geologist in our story. For example, one or more of the geologists in this broad network may have found the sand flower to be the missing link in their research. For others, exposure to the sand flower might have sparked a new interest in the phenomenon, leading them in fruitful new directions.

Then again, the professor's query about the sand flower might have been completely overlooked by the busy geologists in the broad network, since the query wasn't directed at any one of them in particular. The query could have been lost in the clutter of an overflowing e-mail inbox or a busy day. Both the rifle-shot and shotgun approaches are essential connection techniques; the most effective approach is often to use both of them in parallel.

All three of these roles experience serendipity from a different perspective. They each had a chance encounter, and each responded with their own creativity to move the query along the chain. But each role joins the story at different times and in different ways. Henry (the initiator) made an unsought discovery of a sand flower, and developed the connections to take it forward. The professor (the router) was presented with an unexpected mystery and happened to know the perfect expert to solve it. The geologist (the receiver) was exposed to a surprise geological phenomenon that may eventually lead to a breakthrough insight in his field. Yet there was nothing fixed about the roles these individuals were playing in the chain—in a different situation Henry might be the receiver, presented with an unusual finding about the Lake Ontario terrain brought to him by the geologist, now playing the router for another scientist. The skill of connection means being ready to take on each role in the serendipity chain when the opportunity presents itself.

And while each of these roles in the chain gets individual value from the connection, what really stands out is how their combined capability is so transformed. They can do together what they could never do apart: tracking and capturing natural beauty through photography, organizing knowledge, and practicing science.

The Department of Good Ideas

The serendipity chain is a naturally occurring phenomenon, especially when driven by passionate individuals like nature photographers. Small businesses find it easy to exercise the skill, revolving as they do around fewer people, all of whom are strongly motivated to discover ways to make the business work. As our organizations get bigger, though, our environments tend to get more insular and less accessible. It becomes palpably harder to foster strong serendipity chains. The good news is that the bureaucratic process of the big company—along with resources and manpower—which so often work against serendipity, can actually be used to strengthen and interconnect these roles inside and outside the organization.

Planned serendipity chains unlock value that might currently be lying dormant within our organization, by connecting the best ideas and discoveries inside our business with people, either internally or externally, who will know exactly what to do with them.

Organizations can practice the skill of connection by modifying their work environments to improve the likelihood and frequency of these chains developing. They may even task individuals with playing roles along the chain, ferreting out and disseminating information to other environments in an attempt to improve the likelihood of making a serendipitous connection. This is an approach that's particularly well suited to larger organizations, as they have the resources available to create roles and build tools that facilitate exactly this kind of planned serendipity.

In fact, one of the most successful generators of serendipity chains that we've encountered happens to be a huge scientific organization, currently running one of the largest physics research projects in the world headquartered in Geneva, Switzerland. The international project is known as the Large Hadron Collider (LHC), a 26 km underground particle accelerator designed to push the very edges of human knowledge about the nature of matter. This project aims to uncover what's often referred to as the "God particle," the as-yet undiscovered Higgs boson particle that physicists have long hoped to find. This would be a critical finding in the field of physics, because quantum theory as it exists today—the result of billions of dollars of research across dozens of countries—assumes that this particle exists. If the scientists at LHC can't find it, they'll have to throw out much of what they think they know.

LHC is the latest project by CERN, the European Organization for Nuclear Research, the professional home to many of the most brilliant physicists and engineers in the world. The almost 10,000 CERN-affiliated scientists, located all over the planet, produce an extraordinary number of innovations and good ideas in a range of fields. Particle physics research pushes against the absolute edge of current scientific knowledge, and in building a machine as complex as the Large Hadron Collider, CERN requires breakthrough inventions and discoveries in virtually every technological domain—from materials science to computation to optics to biology.

Many of these innovations also turn out to be well suited for commercial use. The problem is nobody knows which ones—least of all the scientists themselves. There are many reasons, but they all come down to a basic fact: CERN scientists pursue their own narrow research goals and personal curiosity, usually without a thought for commercial needs. As Jean-Marie Le Goff, head of CERN's Technology Transfer Office, explains: "We don't develop products, we develop technologies and some of these are just too advanced, too costly, and too far removed from daily life for there to be market interest. So, it is a question of timing."

Nowhere is this clearer than in the most well-known case of an invention from CERN breaking into the mainstream—the World Wide Web. From the standpoint of bureaucrats overseeing CERN, the emergence of the global computer network was serendipity pure and simple, completely unexpected, and its eventual dominance in mass media even more surprising.

CERN's Technology Transfer Office (TTO) was established in 2000 to ensure that no good ideas—like those that led to the Web—go to waste, and to "promote, support and maximize knowledge and technology transfer from CERN to society." The TTO's job is to systematically create connections between its hundreds of labs and the outside world. It has been enormously successful in doing so, with many projects coming to market as public-private partnerships: Agile software (as discussed in the previous chapter), solar thermal collectors, Medipix for advanced material research, medical imagery, and solar panel plants, just to name a few.

TTO is by no means unique. It has become increasingly common for large public R&D organizations to formalize the dissemination of new technologies to be re-used in other public arenas as well as the private sector. Doing this effectively may be the price of political viability of mega-projects like the Large Hadron Collider. They have to either get good at planned serendipity or risk losing their funding. As a 2005 report for the British National Space Centre explained:

Knowledge Transfer opportunities abound, but ... rarely is the matching of the donor and recipient a smooth process and serendipity is often a major factor in successful cases. Therefore, the major challenge for Knowledge Transfer organizations is to improve the chances of serendipity by providing appropriate support structures and resources. *[emphasis ours]*

CERN's TTO demonstrates how the skill of connection can become an organizational practice, and a profitable one. TTO delivers financial multipliers of 3x or more to private industry for every dollar invested in the initiative. This is achieved by putting formal process and structure around the three roles of the serendipity chain—the initiator, the router, and the receiver. Individuals on their own may find themselves playing any one of the roles depending on their circumstances, but at the level of the organization these roles are likely to be fixed as functional units. When done well, these fixed roles provide connection on tap to everyone in the company. It's planned serendipity at scale. The model that CERN has developed with the TTO provides useful insight into how we can achieve similar results with our own businesses.

Here's what the organizational version of these roles looks like:

- **Scientists = Initiators:** The scientists, working under the umbrella of CERN's overall research goals, are the drivers of new ideas and technologies. They are where serendipity chains begin inside the organization.

Often, they're responding to a stated need from another group. For instance, in the mid 1990s the collider project needed advanced detectors to track and visualize the paths of the otherwise invisible Higgs boson particles in a way that was completely noise-free. An electronics team set to work on the problem. In assembling the new chip, it struck one of the researchers, Michael Campbell, that this detector could also be put to good use in medical imaging. Medicine may seem a world apart from particle physics, but in fact many CERN breakthroughs have made their way into medical innovations over the years, from PET scans to cancer therapy. However, recognizing the potential was only the first step: Campbell had neither the background in medical imaging nor the ability to commercialize a product.

Luckily, he didn't need this background. He was able to link up with like-minded scientists within the organization to develop the idea for a new medical imaging technology. This was the first step in forming one of CERN's greatest technology transfer successes, Medipix. Today CERN provides an internal network, INET, that reinforces this kind of sharing between its researchers. Representatives inside each lab are tasked with tracking and communicating new developments that percolate out of their groups. By anointing people to broadcast the expected and unexpected advances their groups have made, CERN has formalized the initial conditions for serendipity to ripple across the organization and out into the world.

- **TTO = Routers:** The overriding purpose of the Technology Transfer Office is to connect the innovations of the scientists, our initiators, with the various organizations who can further develop those innovations (the receivers, as we'll show next). They are routers.

TTO has a double-sided problem. On the one hand, they have to plumb the ideas of inventors for viable, licensable technology, supporting breakthroughs like the Medipix chip, making sure that the intellectual property is appropriately protected by licenses and patents before sending it out into the world. In other words, they have to build a network of initiators. On the other hand, they have to build relationships with the outside world to find the enterprises—receivers—that have a ready use for this bounty of ideas and inventions.

TTO relies on their networks of initiators and receivers. But they recognize that a centralized router function in an organization as large as CERN is likely to lead to many missed opportunities. So besides building their own internal and external networks, they invest heavily in a range of knowledge exchange networks that allow people inside CERN to connect with knowledge exchange groups at other businesses and research organizations. Their approach as a router is, essentially, to get the right ideas and information from the initiators to the receivers by any means necessary, wielding any technology that does the trick.

On top of these networks, TTO takes both rifle and shotgun approaches to connecting initiators and receivers. Through their many contractor and co-development relationships they often have a good idea when there's a fit between an outside company—a receiver—and a technology being developed within CERN, which allows them to use the rifle-shot approach. Not only can TTO match-make, but they can also create the conditions for true R&D partnerships where prototypes can be built in collaboration between the external company and CERN.

Essential to their strategy is their shotgun-like ability to blast new ideas or licensing opportunities to thousands of related companies that connect to the many networks they're connected to. They also frequently hold industry events where CERN can present their latest technology breakthrough to a wide range of professionals.

When all is said and done, TTO is a cocktail party host writ large, knowing all the most interesting people and what they're working on, bringing them together at just the right time and place whenever and wherever they can. By using their skill of connection, TTO is able to find many more needles in their haystack of possible technology transfers.

- **Enterprises = Receivers:** From the perspective of knowledge transfer, the receivers are the commercial and agency partners that want to license CERN technologies or learn from its accrued knowledge. Across all of the organization's member countries—twenty-one and counting—there are many companies large and small that are working in industries that could benefit from an injection of bleeding-edge innovation. But finding usable and appropriate technologies to adopt from CERN's imposing database is no easy task. Some of these companies already have relationships with CERN as contractors or existing licensers, but the vast majority does not, which make the activities of the TTO all the more important.

Like the initiators, the receivers also have their own networks, sometimes directly mediated by CERN, sometimes not. One example is the independent Enterprise Europe Network, designed to help small businesses in the European Union connect to international partners. By pulling together large numbers of EU companies, organizing them by sector and technology concern, and creating a communications infrastructure around them, this network creates the conditions for receivers to be reachable by routers in search of a match.

The receivers make it easier for the right information from CERN to find them. For example, having an existing network of medical imaging companies on hand makes it much easier to know where to turn when a scientist shows up with a next-generation photon detector one day.

As CERN shows us, building large-scale serendipity chains is a focused, long-term effort involving the relentless creation of practical networks within and without, all with the goal of fostering the conditions for open communication. CERN's approach shows us how developing the skill of connection into an organization-wide capability can amplify any single instance of serendipity, like the medical use of a collider part, into a self-reinforcing phenomenon, such as a web of R&D partnerships with the medical imaging industry.

The Best Place to Find a Needle

Not long ago the best place to find a needle was somewhere you knew you could find it, like a pin cushion, with the other needles. Consolidating all similar things in one place—whether it was needles, or architectural blueprints, or party clowns—was the safest and best strategy for everyone, because otherwise it was just too hard to find something when you needed it. Well, that was then. Today, in the Internet age, the best place to find the needle you're looking for is in a huge haystack.

Systematically cataloging the world around us is rarely any help in finding what we're looking for. There's simply too much out there, and it's changing too fast. It's only by maximizing our ability to connect to everything else that we stand a chance to find what we need. The most effective way to do this is to learn to play each of the three roles of the serendipity chain, whether inside of a large-scale organizational effort, in a small group, or on our own. It's in these roles that we are able to find needles by creating connection just when we need it, ultimately making every link in the chain more valuable.

The skill of connection gives us form and structure for engaging in this network of relationships. It is through our personal ties, the strong and particularly the weak variety, that many of the unsought discoveries we didn't know we needed show up in the first place. Practicing this skill means being a good citizen of serendipity, ready and able to initiate a relationship based on a surprise or insight; to route another person's request when we are the person best suited to doing so; or to openly receive a query or idea when it serendipitously comes knocking at our front door.

Connection is how we play our part in linking every person in the world to every other person, as situations require. In our fast-changing, chaotic world this is what creates fertile ground for serendipity. Our connections ensure that when we're partway through searching through our big stack of hay, instead of finding the needle we'll stumble on a hundred-dollar bill. Or a gold watch. Or the farmer's daughter. Even with connections, we never know exactly what we'll find until we find it, but thanks to the skill of connection we can always be certain that, with a little help from everybody on the planet, it will find us.

8

Skill: Permeability
Storming the Castle

"When we try to pick out anything by itself, we find it hitched to everything else in the universe."
— JOHN MUIR

The "do it yourself" movement is all the rage right now. Just spend a few minutes hanging out on any DIY-devoted website, and you'll quickly find a world filled with talented, crafty individuals who sew their own pillows, felt their own sweaters, build their own birdhouses, and solder their own light fixtures. They're always looking for ways to craft their wares in a manner that gives them more life and personality than mass-produced products. They don't just do this for their own personal use—they often sell their lovingly crafted items on popular websites like Etsy.com, which bills itself as "the world's handmade marketplace."

April Winchell is a fan of the art of crafting and the people who practice it—or rather, Winchell is a fan of crafters when they're at their worst. If a crafter's light personal touch gets a tad too heavy, Winchell is ready to call them out on her blog Regretsy, a daily compendium of the funniest, worst, and most bizarre items that show up for sale on Etsy. Billing Regretsy as "Where DIY meets WTF," and writing under the pseudonym "Helen Killer," Winchell eviscerates the creations of crafters who post products like a wind chime made from discarded beer bottle caps, a used Doritos nacho cheese wrapper "upcycled" into an iPod holder, and a beer cozy made out of a taxidermied squirrel.

Regretsy has been incredibly popular, so much so that Winchell was able to parlay her success into a book deal, publishing a "Best of" collection in 2010. Not bad for a side project, since Regretsy isn't even her day job. She's also an accomplished radio writer/producer/director in Los Angeles, California, a former member of the well-known improv comedy troupe The Groundlings, and has played the voice of a number of characters in animated television shows like *King of the Hill, Phineas & Ferb,* and *Mickey Mouse Clubhouse.*

The other notable fact about Winchell is that she has her own army.

Like so many on the Internet, Winchell mocks because she loves. As her site rose in fame and attention she looked for a way to leverage her success to give back to her growing community. "April's Army" was her answer. A longtime supporter of charitable causes, Winchell built her army, consisting of individual Etsy sellers, with the support of her readers. Every month since April 2011, members of the army sell one of their handmade items to raise money for Regretsy's charity fund, which makes donations to Etsy sellers who need financial assistance.

The other thing armies are good for, of course, is going to war—as PayPal, the online payments arm of the auction site eBay, discovered in December of 2011. Winchell had been using PayPal to collect donations for a Secret Santa gift campaign for two hundred needy children, making use of a "Donate" button that PayPal offers its customers to use for acts of charitable giving. The Secret Santa campaign quickly blew past Winchell's initial expectations, and she found herself collecting so many donations so quickly that she happily informed her community that Regretsy would be able to provide not only toys but also a monetary gift to help each family with the holidays.

What PayPal did next earned it a place on Santa's "naughty" list. Because of the large amount Regretsy was raising as well as the speed with which it was being collected, PayPal flagged and froze its account. Winchell found she was unable to access any of the donated funds.

PayPal informed her that she had violated PayPal's rules for using the "Donate" button, which she was told was only supposed to be used by nonprofit organizations (though this turned out to be untrue). Undeterred, Winchell, who by this point had already purchased the toys, decided to go the traditional PayPal route and offer them for sale via the Regretsy site using the PayPal "Purchase" button instead. Charitable individuals could buy a toy for a family in need directly from Regretsy, and Winchell would ship the toy to one of the families in need as a gift.

PayPal quickly put a halt to that approach as well. Winchell reached out to PayPal to once again restore her account but was blocked in her attempt by a chilly customer service agent who, over the course of their conversation, gave her multiple unsatisfying reasons for why the funds would not be restored. Worse, PayPal demanded that she refund all the funds that she had collected up to that point, and informed her they were *keeping the transaction fees associated with each sale*, thus ensuring that the only entity getting any money from Regretsy's Christmas donation drive was PayPal. Finally, just to make sure they had gotten their point across, PayPal froze Winchell's unrelated personal account as well.

If only PayPal had realized that Winchell had an army at her back. With each new development, Winchell updated members of Regretsy and April's Army via her blog. Moments after sharing the news of PayPal's final offense, word began to spread, first to loyal members of her army, and then, through various social media tools, well outside her usual community. Children denied! Christmas ruined! A righteous cause quashed by corporate greed! The Consumerist, a consumer watchdog website, was one of the first to report on the story, and from there it was picked up first by technology bloggers like The Next Web and Venturebeat, and then by mainstream media like CNN and MSNBC.

Not content to merely complain, April's Army flooded PayPal's Facebook wall with the goal of shutting down all other communication there except for posts expressing their frustration over Winchell's situation. Other community members began a petition on the site Change.org insisting PayPal reverse its decision, which quickly gathered over fourteen hundred signers.

As the onslaught escalated and the publicity worsened, PayPal was forced to respond. After several days of public humiliation, the company reversed its position, unfroze Winchell's accounts, and a company executive called her to apologize directly. They also refunded the service charges on the transactions, and even issued a statement on the PayPal blog announcing that they would make a donation of their own to each of the needy families on Winchell's list.

Complete triumph for April's army, right? Not according to Winchell. Her blog post announcing PayPal's reversal doesn't read like a victory speech—more like a lament for what should have been. "I am a good, solid customer," she writes. "I do a lot of business with PayPal. But the days of a company rewarding you for your loyalty are just over. No one knows how to treat you anymore. No one cares."

None of this should have happened. Winchell and members of April's Army are PayPal's customers, after all, not their enemies. They rely on PayPal to run their companies. They don't want a contentious relationship with such a crucial partner—they just don't feel like they have any other choice but to fight back.

By the end of the ordeal, despite PayPal's backpedaling, Winchell evinces no confidence that the changes will stick:

> *Do I think all of this will make a difference? Do I think this will usher in a new era of accountability and raise the level of service PayPal provides their customers?*
> *Hell no.*
> *But I will say this:* we got someone to pay attention.

But these are PayPal's customers. Why wasn't PayPal already paying attention?

Soaking It All In

PayPal owes its dominance in the world of online payments in part due to its early arrival on the Internet scene. You'd think that would mean they're primed to deal with just this kind of customer revolt—they should be the standouts, given how long they've had to engage with and adapt to all sorts of customer situations online. But they aren't. The website PayPalSucks.com has, as of this writing, 11,675 individual topics under discussion on its forum under the header "Horror Stories: PayPal Did It!" The site does a thorough job of educating visitors to the site on how to deal with PayPal when something goes wrong. If April's Army engaged in a one-time skirmish, PayPalSucks.com is the frontline of a ceaseless war that aims to pressure PayPal to change what they view as its anti-customer policies. It's a war that doesn't seem likely to end anytime soon.

To be fair to PayPal, they're not the only ones that struggle with this issue—PayPalSucks.com is part of a long tradition of *Company-Name*Sucks.com sites on the Web. PayPal isn't even particularly exceptional in the way that they relate—or completely fail to relate—to their customers. As anyone who has ever found themselves screaming at the byzantine phone tree of their electrical utility or cell phone service provider can tell you, most companies do everything in their power to keep customers at bay. Businesses architect entire systems designed for what the customer contact industry refers to as "customer deflection"—finding ways to distance the company from the customer, deterring customers from ever interacting directly with a human being inside the company by putting layers and layers of technological defense in between them.

Many companies run their businesses like PayPal does—like a castle, fortified with walls designed to keep information and engagement with the outside world at a minimum. Most take this approach because they see it as the only way to effectively manage their business. But in doing so they shut out all the potential serendipity that comes from paying attention to what's going on beyond their castle walls. There is a more humane and serendipity-friendly approach: exercising what we call the skill of permeability.

We've shown how you can plan for serendipity by structuring your environments to continually generate chance collisions. Cultural, organizational, and physical changes open the door for you to see unexpected possibilities and connect them together in ways you might not have been able to otherwise. But perhaps the most reliable way to invite serendipity into your organization is to open up to people and ideas outside of its walls, particularly those who have a vested interest in what you do or make.

In other words, your customers.

All companies interact with their customers to some extent, but we're talking about more than just conducting focus groups or taking sales calls. We're also going well beyond traditional customer service, which consists primarily of responding to inbound requests from customers post-purchase, most often because something didn't work right. Instead, the skill of permeability is the ability to seamlessly and constantly interact with your customers, to engage with them throughout their entire product or service experience, and to weave the insights generated by these interactions and engagement into the daily practice and outcomes of your business.

The high castle walls we build around companies need to come down. We have more to gain by embracing our customers and finding effective ways to allow their intentions, desires, and knowledge to flow into our business than by of blindly shutting them out. Permeability means maintaining a well-defined structure while still allowing other materials to flow in and out. Like a sponge, which continually ingests and expels water in order to hold its shape, the skill of permeability breathes life into our organizations by letting new ideas flow in when we thoughtfully open ourselves up to the wide world that exists outside.

Permeability is a skill that every single employee can and should learn—not just the customer service team tasked with dealing with customer problems. There are surprises and insights out there, living within our customers, and permeability is the skill that allows us to get at them reliably. Any one of them could be the spark that leads to the next product breakthrough or marketing coup. Any of them could lead to serendipity.

You're So Far Away from Me

Before we can develop the skill of permeability to allow customers into our business, we first need to understand why we built these castle walls in the first place. As frustrating as it is to read about what happened to Regretsy, the real question to ask is why it happened at all. What kind of company sets out to alienate and isolate its best customers the way that PayPal alienated Regretsy?

Practically speaking, it doesn't make any sense for a business to bite the many hands that feed it, but dehumanizing customer deflection practices—which often spur customers to anger, and sometimes even incite an entire mob—still rule the day. Contrary though it is to customer satisfaction, policies of customer deflection, and the distance they put between companies and their customers, are the natural outcome of (usually) well-intentioned decisions about the best way to manage a thriving business.

Scale is one reason why companies engage in these deflection practices. An intensive focus on customer service and responsiveness is a hallmark of many newly created businesses. Ask any small business founder who they have on their customer service team and they're likely to respond "everybody." But in customer relationships as in so many areas of business, the qualities that generate our initial success suffer when we begin to scale. We start to formally segment responsibilities across the employee base, and "customer service" becomes one department among many. While this segmentation allows the business to manage its growth predictably—and may help it to deliver products and services to its customers at lower cost—it also has the unfortunate side effect of cutting employees off from the customers they are ostensibly working to support.

Compounding this problem, the Web has opened up the possibility for many businesses to achieve "Internet scale"; that is, whereas before most companies were limited in the size and scope of their market by factors like physical location and marketing budget, the Web has removed many of these traditional barriers, opening up a worldwide market for goods and services. Witness web startups that manage to acquire millions of users in years and sometimes months, or e-commerce companies that launch and reach millions in revenue before they've had a chance to blink. In the face of such an onslaught of success and the inevitable customer issues that come with it, it's not surprising to see companies building high walls around themselves. The clamor of external voices becomes so loud that, were the company to attempt to listen and respond to everyone, hardly anything else would get done. In these situations, deflection seems like the only reasonable option.

Costs also factor in companies' decisions to invest in deflection practices. Each new customer comes with a customer service cost attached. Ask an executive at any major consumer products company, and she will probably be able to tell you in real dollar terms exactly how much each customer service phone call costs the business. This is less of an issue at the beginning of a company's life, when these costs either aren't calculated into any financial assumptions or are borne as a necessary part of building the business. But in conjunction with scale, customer service costs become significant, and because they almost always come after the customer has already paid, these costs are rarely seen as anything but a loss to be minimized. On the face of it, automated customer deflection tools seem far cheaper than dealing directly with customers who can just pick up the phone or shoot off an e-mail whenever the whim strikes them!

Yet another reason deflection practices have become common is that luck-dampening need for process and control. Large and complex technology systems have been developed over the last twenty years under the moniker "customer relationship management," also known as CRM, with the explicit goal of helping companies catalog and communicate with their customers in a highly targeted fashion. CRM systems allow corporations to collect all sorts of personal information on customers and then use this information to tailor individual messages to each one, designed to intercept them at exactly the right moment to increase the likelihood of a sale.

CRM has become a multibillion dollar industry, suggesting, you might think, that businesses take their customer relationships quite seriously. The CEO of Get Satisfaction, Wendy Lea, a veteran of the CRM industry, explains why this isn't exactly the case: "I used to be in customer relationship management, and we really weren't helping companies get to know their customers better. We were helping companies forecast their sales better. It was about efficiency, not effectiveness—better targeting our customers with marketing messages. It wasn't about honesty and transparency; it wasn't about genuine communication; it was about control."

Mash together all of these reasons why deflection practices are adopted by companies—scale, cost, and process and control—and you end up with a situation that looks much like the one that transpired between PayPal and Regretsy. A company that engages with customer distancing tools ends up with employees who feel distant from their customers. Told to prize cost-savings over conversation and automation over authenticity, it's almost inevitable that customer service teams like PayPal's end up de-humanizing and mistreating their customers. And taking toys away from kids at Christmas.

At the end of her ordeal, Winchell laments the extent of the damage done by the distance companies create between themselves and customers:

> *We see the erosion of customer care in every sector. No one knows your name. No one makes eye contact. No one thanks you. Even doctors are practicing a completely different kind of medicine now. They have to see so many people to make the same money they used to that they've become more like mechanics. They forget your cancer is attached to a person. And PayPal forgets your fees are attached to people who are trying to make a living, or facilitate something good for other people.*

But there is an alternative. If we can learn to see the value our customers bring to our business across the lifetime of their relationship with us, and do it in a way that doesn't squeeze our company's precious resources of either money or time, we can re-connect our entire workforce with our customers, and make more room for serendipity along the way.

Ride on the Cluetrain

It's within our power to engage with our best customers rather than ignore them—and to do so well before a situation has deteriorated as completely as the one between PayPal and Regretsy did. Our choice, as organizations, is whether or not we find better ways to reach out to our customers and communicate with them on a recurring basis, without sacrificing speed, scale, or productivity gains in the process. When it comes to creating the conditions for serendipity to thrive, this kind of interaction is greatly beneficial; for the long-term health of our business in a highly networked world, it's critical.

According to Lea, the whole strategy of deflection and scripted customer interactions through tightly controlled channels like phone trees and e-mail ticketing systems is obsolete. "The old style of managing people, process, and technology has been exposed and exploded by the Internet. A new generation of customers is comfortable being online. They want answers from companies in a fast, friendly, and conversational manner, and they want to be able to communicate with these companies whenever and wherever they happen to be."

Lea's comments echo those made by the authors of *The Cluetrain Manifesto*, the seminal work on Internet marketing from 2001 that anticipated many of the changes the Web would foist upon businesses as they made their way onto the digital landscape. "Markets are conversations," the authors of the *Manifesto* announced, and thanks to the Internet, "markets are getting more connected and more powerfully vocal every day." The days of being able to simply broadcast a message to customers and expect them to willingly take it are over, they declared. Instead,

Every product you can name, from fashion to office supplies, can be discussed, argued over, researched, and bought as part of a vast conversation among the people interested in it.... Finding themselves connected to one another in the market doesn't

enable customers just to learn the truth behind product claims. . . .
These voices are telling one another the truth based on their real
experiences, unlike the corporate messages that aim at presenting
what we can generously call a best-case scenario . . . . The tinny,
self-absorbed voices of business-as-usual sound especially empty in
contrast to the rich conversations emanating from the Web.

When it was released, *The Cluetrain Manifesto* made claims so far
outside of what we understood then to be "the norm," that it was
easy to dismiss it as an over-the-top, radical rant. A short decade
later, it's remarkable how thoroughly the commercial landscape has
transformed in exactly the way its authors predicted. Businesses large
and small have had to come to grips with the dominant voice of
their customers. Whether it's a frustrated customer review on the local
business directory Yelp or an angry tweet seen by someone's 100 closest
friends, the messages customers send about the businesses they frequent
make an impact. And, of course, they also occasionally blossom into
full-scale, Web-wide customer revolt.

Sadly, the response from inside our high castle walls to this onrush
of customers' voices has mostly been to pull the drawbridge up a little
higher. Turns out the Cluetrain gang saw that one coming, too. They
write: "Many companies fear these changes, seeing in them only a
devastating loss of control. But control is a losing game in a global
marketplace where the range of customer choice is already staggering."

Lea agrees. Instead of fearing this change, she believes, companies
should embrace it. Adopting this mindset isn't even particularly new,
according to Lea, but harkens back to the way commerce used to work.
"The need is ages old," she says. "Local businesses always knew their
customers. They had conversations early and often. A relationship built
through consistent exposure to each other, using natural language to
discuss the things that matter most to them."

Once companies embrace a new approach to talking to their
customers, a whole world of benefits opens up to them that had
previously been hidden away. Yes, some customers will show up with

complaints and problems. But opening your business up to connect with your customers doesn't just mean you get negative feedback from customers. It also opens you up to your customers' intelligence, inventiveness, creativity, and excitement.

All of these qualities—and the knowledge that rides along with them—come from customers who have willingly chosen to engage with your product or service and want to share that experience back with you. Who knows what insights will serendipitously arise as a result? Companies that practice the skill of permeability are the ones primed to get just these kinds of benefits from this new world of company-customer connection.

Satisfaction Guaranteed

In case it isn't already obvious, as two of the cofounders of a company dedicated to bringing companies and customers closer together, the skill of permeability is near and dear to our hearts. Even when we dreamt up the idea for Get Satisfaction back in 2006 it was clear that the prevailing customer service philosophies, focused around customer deflection practices, were going to be worse than useless in the new social environment that was emerging online. Customers everywhere could be found scattered around the Web—talking, sharing, exchanging tips and ideas—and some had already begun to use all these new online technologies like blogs, social networks, and forums to get closer to the companies that mattered to them.

We began Get Satisfaction because we saw there was an opening in the market for a tool focused specifically on amplifying this company-customer communication—one that would allow customers to be better heard, and would bring value to the businesses that used it at the same time. Instead of deflecting customers, Get Satisfaction would help companies embrace them in a meaningful but still cost-effective way.

The way we saw the problem was simple: Technology had given customers a stronger voice at the same time it had made companies far more aware of those voices—more than ever before—and existing customer service tools weren't prepared to handle these loud, insistent conversations. But technology was also what we could use to fix this situation. We could use the Web to build a sponge-like, semi-permeable membrane for companies, allowing customers to flow in and out of these businesses appropriately. Not just another customer support product but a new kind of communication layer between companies and customers, one that allowed customers a chance to come in and hang out with a business in a way that hadn't previously been possible.

The skill of permeability is a natural outgrowth of the Internet, which makes it as easy for individuals to express themselves as a big organization. Get Satisfaction was our attempt to get businesses to listen and interact with these increasingly empowered individuals. Companies wouldn't need to throw out their existing tools or completely overhaul their approach to customer service—that would be as foolish as it would be impossible. Instead, they would be able to poke some holes in the walls of their castle to let the ideas flow in and out.

That said, a leaky castle isn't the best metaphor to use when you're selling a product, so instead we told our customers to treat Get Satisfaction as if it were a hotel lobby: a public/private online environment, owned by the company but welcoming to anyone who wanted to come inside. Maybe the customer had a specific issue and needed to connect with the concierge—sometimes, a customer service person but other times the CEO, herself—who would help them figure out the best way to resolve their issue. Or maybe a customer just wanted to come in and spend some quality time sharing with and learning from other customers. They might even stumble across the person of their dreams and fall in love. (We're not kidding! Passion is an appealing quality in people. When you give your customers room to express themselves to each other around the products you make that they care about, anything can happen.)

This was something besides customer service; this was customer community. It provided a value that was different from what companies got from traditional customer interaction tools. There are so many pressing concerns that customers bring to our attentions—so many fires to put out on a daily basis—that the customer service team is naturally going to focus on those. The few customer suggestions and insights that would help a company think innovatively about its product and its market tend to fall through the cracks in the traditional customer service dashboard. But by adding community into the mix, that's no longer an issue. Those suggestions don't get buried in a customer community—those issues are the *point* of the community, and fully exposed to the company's benefit.

We've seen companies hone the skill of permeability successfully time and again with Get Satisfaction. What follows are a few of our favorite examples.

Pampers

When you think about the kinds of products and services that incite passion in their customers, you probably think about people who love talking about the latest car or mobile phone they've bought and can't wait to show off. But you'd be surprised—people want to talk about any product or service that affects their lives on a regular basis. Like diapers.

Pampers, the division of the consumer packaged goods powerhouse Procter & Gamble that makes diapers and other baby-care items, culti-vated a thriving, engaged customer community around their products. As any new parent knows, every decision related to your baby can feel like life or death, especially choosing the right product to cling to junior's sensitive skin all day and night.

This makes Pampers parents the kind of customer a brand manager at a company like Proctor & Gamble would refer to as "high engage-ment": strongly invested, very concerned with making smart decisions, and therefore likely to spend a significant amount of time researching all the available options before making a purchase. In other words, exactly the kind of passionate customer who's likely to participate when pre-sented with the chance to connect with other customers and employees online.

"Pampers provides good customer service and support as a founda-tion," according to Scott Hirsch, Vice President for Business Develop-ment at Get Satisfaction. "For Pampers that means resolving customer complaints around product issues like 'the tabs fell off my diapers,' or 'the box only had eight diapers when it was supposed to have ten.' Those issues need to get resolved, but once that happens you can have more meaningful conversations with that customer, on issues that aren't oriented to pure service and support."

Instead, on the Pampers Get Satisfaction community parents ask questions that cut to the heart of the worries and challenges that they face, like moms asking other moms how to get a teething baby to sleep through the night, or when and how to get started on potty training. That's the type of conversation that supports everything a brand like Pampers stands for, but without having to slap customers in the face with an obnoxious, unwanted marketing message. Instead, Pampers "markets" to its customers by giving them the space and opportunity to have a conversation with each other.

Hosting this open conversation between your customers out on the Web has an impact on employees inside the organization, too. Even employees who aren't participating can see and benefit from the conversations that are happening. With a traditional customer service system, like a phone tree or a "trouble ticket" application that takes a support e-mail and turns it into a number, only two people generally see the conversation that takes place: the person complaining and the person resolving the complaint. But when the conversation happens publicly on the Web, any person who works at Pampers can monitor and potentially respond to what's being said. It can become part of their workflow and knowledge intake without requiring a huge additional amount of effort or interrupting other critical work.

"It gives Pampers employees the ability to see what their customers care about, and the potential exists for one of those conversations to spark something inside the organization, a way of seeing something that might not have happened otherwise," according to Hirsch. That's the spark of serendipity.

Whole Foods

Another useful effect of developing the skill of permeability inside your company is that it doesn't just allow knowledge to better flow *into* your organization—it also allows it to better flow *out*. There's a ton of deep, subject-specific knowledge stuffed away in the brains of the employees inside any organization. How could there not be? It's their job to know—that's why you hired them, that's what they spend the majority of their days thinking about, and in the best cases, it's what they are passionate about as well. The opportunity to share that knowledge with customers that want to hear it can be powerfully motivating for employees.

We first realized this at Get Satisfaction while watching the interactions taking place between customers and employees of Whole Foods Market. Whole Foods is the leading natural and organic grocery chain in the U.S., and its customers, like Pampers', are highly engaged with the products Whole Foods stocks. Participants in the chain's online community have a variety of questions about how the business is run, ranging from basic queries about future store locations to more specific ones about the types of organic fruit that the company buys and the way that it chooses which charitable organizations to donate to.

Back in 2008, a customer asked a question on the Whole Foods community about the bottled water that the store sold. She asked, "Which water do you sell that is the most pure? Is your 365 brand water really Crystal Geyser? And which type of Crystal Geyser is it?"

Teresa, a Whole Foods employee, jumped in to respond, explaining how the bottled water program at Whole Foods works. It's an amazing response—six paragraphs and 500 words long—addressing not only the different types of water and the various sources Whole Foods gets them from, but even delving into issues around the different filtration processes used for each kind of water, including some of the science behind filtration and the work the chain has done to meet governmental regulations.

What's notable about Teresa's response is not just the level of detailed concern she shows about bottled water (though that is impressive). It's that Teresa isn't a member of the "customer service" team. She stated at the beginning of her response that she's "with the Private Label division of Whole Foods Market"—and yet the online community platform allowed her to monitor customer concerns and choose to get involved when she came across a question that she knew something—or in this case, a lot—about.

Her response is far more valuable than the rote answer a customer service agent would have provided. Even a concerned customer service rep isn't going to know as much about bottled water as somebody who works in the division that produces it. The permeable nature of the Get Satisfaction platform allowed Teresa to share her work knowledge with both that customer and any others that happened across the question, bridging the distance between her and her customers in a way that hadn't been possible previously. She poked a hole in the castle walls and (bottled) water flowed through.

Teresa's response lives on online and continues to benefit Whole Foods long after she first answered. When someone searches Google for "Whole Foods" and "bottled water" together, Teresa's response is right on the first page of results. The answer will always be there, available to anyone who decides to go looking—or serendipitously stumbles across it without knowing it was exactly what they needed.

Timbuk2

Timbuk2 makes custom bags—backpacks, tote bags, travel bags, and most frequently, bike messenger bags. In fact, they're fanatical about bike messenger bags. As they write on their site, "We were born in a San Francisco garage and bred on the backs of messengers in the city streets. For 20 years, we've been building bags and accessories for urban adventures with a simple philosophy—create good-looking, tough-as-Hell bags you can truly make your own."

"The kind of organizational focus and mission that a company like Timbuk2 has is critical for companies," according to Hirsch from Get Satisfaction. "A well-defined mission keeps you on track and helps you figure out who your customers are. But this intense organizational focus can also create problems, because you might not realize that there are adjacent, underserved markets that you could be in that would still be on brand for you. You can miss huge business opportunities as a result of tunnel vision."

Hirsch saw an example of this first-hand when Timbuk2 started using Get Satisfaction. Timbuk2's brand, based in its two-decade-old bike messenger history, is centered around a young, hip, urban, cutting-edge in a tattooed, screw-the-man kind of lifestyle. As a result, Hirsch explains, their products tend to be "masculine and aggressive." Although they're intended to be highly customizable and even hackable, Timbuk2 bags aren't warm and fuzzy. They were made for the streets.

This gritty self-image is a big part of why Timbuk2 has been so successful holding on to and expanding their customer base for as long as they have. But when you're used to thinking of your customer as a twenty-something bike messenger, it can be hard to realize she might also be a mom.

"Timbuk2 has a type of customer they probably didn't used to think about as much—the skate-punk mom, who goes to Burning Man but also buys organic groceries and has two kids," says Hirsch. "She loves Timbuk2, has a messenger bag she's probably been using since she *was* a bike messenger, but then she grew up and had kids and now she needs a diaper bag, too."

When one of these moms asked Timbuk2 whether they would ever make a diaper bag in the Timbuk2 Get Satisfaction community, something special happened. The initial response from the company was negative. What kind of bike messenger needs a diaper bag? But then, as the community—both Timbuk2 employees and their customers—explored the topic together, the group perspective evolved.

Turns out their customers didn't want a special diaper bag—certainly not one that would be pink, or has a rattle, or any of the other things that are traditionally associated with other diaper bags. In fact, the community discussion showed that they already knew exactly what they wanted, because a bunch of moms had already done just the sort of thing you'd expect from a Timbuk2 mom: they had hacked their existing messenger bags to make diaper bags. "Moms came in and posted pictures," according to Hirsch, "saying 'here's a hack kit I built so that you can put a baby bottle where the cell phone is supposed to go,' and, 'the pocket for your note pad is perfect for holding two diapers.'"

"This is an on-brand conversation about exactly what the customers want," says Hirsch. In response, instead of developing an entirely new product, Timbuk2 created a "Diaper bag hack kit," and posted it on their Web site, also making space for other moms to show off their own diaper bag hacks. Pure marketing gold, concludes Hirsch. He explains that, instead of investing in an expensive and off-target product development process to make an entirely new type of diaper bag or, worse, missing out on an entire market, Timbuk2 gets "a product extension, a new brand experience, and a new persona to include in their brand experience. At zero cost. Just for talking to their customers about it."

Feedback Formula

How Timbuk2 developed its diaper bag hack kit isn't a traditional customer service story. The story doesn't have anything to do with resolving customer issues in a way that makes them happy—or at least less angry. Instead, it's about how a company and its customers, together, came up with an idea that changed the way the organization related to its customers overall, and affected the way it would interact with them in the future.

Getting to this kind of product insight from your customers takes work—more work than just putting up a page on your Web site requesting feedback and waiting for the brilliant ideas to appear. There are thousands of such pages on web sites devoted to gathering feedback from customers, and they do generate many millions of ideas and suggestions for businesses large and small, using Get Satisfaction or any number of other tools that people have developed to add some permeability to their businesses.

The idea that customers are better product designers than the professionals is a myth—in practice that's rarely the case. Most readers will have heard the old Henry Ford line about designing the first Model T automobile: "If I'd asked customers what they wanted they would've said a faster horse."

This, however, doesn't mean product feedback isn't valuable—it just means that we have to find a different way of looking at it in order to extract that value. In our experience as product developers—and in our observations of thousands of customer communities—there are a few general categories you can slot customer feedback into in order to better get at the value it holds: actionable suggestions, obvious feedback, and clues.

Actionable Suggestions

A vanishingly small portion of the time (far less than 1 percent in our experience), customers will offer ideas that are truly novel and useful. The popular mythology around the value of user feedback is concentrated in this category.

The prospect of an idea being dropped into your lap by an outsider rather than developed in-house at a hard cost is so appealing that we continually hope for this cheap innovation to materialize. That's understandable, given that when it appears, a novel, actionable suggestion is pure gold. The challenge, as with all serendipitous findings, is recognizing it amidst all the noise for the gift that it is, and being willing to act on it (as discussed in Chapters 3 and 4). Still, even for the most prepared, it's a rare occurrence.

There are a few reasons why so few novel ideas are born from user feedback. First, internal product teams are idea-generation machines. In the case of Get Satisfaction, we joke that 95 percent of all the ideas that we've adopted to grow and run our business over the past five years made it onto our whiteboard in the first three months of the company's life. Even today the company has still only built out a fraction of all the ideas that showed up on the whiteboard in those early months.

Second, many novel customer ideas aren't useful because they're too narrowly focused or are incompatible with the company's business strategy. A customer might want your product to work seamlessly with one of your competitor's products because it would make the customer's life easier, without taking into consideration how doing so could affect your sales and the viability of your business in the long run. These types of ideas might be interesting, but taken at face value they don't help much. However, they can sometimes be put to other uses.

Obvious Feedback

In the Get Satisfaction community we maintain for our own product, we've had the suggestion "You should internationalize your interface" posted dozens of times. Now, we didn't mind the nudge—we would never want our Francophile friends to think we don't love hearing from them (or any other brand of linguaphile.) But from the standpoint of the idea itself, it falls squarely into the "no duh" category.

While customer ideas like this one may not be actionable unto themselves—they're likely to be in your service or product development plans already—it is still valuable to have the pitter-patter of anxious customers exerting pressure on your development process. They can also provide a good opportunity to better understand the deeper needs of these customers: What languages are most important to translate into? Is language a user-preference or is it defined by each community? Are people willing to help translate?

The tendency in a busy product team is to dismiss or ignore an obvious suggestion, often because the team is self-conscious that they haven't gotten around to it yet ("it's been on the roadmap for a year—how embarrassing"). Instead, look at idea discussions as a way to collect user requirements for the feature or product you already know you want to build, even if you don't get around to actually building it for a year.

Clues

A huge portion of user feedback isn't either novel or obvious. At first glance it may look like noise—offbeat suggestions or ideas that don't quite make sense to you or your business. "Add spellcheck to posting topics" and "Allow anonymous posting" are examples of one-off suggestions that were posted on our own community. The ideas have merit, but we're unlikely to support them anytime soon.

While individually these suggestions might not be useful, if many people make the same suggestion, or if the same type of suggestion appears in different contexts over time, it might point the way to an underlying issue that does need to be addressed. The wide range of customer input available in your community can become the basis for uncovering deeper problems and customer needs.

Take the suggestion that we allow anonymous posting. When using Get Satisfaction, customers are asked to sign up and give their real name before they can give feedback to a particular company. The customer who asked us to implement anonymity believed it would make it easier and faster to post new ideas, which would improve the quantity of ideas people were willing to share.

What this customer didn't know is that we've actually tried implementing anonymous posting in the past, and it was a disaster. Anonymity in the community became a giant invitation to spammers to overwhelm the people who just wanted to have a conversation. Perhaps surprisingly, the quantity of usable customer input did not noticeably improve. It also challenged our core objective of creating stronger relationships between companies and their customers, since that's harder to do when one of them is hiding behind a pseudonym.

We sympathized with this customer's goal of removing barriers to providing feedback in the community. The tension between this customer's desires (echoed by others) and what we as a company considered a viable business decision prompted us to stop and investigate more thoroughly the underlying issue driving their suggestions.

In this case, our job was to identify the deeper need behind the suggestion: if customers wanted us to do more to remove barriers to posting, then we should look for methods besides anonymity that would allow us to achieve that goal. After much consideration, we decided we could remove a barrier to posting by adding authentication through Facebook Connect, allowing customers to log in to Get Satisfaction using their existing Facebook account with just one click of a button. This approach gave us the benefit of authenticating the customer as a real person, while also eliminating almost the entire account creation process. In the end, we were able to make the posting process simpler than it had ever been while also solving the real problem our customers were trying to communicate—not just the solution they felt was most obvious and that we already knew wouldn't work.

We always need to be ready to engage with our customers to draw out their best ideas, but being truly adept at the skill of permeability means we're also willing to look beneath the surface of what they're saying to draw out the hidden value. When we manage to do this organizationally—when we've learned to skillfully practice permeability as an entire company—we move towards fully integrating our customers' lives into our experience at work. Organizations that master permeability become empathetic, connected to their customers in a deep and intertwined way. By practicing this skill of planned serendipity, when our customers stumble onto something interesting, we stumble along with them.

Patients and Patience

We've shown you how to storm your company's castle—how to bring down the castle walls and let customers in—and how to figure out how to extract value from the feedback these customers share with you. Whether they offer an actionable idea, an obvious suggestion, or a hidden clue, you can turn their suggestions into all kinds of serendipitous benefit.

But while storming the castle sounds easy enough—and you might even feel like it's a no-brainer to do so—it can actually be very hard to put into practice. Nowhere is this more true than if you work in a large, fortress-like business, where the castle walls reach so high it sometimes seems like you can't even see the top—much less imagine them coming down. In a company like this, developing the skill of permeability might seem so far out of reach as to be close to impossible.

For all the value that collapsing the distance between companies and customers promises, the truth is that, as Doc Searls, one of *The Cluetrain Manifesto*'s authors, recently put it, "We have certainly made a great deal of progress—a lot of companies are more eager to talk to and engage with customers than before—but the old ethos has not died easily. We still encounter it everywhere . . . . We always have a choice between love and fear, and we're still choosing fear a great deal of the time."

Despite all our talk about wanting to be close to customers, we are still afraid of letting them in. Change is hard, and organizational change is hardest. But it can be done. Even doctors are beginning to employ the skill of permeability to better serve their patients. A new practice called "narrative medicine" has begun to transform the heavily analytic medical environment, normally so resistant to change.

Doctors lean on deduction to rule in or out a disease based on a patient's symptoms. But they often hit a wall when they're confronted with conflicting or inconclusive data. Patients are seen as complex problems to solve, with combinations of lifestyle, medical histories, and epidemiological factors, some known, some unknown. Doctors aim for an objective review of all the available data for each patient to get to the bottom of their symptoms.

Alas, this approach combined with the fast pace and insurance-centric systems of medical practice have created a doctor-patient relationship that can be cursory, checklist-oriented, and transactional. Modern medicine at its worst dehumanizes patients, often with the justification that the distance that it creates between patient and doctor allows doctors to see the medical facts objectively.

The idea for "narrative medicine" was developed by Columbia University's Dr. Rita Charon, who believed there was a better way to get at the facts of a patient's case by looking at it *subjectively*. Charon, a doctor who has also had a long love affair with the language arts, noticed that "sickness unfolds in stories." She developed the narrative medicine approach for doctors to better track, capture, and respond to their patients' stories.

Her technique helps practitioners treat the whole person, rather than just the illness. "Before there was no way to capture, open up, and honor the experiences of those in our care," she explains. Doctors who practice narrative medicine use "parallel charts." The patient's story—what they experience and their reactions to their treatment—sits alongside the traditional data-centric chart. Parallel charts require doctors to add literary interpretation to their diagnostic process. This approach allows doctors to find a way to infer problems in a way that hard data alone doesn't. It gives the qualitative data license to ride alongside the quantitative both on doctors' charts as well as in their heads, making it almost inevitable that new kinds of connections will be made.

It's a radical departure from the traditional approach to diagnosing a patient, but one that is reducing unnecessary tests and ineffective treatments. Doctors know things "that we don't know we know," according to Charon, and narrative medicine helps bring that knowledge to the forefront. The act of writing keeps a doctor's ability to see from "falling prey to boredom, fear, censure, or simply being overlooked." Invariably, when doctors and nurses write about their patients, "they have 'aha' moments," she says.

Our companies can learn a lot from the parallel charts approach to "treating the whole patient." Customers are already sharing their stories with us, if we have ears to listen. Narrative medicine reminds us that while systems are important, the minds and personalities that inhabit them are more so. This approach transforms the relationship doctors have with their patients, making it more intimate and giving doctors an opportunity to see the whole patient in a way that can lead to serendipitous breakthroughs.

The idea of the "parallel chart" in medicine is a small change made in one of the hardest environments in the world to change—a system where risk aversion conspires with the high-pressure work to make change supremely difficult. But it works. If the practice of medicine—arguably a much more rigid, conservative environment than even the most traditional of old-line businesses—can start to let their patients permeate their work, what excuse do we have not to do the same with our customers?

9

Skill: Attraction
Magnetic Fields

"Fortune favors the bold."
— LATIN PROVERB

What would it look like if an organization were designed from the ground up with all the principles of planned serendipity in mind? So far, we've discussed each skill on its own. But how do they fit together into a single, coherent experience?

For that answer, we can look to an experimental school based in San Francisco called Brightworks. The school is based on the premise that kids are not empty vessels to be filled up with learning by enlightened teachers, the default assumption of modern schooling, but rather that they are born voracious, self-directed learners who only need supportive environments, mentors, and light structure in order to become accomplished students.

Serendipity is built into Brightworks' DNA. You could even say it's their prime directive. As the school's founder, Gever Tulley, puts it, "The opportunities for engaged learning are inversely proportional to the knowability of the outcome." At Brightworks, students are asked and expected to work on their own and in groups to complete projects they've designed themselves and execute together. Gever had observed from his previous instructional experience that subjecting students to preplanned lessons "draws a foregone conclusion in the minds of the kids—nothing to discover, only steps to be followed." By contrast, he says, at Brightworks "the best engagement we get from the students is when they're forced to deviate from the recipe to accommodate the materials on hand."

Like many of the other lucky organizations we've visited in this book, Brightworks is readily accessible to anybody curious enough to step through its front doors. A particularly good time to visit was the evening of December 16, 2011, when, like many schools, Brightworks was celebrating the last day before winter break. Visitors who stepped inside the 10,000-square-foot warehouse that night quickly saw that Brightworks was like few other schools. Except for a small office area in one corner, the school is one wide-open space, hangar-like, with makeshift areas defined by handmade walls of plywood and butcher paper. Off to one side sits a full-sized shipping container re-purposed to hold shop equipment like power saws, blow torches, and drill presses. Even the kitchen is open to view, where on this particular evening the staff and students were preparing plates of appetizers for the people coming to see the final presentation of the students' work.

The warehouse was lit up like a Christmas tree, with stations set up at tables around the room, each manned by a few of the school's twenty students, aged six to twelve. Many of the kids were beside themselves with excitement about the opportunity to present their projects to the wider school community—parents, relatives, friends, and anybody else curious enough to know how this unusual private school operates.

At a few minutes after 7 P.M., the fifty or so adults and twenty kids gathered around a makeshift movie screen for a presentation from a group of students. "We've worked long and hard on this over the last three weeks," one of the kids, Kaia, age eight, said. "We hope you enjoy it." The lights dimmed and the video began. "Zompples: A Love Story," read the title. Dance music began playing as an intricate stop-motion movie unfolded on the screen—characters made of Legos dancing at an outdoor party, followed by a deep-focus shot, in which cows grazed in the background, then a tiny DJ spinning on Legos turntables. The audience emitted an audible gasp—it was a surprisingly high-quality production. As the two-and-a-half-minute video—"a love story with zombie complications," according to the students' description—continued, the crowd broke into spontaneous applause and belly laughs several times. The short movie was genuinely entertaining and impressive considering it was made by four kids ranging in age from seven to nine.

After the film, the students provided a live demonstration of the stop-motion process: how characters had to be adjusted frame by frame, how they tested different rates of image capture to get the most fluid movement given the available time they had to complete the project, how they discovered the difficult challenge of lighting a scene as they began to film. The presentation ended with the kids performing a live zombie rap, including beat boxing, and a brief talk by Mark Korh, the adult who had guided the young team, who explained the experience of mentoring the kids through their multistep production cycle.

This presentation is just one of five made by Brightworks' twenty students that night, who are now in the final part—the "exposition stage"—of the six- to eight-week learning experience that Brightworks calls an "arc." Every arc is oriented around a theme, an area on which students focus for several weeks, first by exploring it and then completing a project that is relevant to it. Some themes are concrete, like "cities." While on this arc, kids met with city designers, played economics simulation games, and toured sewage treatment facilities. Then, they worked together to construct "kid city," a full-scale, two-story building with a custom room for every student. Other themes are more abstract, such as the theme for the arc that resulted in this zombie love story—"by hand"—in which students explore the role of the hand in art, science, and society.

Back in the warehouse, the kids continue to give final presentations on their projects. A six-year old carries around a laptop so that a bedridden student can watch the presentations from home via a live Skype feed. One group of students has chosen to hand-build boats, and they've set up a boat lab in the warehouse to test their scale models. As part of their project, they launched and rode in their boats on one of the city's lakes. Another two-student group has made an interactive comic book that combines hand-drawn art and laser-cut wooden puzzle pieces. (At the end of their presentation, the artist, Henry, offers to draw any attendee as their favorite superhero.) There is a collaborative felting and quilting project and also a "cooking as chemistry" project. In every case, the projects are the result of the unbridled curiosity and collaboration of the students—conceived, designed, and implemented entirely by them, with active guidance by staff and members of the wider community.

Brightworks allows every student to pursue the things that have sparked their interest, no matter how obscure. All lessons emerge from the loosely guided experiences of the kids, not the other way around. This means the collaborators—Brightworks' term for the teachers—often do not know when or what the next lesson will be until the circumstances for it have presented themselves. The stop-motion movie team spent a week developing story ideas, writing the script, and doing production tests that exercised their math skills (e.g., how many shots do we need at thirty frames per second if we move the characters four times per second?). The boat team learned about materials science and water displacement, while the cooking-as-chemistry team learned about viscosity, acids and bases, the five base flavors, and boiling points. What may be controversial elsewhere is accepted wisdom here: there are no tests and there is no assigned homework. Instead the kids are devoted to completing their projects on time in order to triumphantly present to the school community during the final exposition phase of every arc.

Brightworks has implemented planned serendipity through and through. They've created not just a space but an entire structure—physical, organizational, cultural—that mixes its students' raw curiosity with intentionally chance encounters with people, places and events, any of which might spark deep interest in the child. But once the children begin their wide-ranging projects, the real challenge for the school and its collaborators begins: they must *attract*, in real time and without fail, the expertise and materials needed to support the students in whatever endeavor they've chosen.

Brightworks is a school of serendipity, made possible *by* serendipity. It's the final skill of attraction that makes any of it possible.

Come Together

Some people and organizations demonstrate an uncanny ability to draw serendipity to themselves. Eerily helpful chance collisions erupt around them at an uncommon rate, but not just because they're moving around and running into opportunities along their path. Rather, these individuals are like magnets, able to express what matters most to them in ways that *attract* a wide range of people and ideas to come their way.

Attraction is the most advanced skill in the planned serendipity toolbox. It's a distinct ability, but one that builds upon every other skill we've discussed. The skill of attraction is what turns a great idea into a world-changing business or a global phenomenon. Listen to the story of any highly successful person or company once they've come into their own, realizing their full potential, and what you'll hear is a story of attraction.

The skill of attraction is what happens when we take our commitment to our project, product, service, or cause—when we find our purpose and stick to it—and then turn it towards the eyes and ears of the public. Attraction changes how the outside world sees and interacts with us. It's how we engage people to change their behavior, transform the environment around them, and produce more serendipity-rich experiences, all in the service of the purpose that we have shared with them. Attraction is how we move the world in our direction.

When playing a video game, achieving all the goals set out for you during a particular period of play often unlocks new opportunities within the game—the player is given new items, greater powers, or the ability to move on to previously unavailable levels of play. This activity in the gaming world is known as "leveling up." The skill of attraction is essentially "leveling up" for planned serendipity: when we succeed in effectively practicing the seven previous skills we've discussed—motion, preparation, divergence, commitment, activation, connection, and permeability—and then successfully project these outwards through the external pursuit of our purpose, we "level up" in our ability to attract serendipity.

As with the other skills of planned serendipity, attraction might seem mystical, but it isn't. When we tease it apart we can see that it works not on the basis of abstract or metaphysical properties, but as the result of publicly expressing ourselves in four practical ways. When used together, these expressions and the actions that accompany them create an irresistible force pulling people and ideas towards us.

Projecting our purpose is the broadcasting of our intent and our goals to the public. Projecting our purpose requires us to loudly and repeatedly share the work we're doing and the reasons we care about it, instead of secretively hiding it away from public view. In the process, this projection reveals the values that motivate our actions, which draws others who share those values towards us.

The talk show host Oprah Winfrey built her entire career by projecting her empathy and desire to make people feel more comfortable with themselves, and that drew towards her an audience that connected with that desire. Target, the U.S. home retails goods chain, built a brand projecting access to designer goods at affordable prices. Amnesty International, a nonprofit organization, built a global organization by projecting the importance of ending political persecution around the world.

Projecting one's purpose in order to make it as big and well known as possible, and to attract the right people and ideas, is foundational to the skill of attraction. On the social Web we engage in public conversations constantly; each conversation provides an opportunity for projecting our purpose.

Building our reputation is how we develop a positive public identity. In *The Power of Pull*, the definitive work on organizational attraction, John Hagel III, John Seely Brown, and Lang Davison put it like this: "By beginning to build a reputation for being helpful, either by resolving existing problems or providing insights that suggest new opportunities, individuals can begin to attract attention from people that matter." We build our reputation by behaving in a consistent manner that allows others to develop trust in us and what we're promoting. Deeds speak louder than words, of course, and this is doubly true when we're acting out in public, with the eyes of the world on us ready to repeat (and retweet) what we do. Reputation means consistently living up to our ideals so that others come to believe in us enough to join our cause.

Reputation is also built by how we recover when we inevitably fail to live up to these ideals. Oprah, for instance, famously excoriated the author James Frey when it was discovered he had fabricated portions of his memoir, *A Million Little Pieces*, after she had promoted it into a nationwide bestseller. What stood out most about this incident is that she followed her public shaming of Frey by voluntarily issued an apology! Oprah felt she had betrayed her spirit of generosity with her one-sided condemnation: "[Mine] was not a position of, 'Let me hear your story. Let me hear your side.' And for that, I apologize." Oprah's ability to reflect back on how her actions embodied her purpose—or in this case, did not—were an example of the kind of behavior that has allowed her to build such an attractive reputation over many years.

Transforming our environment is how we change what people believe is possible by putting ourselves forth as a role model for others to follow, in pursuit of a new and audacious goal. Providing a shining example to others turns us into a center of gravity, attracting those who aspire to make similar change in the world.

Amnesty International invented a new way to fight for the cause of human rights, developing a highly effective process for shaming despotic governments into freeing the prisoners of conscience they had imprisoned. They transformed their environment by creating an umbrella organization that gave conceptual and material support to thousands of local groups across the planet, each of which mobilized and joined voluntarily because they were attracted to the organization's cause. Through a process designed by Amnesty International called "Urgent Action," these distributed groups of individuals were able to focus their collective attention on a particular prisoner or situation to maximize the effect of their individual actions. Amnesty International achieved such success that the organization was awarded the Nobel Peace Prize in 1977. Their focus and sense of purpose created a whole new way of seeing the power of a human rights movement—one that was activist and able to outmaneuver governments through innovation. In doing so, Amnesty International transformed the world.

Amplifying our message is when our purpose, having found a receptive environment and a willing group of participants drawn to our cause, creates a positive feedback loop that grows and extends our message, as if on its own accord, well beyond anything we could have managed or achieved on our own. Individuals that master this amplification get more and more return for less and less (relative) effort, as others who have taken up the cause find reasons to broadcast and thereby amplify its message themselves.

We have all experienced the end result of amplification any time we find ourselves talking about some subject—a product, an idea, a person—because everybody else is talking about it. We become part of the whirlwind that is amplifying the frequency of this subject. This is how trends occur—whether it's a new hit song, a suddenly popular type of handbag, or the constant change in the flare of the openings at the bottom of a pair of blue jeans. But while trends come and go, amplification, when applied to people or businesses, can lead to long-lasting ubiquity in precisely the areas in which we wish to achieve success.

Combining these activities of attraction with the other seven skills of planned serendipity allows us to truly "level up" in our ability to generate luck. This is when we achieve escape velocity, the all-important inflection point where we (or our projects or our companies) are propelled forward by the accumulation of everything that came before. When we look back on the story of Brightworks, we can see that reaching this point was precisely what allowed Gever to create the school of his (and, it turned out, many others') dreams.

A Teachable Moment

Gever, Brightworks' founder, starting without significant funding or institutional backing, has relied heavily on the skill of attraction to build his one-of-a-kind educational community, taking advantage of every one of the activities we've outlined above.

Brightworks is a startup at heart, and many startups in a similar position remain in "stealth mode" until such time as they're ready for their big launch—a dramatic reveal that coincides with a broad PR campaign. Stealth mode allows a company to fly under its competitors' radar and, more relevant to a new, unfunded school like Brightworks, provides a wide margin for error when they experience the inevitable setbacks.

Instead, Gever broadcast his vision everywhere he could. At conference talks, on guest blog posts, and in educator workshops he projected Brightworks' purpose—to put experience in front of lessons, and to put the kids' curiosity (and serendipity) in the driver's seat.

The sheer scale of Gever's vision was audacious for such a speculative project, but he benefited enormously by being public about his vision. Gever's transformational purpose with the new school became well known, even though at first the project existed only in his head. What he said resonated with parents—people who felt trapped by what they saw as a failing public school system suddenly saw whole new educational directions that seemed not only possible but urgently needed. Gever's vision, conceived in collaboration with other educators, re-imagined the experiential learning ideals pioneered by people like Maria Montessori for parents in an urban, technology-rich culture. This mix of solid historical grounding with audacious, future-looking vision made it easy to find early believers to buy into the school's nascent vision.

As they planned the school in early 2011, Gever and his team discovered there was a tremendous appetite for radical new alternatives like Brightworks. Families thirty miles away applied for the limited slots. Even with no advertising or "school tours" of the type typically taken by families to compare school options, people of all economic backgrounds were finding Brightworks. The ultimate power of Gever's transformative vision was that the parents that found Gever and Brightworks were those who were willing to put aside any hesitation about sending their children into a new, untested environment.

Underlying this transformational idea, of course, was the reputation that Gever had earned over the decades of his career, first as a software engineer, then as the renowned founder of the Tinkering School (a summer program that was the rough prototype for what eventually became Brightworks), and finally as the author of *Fifty Dangerous Things (You Should Let Your Children Do)*. His projects had led to an invitation to present a talk at TED, the global conference celebrating innovative ideas, which was ultimately viewed by tens of thousands of people as an online video. Because of his long history pursuing similar projects, people felt they could trust Gever to realize the vision, and that he would be straight with them along the way.

For Brightworks to succeed, it depended on the amplifying power provided by widening circles of participation from parents, educators, and subject matter experts who had bought into the school's approach and wanted to share it with others. Like ripples on a pond, each new person who got involved spread the word about the school further and further—all from the single pebble of Gever's original purpose. Parents who had bought into Gever's vision found themselves not only proselytizing on behalf of the school, but looking for ways they could bring others in to participate so they could spread the message as well. Mark Kohr, the parent who helped Brightworks' students create the stop-motion zombie film, was a video director who had worked on music videos and feature films, including *The Nightmare Before Christmas*. His enthusiasm for the project drew other talented filmmakers to the school, some of whom were among the most vocal in their praise of the final version of the film they saw at demo night.

By aligning every activity with the other seven skills of planned serendipity, Brightworks has compounded the effect of the skill of attraction. They have built in:

- Motion, by designing a space and an arc-based framework that maximizes physical and conceptual movement
- Preparation, by focusing on breeding and feeding obsessive curiosity in students and the community at large, avoiding conventional

wisdom, and creating project opportunities that allow students to "arrest exceptions"

- Divergence, by minimizing lesson plans and fixed agendas to allow for changing circumstances
- Commitment, by requiring the students to make a declaration during each arc to pursue their projects with absolute conviction
- Activation, by designing experiences that trigger students' impulse to investigate the unusual; for instance, the school hosts artists-in-residence in an open studio within the warehouse, encouraging students to interact with the artists on their own terms
- Connection, as the school sees itself as a mediator between networks of students on one side, and the wider community of practitioners/experts on the other, finding serendipitous opportunities for learning wherever possible along the chain
- Permeability, by inviting outsiders to participate in the Brightworks community, both as project mentors and as enthusiastic audiences during student demo days

All of the above activities that Brightworks undertakes have one fundamental thing in common: the results they achieve can be tied directly back to Gever's passion, purpose, and tenacious commitment to his school and the philosophy of learning that it represents. In each and every case, people, ideas, and opportunities are drawn to Gever because what he is saying and doing mean something to them—because Gever himself embodies this meaning and broadcasts it outward as far as he can.

How is it, though, that this kind of commitment creates such belief in the Brightworks community that they are willing to sacrifice their own time and give so much of their own experience over to the school and the vision it represents? Why is it that Gever's strong sense of meaning compels them to take such extraordinary measures to participate in his initiatives? What is it about Gever and the way he has communicated his goals that has managed to attract so many people?

Where There's a Will

The skill of attraction can seem magical to those who see only its aftereffects. People who wield this skill effectively, like Gever, are pied-piper-like in their ability to draw people, ideas, and opportunities towards themselves. But our attraction to people who successfully broadcast their purpose outwards is supported by science.

The studies undertaken in this area are as interesting for their design as they are for their results. How exactly would a scientist test "attraction"?

The Viennese psychologist and brain surgeon, Viktor Frankl, was the first to answer this question. His pioneering 1946 work, *Man's Search for Meaning*, chronicles his own experiences as a prisoner of a Nazi concentration camp. From this trying experience, Frankl developed his theory that humans are fundamentally driven by a *will to meaning*—the desire to find meaning in life. His work was groundbreaking, a new explanation for the powerful motivations underlying human behavior.

In 2011, a group of researchers from Florida State University and Southern Utah University tested Frankl's concept of "will to meaning" in relation to interpersonal dynamics. Their hypothesis was that people are strongly attracted to others who have a strong sense of meaning in life, "at least in part to satisfy the drive to find meaning." As they described it, their goal was to understand what it meant for someone to have a "magnetic personality."

Previous research had shown that people reported a strong sense of meaning in life when they had close relationships with others. By contrast, the lack of personal relationships made it more likely that people would report that life was "utterly meaningless." This was proved to be true across many cultures. The two studies developed by these researchers were designed to determine if the inverse of these previous results was true—whether or not an individual's expressed sense of meaning actually made them *more attractive* to others.

The first of the studies started by interviewing seventy subjects to assess the extent to which they felt their life had meaning. The study also measured the subjects' level of self-esteem, in order to determine whether either of these—their strong sense of meaning or their self-esteem—had a noticeable effect on the ability of the subjects to attract others' interest. The subjects were then seated in a room with a friend they had brought along with them and the two were videotaped having a free-ranging, five-minute conversation about their friendship. Afterwards, a separate group of individuals were asked to watch the videos and then rate their response to the question, "How much would you like to be friends with this person?"

The results were unambiguous. People in the group that rated the conversations were attracted to those subjects whose initial interviews had indicated that they had a stronger sense of meaning, while self-esteem had virtually no effect on their ratings.

In their second study, the researchers' goal was to take into account additional factors in determining the subjects' ability to attract: happiness, extraversion, agreeableness, conscientiousness, neuroticism, openness, and extrinsic and intrinsic religiosity. For this study, along with the initial interview to assess their sense of meaning, seventy-two subjects were each videotaped delivering a ten-second introduction about themselves. The researchers' instruction for this introduction was simple: "You may want to mention your first name, your major, your hobbies, or anything else you might say when meeting someone for the first time." The ten-second video introductions were then shown in random order to the group of raters, who evaluated them on a scale of one to seven on three criteria: likeability, friendship appeal, and conversational appeal. They also asked each rater to assess how meaningful they thought each subject's life was, as well as how physically attractive they were.

Across the board the subjects who had been assessed as having more meaning in life were viewed as "more likable, better potential friends, [and] more desirable conversation partners." While the research found extraversion also linked to interpersonal appeal, none of the other factors was strongly correlated—not happiness, not religiosity, not openness, and not physical attractiveness.

The conclusion is clear: to win friends and influence others, there is no substitute for living a meaningful life.

But to truly master the skill of attraction, we need to do more than just find our meaning. We need to make something with it, and then put it out into the world with all the courage and determination we can muster.

Hack Things Better

Jane ni Dhulchaointigh, the founder and CEO of an unusual London-based company called Sugru, has certainly experienced the way purpose and meaning in business blossom into attraction. Originally trained as a sculptor, Jane returned to school in 2003 to study commercial product design at the Royal College of Art. It was a switch that proved more difficult than expected, given her instinct to follow her own unpredictable interests over solving a narrowly defined product problem. Before long, her background in sculpture combined with her insatiable curiosity led her to begin experimenting with new materials. She explains:

> *I was destroying things and putting them back together: chipping blocks of wood apart and putting them back together with other materials. . . . One experiment I did was combining silicone caulk with very fine wood dust from the workshop. From that combination I made these fancy wooden balls. I found it fascinating that you could make something that looked like wood but had other properties—if you threw them on the floor they'd bounce.*

As was the case with Spence Silver and the discovery of his special adhesive that eventually led to the creation of Post-it Notes, Jane's early explorations with her own type of curious, semi-adhesive material was more about her fascination with the possibility of what she could make than about a specific purpose to which it could be put. Still, as her discovery started to take shape, she began to wonder what it might actually be good for. The answer, unsurprisingly, came via serendipity. Jane's boyfriend noticed that she had been using her funny rubber to repair or customize things around the house—enlarging a sink plug that was too small, or making a more ergonomic knife handle. It had been so natural for her to use the rubber in this way that she hadn't even registered the potential in what she was doing. It was only when her boyfriend drew her attention to it that she saw the opportunity in a flash.

Jane had a product idea that mapped perfectly to a deeply held conviction that meant a lot to her: she hated waste. She was fed up with it and knew she wasn't alone. "In the past, some people would have thought that repairing something is a compromise because you couldn't afford to buy it new again," Jane said. "But now there are increasing numbers of people who would rather repair or reuse than throw something out and needlessly buy something new because of the waste involved. Unchecked consumerism, not repairing our old stuff, has become the *un*acceptable choice for us."

Jane decided she would make a kind of space-age rubber that anyone could mold into a desired shape by hand and that would stick to any surface. It would have all the great benefits of silicone: weather-proof, UV-stable, dishwasher proof, very clean. "Every granny who finds it hard to open a jam jar can manipulate this material," she said. "Anyone who has a stiff part on their bike can adapt it to be whatever the bike needs."

She even came up with a tagline that summed up the concept and its DIY ethos perfectly: "Hack Things Better."

The only problem was that the material didn't actually exist yet. The makeshift version Jane had been playing with had all kinds of problems: it didn't adhere to enough surfaces, it had a terribly short shelf-life, and it was too high maintenance to make a successful commercial product.

Undeterred, Jane projected her vision and her initial prototype as broadly as she could, telling anyone who would listen about it. Eventually, she got some attention, attracting local press mentions, a set of science advisors, and a grant from the National Endowment for Science, Technology, and Arts. The grant wasn't huge, a mere £35,000, but it was enough to start testing materials—as long as Jane did the testing herself. To do that, she realized, she would have to be trained as a lab technician and set up her own laboratory. This former art student had become an accidental materials scientist.

It took her two years of painstaking trial-and-error, but eventually she created a brand new, patented class of silicone. Only Jane's immovable sense of purpose kept her going through month after month of laborious formulation and failure, long before her commitment would bear fruit.

Attraction works by pulling in people, organizations, and ideas that have a natural affinity with you. But as is the case with commitment, attraction is strongest when it actively repels those things that are poor fits with your purpose—making room for the self-selected people and ideas that find their way to you. This is precisely what happened to Jane.

As she made progress with her new silicone, she began to approach business partners. Many people told Jane that her only hope of building a proper company—the only way to get her product into the hands of customers—was to forge relationships with multinational companies. It was only through them, these advisors insisted, that her new material would get the distribution, product integration, and credibility it deserved. Jane listened carefully to these experienced voices, put on her nicest business suit, and went out to charm the big brands and glue companies with a no-nonsense, sensible presentation of her new silicone adhesive. Then she waited. And waited.

Where was her so-called skill of attraction now? These were big companies, and Jane knew that meant they moved more slowly than she could, but this was something else. When she met them they hadn't responded to her vision and product in the same effusive way that so many people had since she first started showing it around. She would tell these big companies how her product would enable anyone to repair or improve their products in unlimited ways, but they kept bringing the conversation back to their existing product lines and sales channels. Her idea meant educating a market. It meant creating a new brand. These big companies had no interest in these pursuits. Did they even get what it meant to "hack things better?"

The cool response she was getting from established companies stood in stark contrast to the regular and repeated requests she was getting from designers and engineers who had seen her prototype. "When is it going to be ready?" they pleaded. That's when it struck her: She was trying to move forward on the path of *most* resistance! Meanwhile, she had evidence of an undeniably attractive force with an audience readymade for the product she wanted to be selling, the brand she wanted to build, around the purpose that had kept her going for years.

A friend suggested an alternative: "Start small and make it good." Simple words, but as it turned out, the right advice for an entrepreneur who had inadvertently mastered the skill of attraction. Jane put the talks with big companies on pause and turned her attention to launching her product.

"With our own brand we could talk about repair in a way that went beyond glue and tape," Jane explains. "We could approach it in a fresh way because we saw that there were more creative people out there like us that cared about the same things."

She decided to create a brand that reflected her team's personality and purpose, and named it Sugru, the Irish word for "play." Jane focused the entire brand experience on embracing and even evangelizing the playful DIY spirit that had inspired her in the first place. She converted Sugru's lab into a production line and was soon churning out foil-wrapped packs of the space-age rubber that she had envisaged six long years earlier.

When Sugru launched in December 2009, Jane and her small team were in for a shock: they sold out their entire initial inventory within a few *hours.* Jane attributes this to the ecstatic review that Sugru received in London's *Daily Telegraph* and noted technology lifestyle publications *WIRED* and *BoingBoing*, and the whirlwind of online attention that ensued.

While the publicity certainly helped, there was something more behind all this attention. It's what explains the constant influx of photos, videos, and testimonials of ingenious uses by customers that have continued in the years since their initial launch. It's what explains how Sugru has so many passionate fans that have amassed on all seven continents, and the reason why this tiny company that had been running on fumes just a few months before its launch ended up on *Time* magazine's top fifty inventions of 2010, twelve spots above the iPad. That something is the skill of attraction.

"People want to find things and people to believe in," Jane says. And Sugru customers clearly believe in both the product and the people behind it. They're responding, at least in part, to Sugru's unselfconscious sense of meaning.

And the attraction is mutual—the company and its customers have developed a truly symbiotic relationship. That "perfect fit" Jane had been seeking for her unusual rubber years ago? Her customers are telling her what it is—or rather, all of the perfect fits they've found. Repairing computers, cables for laptop chargers, phones, and outdoor equipment have emerged as the leading uses for her one-of-a-kind product. Jane is finding the company being pulled by customers in directions she could never have imagined, but in each case the path is perfectly aligned with the company's purpose.

What we learn from Sugru's experience with attraction is that the wrong choices just don't stick, whereas the right ones can't do anything but. When we're passionate, committed, outgoing, and believe in the transformative nature of what we're doing, the best and highest purpose for our work reveals itself to us, and the rest just falls away.

Come Out and Play

While Sugru was refining its product strategy with the help of the fanatical customers it had attracted, another company was using the skill of attraction to uncover its own surprising—some would say radical—business model. In fact, there's a good chance the company wouldn't be around today had they not proven to be masters of the skill.

Fifteen million people and counting currently use Foursquare, a mobile application that allows them to "check-in" wherever they happen to be at any moment—whether it's a bar, restaurant, movie theater, hair salon, drugstore, or their bedroom. When a user of the app checks in on their smartphone, their location is broadcast to a select list of their friends, who can pull up the same app on their own phones and instantly see exactly where all their friends are located, wherever they might be scattered across any particular city. In other words, Foursquare is an application designed to facilitate serendipitous encounters, and we can personally attest to the amazing experience of opening it up and realizing that somebody you really like but haven't seen for a while is hanging out at the bar next door—or, sometimes, at the same one you're already in.

Foursquare is one of those online services that seems like it came from out of nowhere and gained huge prominence overnight. It went from something no one had ever heard of when it was launched at the South by Southwest (SXSW) Festival in Austin, Texas, in March 2009, to something that seemingly everybody knew about in no time flat, gaining such cultural omnipresence that it recently made an appearance in an AT&T commercial as well as on the laptop of a character in the television show *Two and a Half Men*.

Yet as Dennis Crowley, one of Foursquare's two founders, will be the first to tell you, nothing about Foursquare's rise to prominence was assured or easy—or particularly fast. Foursquare is the kind of service that people in Silicon Valley sometimes refer to as a "ten-year overnight success"—a product that from the outside looks like a genius idea that skyrocketed to success as if by magic, but in reality was the result of a relentless focus on solving a particular problem over many years.

In the case of Foursquare, the question that dogged Dennis for over a decade, and that drove Foursquare's development and ultimately attracted such a devoted following, was this: "How can I get my friends free drinks?"

A true New Yorker at heart, Dennis has always liked to go out late at night, ever since he first moved to the city in 1998. It's no surprise, then, that he ended up creating a service that helps you find other friends at bars, a problem he's been obsessed with ever since he got laid off from his first job after college.

His first attempt at solving the problem came in 2001, when, after losing his dot com job, he found himself with a lot of free time on his hands in a dense urban environment where many of the people he knew were also out of work. They, too, were hanging around out in the city, somewhere.

"Why should I go watch the baseball game in the bar by myself," Dennis asked, "when one of my friends is probably already watching it somewhere else? We're all around the city and none of us have jobs. Some of us are in Central Park. Some of us are in coffee shops. Some of us are hanging out in bars in the middle of the day. That's where the check-in idea came from. If people can self-report their location, then it would make it easier for us to meet up." Dennis built a few prototypes to test his ideas, but these original attempts to solve the problem didn't get very far past the interesting experiment stage. Still, the idea was lodged in his brain, and he continued to re-visit it as the opportunity arose.

His second attempt was more successful. Dubbed Dodgeball, it was the output of his 2004 NYU grad school thesis project. Dodge- ball was essentially an SMS-based version of what would later become Foursquare, with a lot less of the functionality. Enough people were carrying cell phones in their pockets by this point that Dodgeball picked up a loyal, though tiny, following. SMS-based checking-in was still clunky, which hindered Dodgeball's adoption by a broader user base, but the product concept was novel and intriguing enough that Dennis and his partner Alex Rainert were able to forge a partnership with Absolut Vodka. Though Absolut wasn't willing to give users free drinks—Dennis' original goal—they did successfully promote Dodge- ball to their customer base in exchange for the Dodgeball team creating a series of Absolut promotions to their user base when they checked in at certain bars.

Between overall interest in the novel nature of the Dodgeball concept and the attention from the Absolut partnership, the team managed to get the attention of several notable publications, including *The New York Times*. The media coverage didn't garner them a ton of additional users, but it did manage to catch the eye of Google, who purchased the two-person company in 2005.

After only two years working for Google, both Dennis and Alex left to take other jobs. But when Dennis heard in early 2009 that Google was shutting down the Dodgeball service for good, he realized he had an opportunity to try again. This time—building on top of the iPhone and other modern platforms—he would get it right with Foursquare.

It's impossible not to admire the allegiance and commitment that Dennis showed through the years to his idea of helping people serendipitously discover each other using the best available technology. But even more impressive is how his persistent dedication and perseverance to this idea has coalesced into an attractive force: people and organizations, whether engineers, investors, or business partners, have increasingly rallied to support his cause. The dedication has accrued to his—and by extension Foursquare's—public reputation, having transformed what everyone thought was possible with a location-based mobile service. And nowhere is that better exemplified than in the way that Foursquare found its business model—or rather, how the business model found Foursquare.

In many startups—including powerhouses like Facebook, LinkedIn, and Twitter—it's common practice to launch first and develop a business model second (or, sometimes, fifth). Grow a huge user base and then figure out how to make money on top of it, the thinking goes. Anathema though that approach might be to conventional business wisdom, it's a common practice for venture-backed online services that have the potential for high initial growth. Figuring out the business model in this way is not easy, however, and finding the best way to make money off one of these services often requires serendipitous intervention.

As Dennis describes it, there was one key moment that helped him define the business Foursquare was in, and it came about as a direct result of practicing the skill of attraction.

Far from being a smash hit out of the gate, the first months after the application's introduction at SXSW were rocky. "We launched like a rocket ship to 4,000 users and then went back down to 500 users, and it was that way for almost six months," according to Dennis. They went looking for investors to help them, but with such small growth in the user base and no clear business model, investors just weren't interested. It was then that Dennis got an e-mail from one of those dedicated initial five hundred users with a link to a photo of a sign at a coffee shop in the Mission district of San Francisco called the Marsh Café. It read "Foursquare Mayor Drinks for Free."

In Foursquare, the person who has checked into a particular location the greatest number of times is dubbed the mayor of that venue. This homemade sign was, essentially, a new kind of loyalty program for frequent visitors to a particular business, but instead of ticking off marks on a card to indicate participation, this one was built entirely on top of the check-in process in Foursquare.

This was Dennis and team's Eureka moment. Not just that they could build a loyalty program on top of their service, but that they could build one that went well beyond the capabilities of previous such programs available to local merchants. "It suddenly became clear that we could be a whole new kind of information channel for local businesses," Dennis said. "If we exposed all the stats we were collecting around check-ins to the merchants, then the merchants would actively participate, and they would be able to give rewards to their customers as a result." Thanks to the attractive pull of their service as well as the careful attention of one of their loyal users and the ingenuity of a scrappy local business, the answer to the question of how to make money appeared before them, just when they weren't looking for it.

"And then," he adds, "it dawned on me. Maybe it took us five or six years to figure out, but we figured it out. This is how you get free drinks with Foursquare. And these days we can all get a lot of other free stuff with Foursquare: sandwiches, $25 off, a bottle of wine on your birthday. People even get to cut the line at the brunch place. It took us a long time to do it, and it's not like we were trying to make it happen, it just kind of happened."

Even after this serendipitous breakthrough, it has taken several years for Dennis, his cofounder Naveen Selvadurai, and their ever-expanding team to begin to realize the potential of this model for Foursquare. But it's working now—at last count they had 600,000 local merchants using the platform. As a result, they no longer have a problem attracting money: Marc Andreessen, the rock star venture capitalist whose musings about luck kicked off the process that led to the book you now have in your hands, is one of their biggest investors. But they're not finished, because their vision has only grown in the years since.

"We're not there yet," says Dennis. "The app needs a lot work. I see the point when we have 50 million users because of all the stuff that Foursquare offers. I just don't know when we'll hit that." And while their future is as uncertain as any startup at their stage, thanks to their commitment and willingness to put it out in the world, serendipity will always be on Foursquare's side.

Or as Dennis puts it, "I really feel good about our chances, because the stuff that we've always been trying to do, we know we're doing it, every single day."

The Creative Act

These three tales of the skill of attraction in action—Brightworks, Sugru, and Foursquare—feature companies near the beginning of their (hopefully) long lives. Each exemplifies their willingness to find a way, over many years and after setback after setback, to deliver an idea into the world. Most of all, they are stories of how their creators, by fully expressing their passion and purpose, were able to exert a pull on others to meaningfully contribute to bringing their creation to life.

The skill of attraction is fundamentally a skill of *creation*, and thus a core component of planned serendipity, which exists at the intersection of chance and creativity. Attraction is the end result of making something you believe in and allowing others to believe in it too. It is the force of your belief that draws others in. This kind of attraction is not just desirable—it's necessary. Without the participation of others and the serendipitous ideas, encounters, and opportunities they bring with them, a vision is unlikely to ever become real.

The social Web has made the skill of attraction easier to develop than ever before. Via online communities and social media, we can announce ourselves and our businesses to the far corners of the world with surprising ease. Too often, though, we dampen the full effects of our public presence in pursuit of a controlled message, or to avoid making waves. Afraid that we might not appear "professional" to the outside world, we aren't willing to show our authentic selves—to share the hopes, desires, dreams, expectations, fears, and half-baked ideas, each of which represent some aspect of our purpose, our values, and our desires.

And yet, as Gever, Jane, and Dennis have shown us, those that have learned to resist these urges are the ones that are able to realize their dreams.

So many of the people, events, and ideas critical to our success are outside our current knowledge, and so much of what matters to our business actually lies outside of our business, in the minds and experiences of others. Yet this last of the eight skills of planned serendipity—the mystical-seeming skill of attraction—allows us to conjure what we need just when we need it. In the end, it is our willingness to be *ourselves*, and to express these selves in all their weird and meaningful glory, that is the ultimate lightning rod for calling forth that which truly matters to us.

10

Unraveling the Double Bind

"Everyone has a plan until they get punched in the face."
— Mike Tyson

We humans are planners. We plan our days, our educations, our careers, our retirements, and everything in between. We plan to nudge hoped-for tomorrows into being. We plan to guard against the unpredictability we know lurks around every corner. Whether or not planning is a formal activity, our minds run overtime visualizing how future scenarios will unfold.

There's nothing wrong with planning. We're naturals at it.

Yet in so many ways it's getting harder to plan, and nowhere more so than in our businesses. We see extreme volatility in our stock market and economic growth projections, whose frightening changes loom over our lives even though they lie completely out of our control. We see volatility in subtler ways as well, like the Internet memes that suddenly and without warning strike water cooler conversations. We see it in the quickening pace of waves of technology and the movement of capital around the world at the speed of light. And, sadly, we see it in the human misery caused by the elimination of entire categories of jobs from once-thriving (or even still-thriving) industries.

We comfort ourselves by imagining that there remains a significant difference between our own seemingly stable lives and jobs and those of extreme risk takers like day traders, aspiring rock stars, or technology start-up founders. But many people in formerly "safe" positions have seen masses of their peers summarily laid off, with no possibility of return. Were their careers less volatile than "risky" pursuits?

We don't even have reliable ways to gauge where uncertainty might flare up next—the past is no help in knowing what tomorrow's disruptions will be. In the two-year period leading to this book, the world digested the 2008 financial collapse, the Tea Party Movement, the rise of social media, a nuclear meltdown in Japan, the Arab Spring uprisings, the London riots, the Occupy Movement, and the EU debt/currency crisis—and these are just a sample. In our highly interconnected, interdependent economy, every one of these incidents had some effect on our lives. What's next?

Disruption doesn't just rob us of stability, however. It also offers opportunities, if we're willing to recognize and act on them—and, yes, *plan* for them.

Survival Skills

We believe that together the eight skills of planned serendipity represent the best possible modus operandi for a world in flux, arming us not just to adapt but also to exert a distinct influence on the direction in which we're all headed. In an environment like the one we now live in, the eight skills are not just habits of successful people and organizations—they're *survival* skills.

For all the chaos of the world, there are just as many, if not more, happy accidents lurking in every direction. These are the chance collisions that matter to us, if only we see them and take advantage of them. This is what we want to plan for—not rote predictability, but the ability to create situations where unexpected possibilities are recognized and acted upon. We can achieve this by mindfully developing each of these skills, in ourselves and in our organizations.

Planned serendipity comes with a real tradeoff—it involves violating the logic of the status quo. It's not easy to graft these eight skills onto an organization designed as a machine and optimized for consistent, predictable growth. The skills of planned serendipity are fundamentally human, not mechanistic—and humans are anything but predictable (at least when we're acting like humans and not the automatons we're often asked to be).

Yet if we wish to adapt to the breakneck speed of change or find new ways to increase our exposure to opportunities for growth, we must learn to look for those things we don't see coming. That which we need but can't predict—chance collisions, happy accidents, and timely serendipities—are the very things most likely to reflect the direction of our ever-changing environment. Embracing and responding to them when they appear can provoke us to evolve successfully as we head into the future, however uncertain it may be.

To Paradox Is Human

This will not be an easy change to make. The machine logic of the industrial age—predictable inputs leads to predictable outputs—is deeply incompatible with the human-scale, improvisational nature of planned serendipity. When we pursue them both at the same time, we inevitably end up in a double bind, where one command contradicts the other—in this case, "be predictable" versus "be creative."

The double bind is a recipe for frustration, angst, and ultimately failure, but only if we fail to escape from it. We can free ourselves from any double bind by replacing its distorted logic with a new way of thinking, like the creators of the Agile software development process did. They resolved the dysfunctional tension between serendipity and predictability by establishing fixed habits that are highly responsive to new information as it appears—in this case, a consistent style of work across the entire team combined with regular weekly software releases.

Because the Agile process anticipates potential changes, new needs, requirements, and chance opportunities that arise during the course of any particular project can easily be integrated into the process, rather than disrupting it. Following a similar approach to Agile's—one that encompasses the skills of planned serendipity, allowing us to plan around the (seemingly) unplannable—is a recipe for developing the confidence we need in the face of rapid change.

In truth, many circumstances that seem irreconcilable are actually two-sided situations that we need to learn to embrace, not suffer through. Instead of treating them as opposing forces, planned serendipity teaches us to view these two sides as complementary. Doing so doesn't erase the paradoxes of our double binds, but it gives us a healthy way of living with them. The skills of planned serendipity turn these apparent contradictions into strengths—constraints that push our creative process forward, instead of stalling it out.

For example, within planned serendipity, there is a constant tension between being open to change and being willing to commit to a path. Aren't these mutually exclusive directives? The trick is to see these ideas not as conflicting, but as two halves of a whole. The skill of divergence—the ability to take a different path than the one originally intended—allows us to see and act on more chance opportunities, but on its own, it can lead to a diffusion of our efforts. We end up doing too many things at once or running a business that doesn't reflect our interests and passions. Commitment frees us from this dilemma: it's through commitment to a meaningful purpose that we are able to determine which of these many potential paths we should take. Planned serendipity allows us to take these two "opposites" and use them together to find serendipitous outcomes in line with our convictions.

Similarly, planned serendipity revolves around making people and organizations more open to the unexpected. But constraints are often necessary if we want to unlock new possibilities. How is it that we can be more open and more constrained at the same time?

When we look at the practical effects of planned serendipity, we find that the areas where we are typically most constrained at work—our office environments, our curiosity, our engagement with customers—benefit the most from being "opened up." These are the areas that we've systematically stripped of spontaneity in the name of order and scalability. Removing the barriers we've put in front of our own creativity opens our eyes to all kinds of unexpected possibilities.

On the flip side, those areas where we've given ourselves too much flexibility—such as an organizational purpose that is stretched so thin that it becomes unrecognizable—make it harder to determine which opportunities are the right ones. Tightening up our sense of purpose makes us willing to say no to the wrong opportunities, while we're all the more likely to say yes to the right ones. Changing or adding the right constraints—looking not for a set rule but assessing every situation with fresh eyes to identify the limitations that unlock better outcomes—is often how we set the stage for serendipity.

Finally, consider the trickiest double bind: implementing metrics of success for serendipity. These two ideas, metrics and luck, couldn't seem to be more in conflict. If serendipity is finding things we're not looking for, how can we ever know what to measure?

It's true that planned serendipity trains us to be suspicious of any metrics-focused management approach designed to shut out "irrelevant information"—we're deluding ourselves if we believe we can always tell ahead of time what's relevant and what isn't. We'll never track luck with the same precision as we can, say, a direct marketing campaign. What we can certainly do, and what many firms do already, is measure our success in cultivating the skills of planned serendipity. There are countless ways of doing this. Here are a few examples:

- In-N-Out Burger, mentioned in Chapter 5 as an example of commitment, measures the extent to which all managers have internalized the company's purpose, through In-N-Out University, its in-house training program.
- Agile software development teams, mentioned in Chapter 6 as an example of activation, often downplay the traditional measure of software success (i.e, whether engineers deliver planned features by a scheduled deadline). Instead, they focus on measuring the average rate at which the team produces new work each period.

From this baseline they spot anomalies in productivity as the rate falls or spikes.

- CERN, mentioned in Chapter 7 as an example of connection, keeps track of how many knowledge and technology transfers they've successfully completed over a given time period, and how successful the transfers have been. This tells them whether they're building the organizational skills for realizing the full value of its many innovations.
- Procter & Gamble, mentioned in Chapter 8 as an example of permeability, mandated in 2000 that 50 percent of new product ideas should originate in whole or part from outside of the company's traditional research and development processes. By tracking the source of each idea and how close the company comes to meeting this goal each year, they've created new key metrics for the company's innovation success rate.
- Sugru, mentioned in Chapter 9 as an example of attraction, tracks the number of stories shared by customers describing how they're using its product, giving them (often surprising) insight into their product's potential uses.

There are as many ways to measure for the skills of planned serendipity as there are businesses. We monitor the frequency of personal side projects among our staff, track new ideas generated after a lunchtime presentation series, and report on cross-functional collaborations spawned by random introductions in the atrium. All of these aim at the same thing: to give us some indication of how prepared we are for serendipity. Do we have eyes to see, ears to hear, or the boldness to act on the unsought finding? As the Greek philosopher Heraclitus pointed out 2,500 years ago, "Unless you expect the unexpected you will never find [truth], for it is hard to discover and hard to attain."

Creation Myth

Planned serendipity, measured and baked into business process, is the ultimate insurance policy for an unknown future. It shifts us from quantifying routine processes to tracking how well we're uncovering new possibilities, an implicit mandate for everyone in our organizations to think creatively. This mandate may be our only hope if we want to adapt to changing circumstances, find new paths forward, and extend our success.

As individuals, we understand this intuitively—and it's reflected in business in the form of R&D, innovation "processes," and skunkworks-style labs. But by revolving our organizations around setting and meeting expectations, we leave little room for the big, unexpected leaps—or, worse, we give them nowhere to go when they do successfully materialize.

Planned serendipity—creativity, interacting with chance—is how we escape this trap, because it centers on what we *don't* know, teaching us to use uncertainty to our advantage. We can never digest all the information out there. We can't review every book ever written related to our project or talk to every person who could shed light on our subject—the web of relatedness is too big. It's not humanly possible to know every case study that would prove or disprove our points. We are at the mercy of our experiences, whether we've sought them out proactively or stumbled upon them in the commotion of our lives. Which of these experiences will end up mattering to our work is impossible to predict—until serendipity strikes and we connect what we *know* to what we've *found*.

For us, writing this book has been a pure exercise in planned serendipity. There are a thousand and one ways to begin a chapter or exemplify a point, and the obvious ways are rarely any good. The daily horror of a blank page is an open invitation for chance to intervene, anything to break the dam that stands between the page and the free flow of words. We never suspect what's going to inspire the next passage—a billboard, a conversation with a foreign visitor, an obituary, a random memory recovered in the shower. It's often an unexpected event that provides the spark that leads to the next stretch of writing. This is how serendipity operates—plenty of hard work before and after, but the critical leaps seem inevitable in retrospect.

All journeys of creation begin like this: a commitment to produce something, a presumptive end date, and no fixed path for getting to the finish. This is the act of creation in its simplest form. There is more that is unknown than known; we must by necessity remain open to discovery, to surprise. The success of the entire endeavor relies on the appearance of serendipity.

Thus, our work—whatever it is any of us choose to do—is first and foremost a reflection of our personalities, characterized by our willingness during the act of creation to embrace what we don't know as well as what we do know. For this reason, planned serendipity is fundamentally personalized, human, based in humility and trust, and deeply at odds with the machine-like regularity of industrial processes at their stereotypical worst.

The truth is that we all, individuals and companies alike, have virtually no control over the big events that shape our lives. But what we *do* control is vital. We have agency about where we choose to apply our time, the things we choose to make, and the philosophy that undergirds these decisions. These are the aspects of life that are, for the most part, within our power. These choices are how we exert our influence in a world in which old-fashioned notions of control no longer work.

In the end, planned serendipity is not a band-aid for our sense of powerlessness. It is a true antidote. We can do much more than just survive in a world we can never fully comprehend; we can *thrive*, but only by willingly embracing the unknown and trusting that we will find what we need when we need it. This is the promise. We can reach unimagined heights when we harness not just *our* skills and desires, but those of anyone and anything we serendipitously stumble upon.

Serendipiography

Commentary and sources for each Get Lucky *chapter, a catalog of serendipitous discovery.*

1: Prepare for the Unpreparable

"Any suggestion otherwise would be heresy."

The subject of our inability to accept the large role of luck in our lives and business has been explored at length (and mathematically) by Nassim Taleb, whose books, *Fooled by Randomness* (W.W. Norton, 2001) and *The Black Swan* (Random House, 2006), explain, in great detail, how self-delusional we are by nature.

"Dr. Spence Silver had taken his first job at the Minnesota Mining & Manufacturing Company."

3M actually owes its very existence to serendipity. As detailed in *Brand of the Tartan: The 3M Story*: "Here was a company of entrepreneurs who thought they were embarking on a mining venture, who discovered that they had nothing of value to mine, and who thereupon became one of the great manufacturing enterprises of America. They began with an asset which turned out to be a liability. Their true assets were very different; they were the qualities of initiative and courage and insight."

Huck, Virginia. *Brand of the Tartan: The 3M Story*. New York: Appleton-Century-Crofts, Inc., 1955.

Additional references used for the Post-it story include these:

*Duguid, S. "First Person: 'We Invented the Post-it Note.'" *Financial Times*, December 3, 2010. http://www.ft.com/cms/s/2/f08e8a9a-fcd7-11df-ae2d-00144feab49a.html#axzz18hyDnyKX

*The Januarist, "Why Are Post-it Notes Yellow?" http://www.thejanuarist.com/why-are-post-it-notes-yellow/. February 25, 2010.

*Green, P. "Post-it: The All-Purpose Note That Stuck." *The New York Times*, July 2, 2007. http://www.nytimes.com/2007/06/29/arts/29iht-postit.1.6413576.html

"The online service we founded with two other partners."

Our partners in Get Satisfaction, who are an integral if not always mentioned part of our story, are Amy Muller and Jonathan Grubb. Amy, Jonathan, and Thor had previously founded a Web consulting firm, Rubyred Labs, and it was this team that developed the Valleyschwag site.

"Luck and the Entrepreneur"

The original post is well worth reading: Andreessen, M. "Luck and the Entrepreneur, Part 1: The Four Kinds of Luck." http://pmarca-archive.posterous.com/luck-and-the-entrepreneur-part-1-the-four-kin. 2007.

"It is never entirely in fashion to mention luck in the same breath as science."

Austin, J. *Chase, Chance, and Creativity: The Lucky Art of Novelty*. Cambridge, MA: MIT Press, 1978.

"Almost 10 percent of the most cited scholarly articles include serendipity as a factor in discovery."

de Rond, M., and Morley, I. *Serendipity: Fortune and the Prepared Mind?*. Cambridge, UK: Cambridge University Press, 2010.

"Joseph Priestley, the discoverer of oxygen"

Priestley, J. *Experiments and Observations on Different Kinds of Air*. (FQ Books, 1775).

For further reading on his remarkable (and often iconoclastic) scientific life, see Steven Johnson's excellent *Invention of Air* (Riverhead Hardcover, 2008).

"The cover of a women's underwear catalog in 1992"

Some of these examples of semantic drift were collected by the Sri Lankan English consultant to the Oxford English Dictionary, Richard Boyle. His full essay on the subject can be found here: http://www.himalmag.com/component/content/article/464-Serendipity-and-Zemblanity.html

"The title he prefers these days is "serendipitologist.""

While there may be only one person in the world with the title of serendipitologist, there are many who deserve it retrospectively. The two most notable are the illustrious physiologist Walter Cannon, who single-handedly popularized the word "serendipity" for scientists in the 1930s; and the sociologist Robert Merton, famous for inventing the term "self-fulfilling prophecy," who wrote (with Elinor Barber) a prescient book about the evolution of the word, *The Travels & Adventures of Serendipity* (Princeton University Press, 2006) in the 1950s.

"Listening to Van Andel talk about his work"

The authors of this book originally discovered Pek van Andel in a search for Walter Cannon's famous 1939 speech on serendipity ("The Role of Chance in Discovery"). One of the scholarly articles databases cross-referenced an article in which he outlines the patterns he has gleaned from his epic collection of thousands of examples of serendipity. His article hops between ideas effortlessly, compressing a book's worth of material into a mere sixteen pages. Even the unwieldy subtitle promises a master class: Serendipity: Origin, History, Domains, Traditions, Appearances, Patterns and Programmability.

Van Andel, P, "Anatomy of the Unsought Finding." *British Journal for the Philosophy of Science*, 1994.

"Science is a madcap endeavor."

The playful idiosyncrasies of scientists and technologists often appear in the cultures of organizations they build for themselves: consider character-studded MIT, with its tradition of ingenious campus pranks called "hacks." One year students awoke to find a campus police car balanced on the top of the Great Dome; another year hundreds of gnomes of various shapes and sizes appeared around the Student Center.

"*No* discovery of a thing you *are* looking for comes under this description."

Pek van Andel has advanced a more audacious psychological hypothesis of the term's genesis. Horace Walpole, born in 1725, grew up in the shadow of his great father, the very first Prime Minister of Great Britain, Sir Robert Walpole. And what a shadow it was! Sir Robert was the first to live in 10 Downing Street, keep the peace to the enrichment of his country, and to this day his twenty-one-year tenure (1721–1742) is the longest of any prime minister.

Horace, therefore, had much to be proud of, except for one thing: he looked nothing like his father. In fact, he looked uncannily like another man, Carr Lord Elvey, a frequent companion of his mother. Could he himself be the enduring evidence of an unfaithful dalliance?

"He must have known it," says van Andel. We can imagine the moment in which he looked into a mirror and saw the familiar face of Lord Elvey staring back at him. This would have hit him like a ton of bricks. After all, a bastard pedigree was no pedigree at all in the eighteenth century. Luckily, everyone had good reason to overlook what was patently clear, most especially the prime minister. To be cuckolded so brazenly would have been shameful.

Hauntingly, one of the princes in the Three Princes of Serendip discovers that a king had "a butler's blood in his veins." In the original Old Persian version of 1302 by Amir Khusrau, the king interrogates his mother, who tearfully confesses her infidelity.

"I cannot free myself from my guessed link between the well-known unintended fathering of Walpole and the fact that he, of all people, created this rhythmic and impossible word. Was he the personification of serendipity?" asked van Andel. Did Walpole have the unsought discovery about his illegitimate parentage in the back of his mind when he coined the word itself?

"I can explain serendipity to a person without saying a single word."

Van Andel, Pek, medical researcher, University of Groningen, personal interview with Thor Muller, September 15, 2011.

His award-winning MRI coitus experiment can be viewed at http://youtu.be/OVAdCKaU3vY.

"A full list of his suitcase books is listed in the notes."

Here are the titles we noted.

Causalités et accidents de la découverte scientifique. Illustration de quelques étapes charactéristiques de l'évolution des sciences by René Taton (1955)

The Decipherment of Linear B by John Chadwick (Cambridge University Press, 1990)

Eingenbung und Tat im musikalischen Schaffen by Julius Bahle (S. Hirzel, 1939)

Essai sur la logique de l'invention dans les sciences by Jacques Picard (Alcan, 1928)

Essai sur les conditions positives de l'invention dans les sciences by Jacques Picard (Alcan, 1928)

Fabuleux hasards, histoire de la découverte de médicaments by Claude Bohuon and Claude Monneret (EDP Sciences, 2009)

L'Imprévu ou la science des objets trouvés by Jean Jacques (Jacob, 1990)

Les yeux du hasard et du genie. Le rôle de la chance dans la découverte by Fernand Lot (Plon, 1956)

Lucky Science: Accidental Discoveries from Gravity to Velcro by Royston Roberts and Jeanie Roberts (Wiley, 1994)

The Mathematician's Mind: The Psychology of Invention in the Mathematical Field by Jacques Hadamard (Princeton University Press, 1945).

Der musikalische Schaffensprozess by Julius Bahle (S. Hirzel, 1936)

La réalité dépasse la fiction by Franck Aycard, A. (Gallimard, 1968)

Psychologie van de wetenschap: Creativiteit, serendipiteit, de persoonlijke factor en de sociale context by Peter van Strien (Amsterdam University Press, 2011)

Savants et découvertes by Louis de Broglie (Michel, 1951)

The School of Padua & The Emergence of Modern Science by John Herman Randall (Editrice Antenore, 1961)

La serendipité: le hasard heureux by Daniéle Bourcier and Pek van Andel (Hermann, 2011)

La serendipité, dans la science, la téchnique, l'art el la droit by Daniéle Bourcier and Pek van Andel (L'Act Mem, 2008)

Serendipities: Language and Lunacy by Umberto Eco (Mariner Books, 1999)

Serendipity & the Three Princes of Serendip; From the Peregrinaggio (Univ. of Oklahoma Press, 1964)

Théorie de l'invention by Paul Souriau (Hachette, 1881)

Three Men in a Boat by Jerome K. Jerome (CreateSpace, 2010) [first published in 1889, the titular men are the antithesis of the Three Princes of Serendip, always running into calamity]

Yersin, un pasteurien en Indochine by Henri Mollaret and Jacqueline Brossolet (Belin, 1993)

Les trois princes de Serendip, by Amir Khorow Dehalvi, traduit par Farideh Rava et présenté par Pek van Andel et Daniéle Bourcier (Hermann, 2011)

"It's much like the boomerang, you see."

A video of Pek van Andel demonstrating the Celtic stone is available at http://youtu.be/MkFKVQdMwXg.

"The scholarly literature on serendipity is overwhelmingly focused on the experience of the individual creative mind."

One of the few books to explore the role and power of serendipity within organizations is the highly recommended *The Power of Pull: How Small Moves, Smartly Made, Can Set Big Things in Motion* (Basic Books, 2010) by John Hagel III, John Seely Brown, and Lang Davison. This book, grounded in business management science, gave us the confidence that planned serendipity, or what they call "shaping serendipity," can be applied to organizations.

"Disneyland with the Death Penalty"

With one of the most memorable titles of any magazine article ever, it's worth crawling into the archives for this one.

Gibson, W. "Disneyland with the Death Penalty." http://www.wired.com/wired/archive/1.04/gibson.html. *WIRED Magazine*, September/October 1993, 1(4).

"Ban on chewing gum would be 'relaxed for people with medical prescriptions.'"

Mydans, S. "Singapore, at 40, Loosens Its Grip." http://www.nytimes.com/2005/08/09/world/asia/09iht-singapore.html. *The New York Times*, August 10, 2005.

"They are overtaken by a profound uneasiness."

The double bind was originally developed to help explain the origins of schizophrenia. The research has shed light into its mechanisms and effects, as we see in chilling case reports like this:

A young man who had fairly well recovered from an acute schizophrenic episode was visited in the hospital by his mother. He was glad to see her and impulsively put his arm around her shoulders, whereupon she stiffened. He withdrew his arm and she asked, "Don't you love me anymore?" He then blushed, and she said, "Dear, you must not be so easily embarrassed and afraid of your feelings." The patient was able to stay with her only a few minutes more and following her departure he assaulted an aide and was put in the tubs.

For more on the double bind, see Gibney, P. "The Double Bind Theory: Still Crazy-Making After All These Years." http://www.psychotherapy.com.au/TheDoubleBindTheory.pdf. *Psychotherapy in Australia*, May 2006, 12(3).

"Evidence of this cultural thaw is appearing all over the city."

Lindt, N. "Expanding the Cultural Realm in Singapore." http://travel.nytimes.com/2011/06/12/travel/singapores-cultural-realm-is-expanding.html. *The New York Times*, June 10, 2011.

2: Skill: Motion—Breaking Out

"Jobs realized that it wasn't enough to simply create a space."

Lehrer, Jonah. "Steve Jobs: Technology Alone Is Not Enough." http://www.newyorker.com/online/blogs/newsdesk/2011/10/steve-jobs-pixar.html. October 7, 2007.

It's worth reading Lehrer's entire post, reprinted here:

On January 30, 1986, shortly after he was forced out of Apple Computer (and years before his return), Steve Jobs bought a small computer manufacturer named Pixar from George Lucas, the director of *Star Wars*. While the Pixar team had produced a few impressive animated shorts for marketing purposes—"The Adventures of Andre and Wally B" is widely credited with spurring Hollywood's interest in digital animation—Jobs was most interested in the Pixar Image Computer, a $125,000 machine capable of generating complex graphic visualizations.

Unfortunately, the expensive computers were a commercial flop. Jobs was forced to extend a personal line of credit to Pixar, which lost more than $8.3 million in 1990 alone. His first post-Apple investment was in danger of failing. "We should have failed," Alvy Ray Smith, a cofounder of Pixar, says in David Price's *The Pixar Touch* (Random House, 2009). "But it seemed to me that Steve would just not suffer a defeat. He couldn't sustain it."

The survival of Pixar, and its subsequent rise, are a revealing case study in Jobs's approach to innovation. Although Jobs's background was in computer hardware, he helped transform Pixar into a movie-making powerhouse, one of the most successful studios in the history of cinema. Since 1995, when the first *Toy Story* was released, Pixar has created twelve feature films. Every one of those films has been a commercial success, with an average international gross of more than $550 million per film. Not even Apple has enjoyed that kind of streak.

When introducing the iPad 2 in March, Jobs summarized his strategy this way: "It is in Apple's DNA that technology alone is not enough—it's technology married with liberal arts, married with the humanities, that yields us the results that make our heart sing." Such platitudes are common in Silicon Valley, where executives routinely introduce shiny gadgets with lofty language. But what set all of Jobs's companies apart, from Pixar to NeXT to Apple, was indeed an insistence that computer scientists must work together with artists and designers, that the best ideas emerge from the intersection of technology and the humanities. "One of the greatest achievements at Pixar was that we brought these two cultures together and got them working side by side," Jobs said in 2003.

This faith in the liberal arts is rooted in Jobs's own biography. He famously dropped out of Reed College his freshman year but continued to audit classes in calligraphy: "I learned about serif and sans serif typefaces, about varying the amount of space between different letter combinations, about what makes great typography great. It was beautiful, historical, artistically subtle in a way that science can't capture, and I found it fascinating." ... "None of this had even a hope of practical application in my life. But ten years later, when we were designing the first Macintosh computer, it all came back to me. And we designed it all into the Mac. It was the first computer with beautiful typography. If I had never dropped in on that single course in college, the Mac would never have had multiple typefaces or proportionally spaced fonts."

Perhaps the clearest demonstration can be seen in the design of the Pixar campus. In November 2000, Jobs purchased an abandoned Del Monte canning factory on sixteen acres in Emeryville, just north of Oakland. The original architectural plan called for three buildings, with separate offices for the computer scientists, the animators, and the Pixar executives. Jobs immediately scrapped it. "We used to joke that the building was Steve's movie," Ed Catmull, the president of Pixar, told the authors last year. Instead of three buildings, there was going to be a single vast space, with an airy atrium at its center. "The philosophy behind this design is that it's good to put the most important function at the heart of the building," Catmull said. "Well, what's our most important function? It's the interaction of our employees. That's why Steve put a big empty space there. He wanted to create an open area for people to always be talking to each other."

Jobs realized, however, that it wasn't enough to simply create a space; he needed to make people go there. As he saw it, the main challenge for Pixar was getting its different cultures to work together, forcing the computer geeks and cartoonists to collaborate. (John Lasseter, the chief creative officer at Pixar, describes the equation this way: "Technology inspires art, and art challenges the technology.") In typical fashion, Jobs saw this as a design problem. He began with the mailboxes, which he shifted to the atrium. Then he moved the meeting rooms to the center of the building, followed by the cafeteria and the coffee bar and the gift shop. But that still wasn't enough: Jobs insisted that the architects locate the only set of bathrooms in the atrium. (He was later forced to compromise on this detail.) In a 2008 conversation, Brad Bird, the director of *The Incredibles* and *Ratatouille*, said, "The atrium initially might seem like a waste of space" .... "But Steve realized that when people run into each other, when they make eye contact, things happen."

That emphasis on consilience, even if it came at the expense of convenience, has always been a defining trait of Steve Jobs. In an age of intellectual fragmentation, Jobs insisted that the best creations occurred when people from disparate fields were connected together, when our distinct ways of seeing the world were brought to bear on a singular problem. It's what happens when a calligrapher designs a computer font and when an animator strikes up a conversation with a programmer at the bathroom sink. The Latin crest of Pixar University says it all: Alienus Non Diutius. Alone no longer.

"Steve's theory worked from day one."

Isaacson, Walter. *Steve Jobs*. New York, NY: Simon & Schuster, 2011.

"Oh, the cubicle"

Our history of the cubicle is drawn from several articles covering both the historical details of the cubicle as well as the cultural values it promoted:

*Franz, David. "The Moral Life of Cubicles," *The New Atlantis*, Number 19, Winter 2008, 132–139.

*Schlosser, Julie. "Trapped in Cubicles," *FORTUNE Magazine*, March 2006.

*Musser, George. "The Origin of Cubicles and the Open-Plan Office." *Scientific American*, August 2009.

"*Cars 2*, released in 2011, was another wildly successful box office hit."

Cars 2 grossed $551 million in box office receipts during its theatrical run, making it the most successful film Pixar has released to date. It was the latest in a long line of blockbuster hits produced by Pixar, arguably one of the most successful studios in Hollywood history. According to their corporate history, the company's 11 feature films "have combined [grossed] more than $6 billion at the worldwide box office. The first 10 feature films, through *Up*, have garnered 35 Academy Award® nominations, nine Oscars®, six Golden Globes® and numerous other accolades."

Cars 2 box office total as of November, 2011 from Box Office Mojo at http://www.boxofficemojo.com/movies/?id=cars2.htm.

Pixar Corporate Overview at http://www.pixar.com/companyinfo/about_us/overview.htm.

"Lays out empirical evidence for the value of bringing different perspectives to bear on problems"

Page, Dr. Scott E. *The Difference: How the Power of Diversity Creates Better Groups, Firms, Schools, and Societies*. Princeton, NJ: Princeton University Press, January 2007.

"The problems we face in the world are very complicated."

In his interview with *The New York Times*, Dr. Page clarifies his definition of "diversity" as meaning "differences in how people think," in order to distinguish it from the more common usage of the word to represent racial, ethnic, and sexual minorities. Explains Page, "Two people can look quite different and think similarly. Having said that, there's certainly a lot of evidence that people's identity groups—ethnic, racial, sexual, age—matter when it comes to diversity in thinking."

Dreifus, Claudia. "In Professor's Model, Diversity = Productivity." *The New York Times*, January 8, 2008.

"Pixar University, a professional-development program"

Hempel, Jessi. "Pixar University: Thinking Outside the Mouse," SFGate.com. http://articles.sfgate.com/2003-06-04/bay-area/17493262_1_pixar-s-emeryville-technical-director-bill-polson-pixar-president-edwin-catmull. June 4, 2003.

"Twitter: Rearranging the Structure"

Costolo lays out his thinking about the ideal organizational structure in a blog post he wrote several years before joining Twitter. This section is adapted from that post.

Costolo, Dick. "Ask the Wizard: No Offices." http://www.burningdoor.com/askthewizard/2007/09/no_offices.html. September 2007.

"Message Bus: Adapting the Ritual"

Narendra Rocherolle, President, Message Bus, personal interview with Lane Becker, November 8, 2011.

"Every Thursday we play a TED talk."

If you would like to do this at your own office, an archive of over one thousand TED Talks is available online at http://www.ted.com/talks.

"Gangplank: Baking It into the Culture"

Derek Neighbors, founder, Gangplank, personal interview with Lane Becker, September 22, 2011.

3: Skill: Preparation—Anatomy of a Geek Brain

"The Case of the Floppy-Eared Rabbits"

Incidentally, this classic case study was co-authored by the husband of Elinor Barber, who was the co-author of Robert Merton's epic book on serendipity. It's a very small world!

Barber, B. and R. Fox. "The Case of the Floppy-Eared Rabbits: An Instance of Serendipity Gained and Serendipity Lost." *American Journal of Sociology*, 1958.

"Dr. Kellner considered it too banal to study seriously."

Kellner and his team did use the floppy-eared symptom as a handy rule of thumb. Floppy ears indicated the dosage was *just right*. This was a useful tip in the lab, but not the kind of thing that gets you written up in the prestigious science journals. In the "Case of the Floppy-Eared Bunnies": Dr. Kellner commented, 'I didn't write it up.' . . . He knew that an applied technological discovery of this sort would not be suitable for publication in the basic science-oriented professional journals to which he and his colleagues submit reports of experimental work.

Kellner went on to found the New York Blood Center in 1964, one of the first reliable blood-supply systems for transfusions for the New York region. Every indication is that it was the result of good sense rather than serendipity.

"Arresting an Exception"

Austin, J. *Chase, Chance, and Creativity: The Lucky Art of Novelty*. Cambridge, MA: MIT Press, 1978.

David Eagleman, a neuroscientist and author, explained the skill of arresting an exception this way: "The exclamation that signals a rich discovery is not 'Eureka!,' but more often 'That's strange.' So that's where I try to position myself, around the 'that's strange' phenomena."

Solomon, A. "An Interview with David Eagleman, Neuroscientist." http://boingboing.net/2011/10/19/an-interview-with-david-eagleman-neuroscientist.html. October 2011.

"The coach who became known as the Zen Master"

For further reading about Phil Jackson, we recommend his book *Sacred Hoops: Spiritual Lessons of a Hardwood Warrior* by P. Jackson and H. Delehanty (New York: Hyperion, 2006). Money quote: "Not only is there a lot more to life than basketball, there's a lot more to basketball than basketball." Another essay dissecting his methods is this one:

Turner, D. "Phil Jackson: Zen and the Counterculture Coach." http://uhra.herts
.ac.uk/dspace/bitstream/2299/1346/1/900740.pdf. 2005.

"Dr. Thomas himself had a geek brain."

Thomas' own educational path suggests that these mental processes can be learned.
In his senior year of college, Thomas took an advanced biology course with Professor
Wilbur Swingle, who delivered two lessons that indelibly affected Thomas' outlook.
First was the notion that "science begins with the admission of ignorance . . . .
an endless frontier." Secondly, he learned that experiments done for the sake of
curiosity often yield the most practical results.

"Perhaps there are more around than we realize."

The works of Lewis Thomas are well worth hunting down, particularly these two:

*Thomas, L. *Lives of a Cell*. New York: Penguin, 1978.

*Thomas, L. *The Youngest Science: Notes of a Medicine Watcher*. New York:
Penguin, 1983.

"Relentlessly focused on amplifying the weird."

Godin, S. *We Are All Weird: The Myth of Mass and the End of Compliance*. New York:
Do You Zoom, 2011. This is a lightning-fast read outlining the rise of the weird from
a marketing perspective.

"Big companies don't innovate"

Dixon, C. "(Founder Stories) Mayor Bloomberg: 'Make Sure You Are the First One
in There Every Day & the Last One to Leave.'" http://techcrunch.com/2011/11/30/
founder-stories-mayor-bloomberg-make-sure-you-are-the-first-one-in-there-
every-day-the-last-one-to-leave/. November 28, 2011.

"Construal level theory (CLT)"

A high-level introduction of this study printed in *Scientific American* is available here: Shapira, O., and Liberman, N. "An Easy Way to Increase Creativity." http://www.scientificamerican.com/article.cfm?id=an-easy-way-to-increase-c.
July 2009.

For a scholarly review of the theory:

Trope, Y., and Liberman, N. "Construal-Level Theory of Psychological Distance." *Psychological Review*, 2010, Vol. 117, No. 2, 440–463. http://www.psych.nyu.edu/trope/Trope%20et%20al.,%202007%20-%20JCP.pdf.

"A prisoner was attempting to escape from a tower."

The solution? He unraveled the rope lengthwise and tied the remaining strands together.

"Surge of interest in the new wave of Internet startups"

One of the major psychological explanations of humor is incongruity theory, which holds that we find something funny when there's a mismatch between what we expect and what happens (typically in a story, a joke, a scenario in life). It can be argued that in many cases the incongruity pushes the concepts at hand into abstraction. Many have commented on the humor (sometimes devilish) displayed by the great minds. Does humor help us rise above the banality of life and make us more creative?

"You need to understand things in order to invent beyond them."

Friedman, T. *The World Is Flat: A Brief History of the Twenty-First Century*. New York: Farrar, Strauss and Giroux, 2005.

"They're just terrible poisonous things during the day at work."

This line is from Jason Fried's 2010 TEDxMidland talk, "Why Work Doesn't Happen at Work." http://www.ted.com/. October 2010.

"Only if the meeting is structured in a way that facilitates psychological distance"

There are many ways to do this. For instance, in *Gamestorming: A Playbook for Innovators, Rulebreakers, and Changemakers* (O'Reilly, 2010), Dave Gray, Sunni Brown. and Dave Macanufo provide dozens of playful methods for fostering the abstract, idea-exploration mode within groups.

"Find your tribe."

It's easy to find the other geeks in your midst if you know what to look for. Odds are good there are lots of people around who bring their obsessions into their work, and who can surprise you with their unexpected perspectives. Here are some of our favorite geek-locating questions, as useful in formal interviews as they are in casual conversation:

"On a scale of 1–10, how weird are you?" The easiest geeks to connect with are the ones who readily admit it. The e-commerce juggernaut Zappos makes bringing "a little weirdness" into its culture a priority. Every employee screening interview includes this question. It's not that they're looking for twisted crazies (they aren't), but they are committed to only hiring people who know and prize their own idiosyncrasies.

"Teach me something you know a lot about." This is a question designed to uncork a person's deeper interests and get them away from what they think you want to hear. Have them tell you about the board game they love to play, a series of fantasy books they've been reading, the Iron Man training they're in the midst of, or anything else that they've expressed a strong interest in. If it's a formal interview, ask them to apply this knowledge to the role you're interviewing them for and watch the sparks fly.

"If you and your family were attacked by Somali pirates and you could only have one weapon, what would it be?" One company we know asks this of all their job candidates. There are no wrong answers, but it is revealing to hear people apply their personality to this open-ended, seemingly irrelevant question. Those with a well-developed geek brain will often come up with an answer you've never heard before.

4: Skill: Divergence—The Garden of Forking Paths

"They have mastered the elusive skill of divergence."

The story came to us through *FastCompany*'s design blog:

Jao, C. "Loyal Dean Turns Cast-Off Wood into Artful Longboards." http://www.fastcodesign.com/1664765/loyal-dean-turns-cast-off-wood-into-artful-longboards. 2011.

Dino Pierone, founder, Loyal Dean, personal interview with Thor Muller, December 1, 2011.

"They'd rather have someone who is strong and wrong than someone who's weak and right."

Clinton, B. "Address by Former U.S. President Bill Clinton to the Democratic Leadership Council." New York University, NY. December 3, 2002.

"The Bias Against Creativity: Why People Desire But Reject Creative Ideas"

Mueller, J. S., Melwani, S., & Goncalo, J. A. (2011). *The Bias Against Creativity: Why People Desire but Reject Creative Ideas*. Electronic edition. Retrieved December 2, 2011, from Cornell University, ILR School site: http://digitalcommons.ilr.cornell.edu/articles/450/

The conclusion the authors reach is worth reiterating: "The field of creativity may need to shift its current focus from identifying how to generate more creative ideas to identifying how to help innovative institutions **recognize and accept creativity** [emphasis ours]."

"Fueling cycle after cycle of innovation and extinction"

Christensen, C. "The Innovator's Dilemma." New York: Harper Paperbacks, 2003.

"It stands as a counter-example to the risk aversion that famously plagues Hollywood."

Michael Lambie, The Nielsen Company, personal interview with Thor Muller, September 10, 2011.

"Most shocking of all was that he launched it four full months before the regular season started."

Hampp, A. "Entertainment A-List No. 1: 'Glee'." *Ad Age*, May 23, 2011. http://adage.com/article/special-report-entertainment-alist/glee-entertainment-a-list-1/227661/.

"This is our branching range."

For further exploration on related concepts, check out the following material:

*The social constructivist Lev Vygotsky and his Zone of Proximal Development (ZPD)

*Stuart Kaufmann's "adjacent possible theory," which was also adapted by Steven Johnson in his *Where Good Ideas Come From* (Riverhead Hardcover, 2010)

*The Cone of Expectations concept of Robert Austin and Lee Devin

*Stochastic processes in probability theory

"Bezos issued an edict that would in very short order transform the company."

Yegge, S. "Stevey's Google Platforms Rant." https://plus.google.com/11267870222-8711889851/posts/eVeouesvaVX. October 12, 2011.

"A triple dose can be absolutely suffocating."

Lynn, G.S., Morone, J.G., and Paulson, A.S. "Marketing and discontinuous innovation: The Probe and Learn Process." http://www.radicalinnovation.com/pdfs/Probe%20and%20Learn.pdf. *California Management Review.* 38(3), Spring, 1996.

5: Skill: Commitment—Burning the Ships

"Everywhere else they're tearing down rain forests. We're showing how to put them back."

The definitive work on Gaviotas is well worth reading for many reasons: the adventure story, the science, and the implicit management lessons.

Weisman, A. *Gaviotas: A Village to Reinvent the World.* White River Junction, VT: Chelsea Green Publishing Company, 1998.

"Commitment . . . involves organizing ourselves around an overriding purpose."

It can be tricky talking about "commitment," let alone "purpose" without being cliché. Most of us don't need another lesson in writing mission statements or finding our true calling, but we certainly could use a crash course in how it can be harnessed to court serendipity. We cringe when we hear such leaden advice as "do what you love and the rest shall follow," in large part because it seems detached from the reality of an economy that can be so unkind to so many career choices and industries. Yet if we adjust the phrase to "Do what you do *for* love, and the rest shall follow," we actually get somewhere. The clarity of our motivations is what matters here, not the domain of our pursuits.

"The other shortcut is the ultimate energy saver: do nothing."

Tierney, R. "Willpower: Rediscovering the Greatest Human Strength,"

http://www.nytimes.com/2011/08/21/magazine/do-you-suffer-from-decision-fatigue.html?_r=1&pagewanted=all.

"That is, unless we counterbalance the sheer quantity of choices with commitment."

There are numerous known ways to counteract decision fatigue, including increasing glucose intake.

"The scales dropped from his eyes, and he saw what he needed to do."

Anderson, R. *Confessions of a Radical Industrialist: Profits, People, Purpose–Doing Business by Respecting the Earth*. New York: St. Martin's Press, 2009.

Anderson, R. *Mid-Course Correction: Toward a Sustainable Enterprise: The Interface Model*. Atlanta, GA: Peregrinzilla Press, 1999.

"Like fall leaves on a forest floor, they were beautiful."

David Oakey Designs. http://www.davidoakeydesigns.com. 2011.

"It had become the top-selling product in the history of the company."

WorldWatch Institute. *State of the World 2008: Innovations for a Sustainable Economy*. New York: W.W. Norton & Company, 2008.

"In-N-Out Burger is a business whose adaptability is actually measured in how *little* it seems to have changed."

It has been described by Bain Consulting as a prime example of an "innovation fulcrum," the point where you lose more by changing than by staying the same.

"Serendipity has consistently struck as a result of this committed focus on quality and the stick-to-itness it represents."

Perman, S. *In-N-Out Burger: A Behind-the-Counter Look at the Fast-Food Chain That Breaks All the Rules*. New York: HarperBusiness, 2009.

"San Francisco's most celebrated garden store."

Flora Grubb, founder, Flora Grubb Gardens, personal interview with Thor Muller, September 29, 2011.

6: Skill: Activation—Church vs. Stadium

"Did you know that physically leaning to the left makes things appear to be smaller?"

http://www.newscientist.com/article/mg21228424.000-leaning-to-the-left-makes-the-world-seem-smaller.html.

"Gene Weingarten, describes his experience of watching the scene unfold . . . ."

Weingarten, G. "Pearls Before Breakfast," *Washington Post*, April 8, 2007. http://www.washingtonpost.com/wp-dyn/content/article/2007/04/04/AR2007040401721.html.

"Its Arts for Transit office established a program called Music Under New York (MUNY)."

http://www.christianfischer.name/music_under_new_york.html.

"Many performers have benefited from this program, including musical saw artist Natalia Paruz, who also writes a blog covering the colorful subway music scene."

http://www.subwaymusicblog.com/.

"The banner gives musicians a back."

Natalia Paruz, personal interview with Thor Muller, December 11, 2011.

"Side-by-side comparison of monochronic and polychronic time."

http://www.tamas.com/samples/source-docs/Hofstede_Hall.pdf.

"Like most estimates made in ignorance, they turn out to be dead wrong."

Much like writing a book, for the record.

"Havel took to roller skating around the palace . . . ."

L, E. "Václav Havel, playwright and president," *The Economist*, December 18, 2011. http://www.economist.com/blogs/easternapproaches/2011/12/václav-havel-memoriam.

"The Most Interesting Meeting in the World."

Keith Messick, VP of Marketing, Keas, personal interview with Thor Muller, November 30, 2011.

"WTF? RTFM, noob!"

Translated: "What the f—? Read the f—ing manual, you ignorant fool!"

"In improv you always have to be listening for the scene to go *anywhere*."

David Cosand and Amy Lamp, Forty Agency. Personal interview with Thor Muller, August 19, 2011.

7: Skill: Connection—Needle in a Haystack

"The popular show *Mythbusters* took this very approach in an episode that aired in 2004."

"Exploding House." *Mythbusters*, episode 23, 2004 season. Original airdate: November 16, 2004.

"For the past thirty years Robert J. Henry has been exploring the wilderness around Lake Ontario."

Robert J. Henry, personal interview with Thor Muller, December 13, 2011.

"Most people (if they noticed it at all) would pause for a moment and go on, never thinking of it again."

Henry, J. "Making Room for Serendipity." Wanderings, June 7, 2008. http://wanderings.edublogs.org/2008/06/07/making-room-for-serendipity/.

"When it comes to solving needle-in-haystack problems, isolation is the enemy."

There is a counter-case: polymaths and solitary explorers have historically achieved maximum success given more time alone with their thoughts.

"Pundits and authors have voiced the fear that the Internet is making us shallower."

Paul Carr and Andrew Keane come to mind as quintessential neo-luddites.

"William Powers . . . . believes that we just need to unplug regularly to reclaim time for ourselves."

Powers, William. *Hamlet's BlackBerry: A Practical Philosophy for Building a Good Life in the Digital Age.* New York: Harper, 2011.

"Adapt to a higher rate of connectedness in our lives."

Better to take the approach that Harvard psychologist Stephen Pinker suggests: "The solution is not to bemoan technology but to develop strategies of self-control, as we do with every other temptation in life. Turn off e-mail or Twitter when you work, put away your BlackBerry at dinner time." Or as Clay Shirky said, "It's not information overload. It's filter failure." (Web 2.0 Expo NY, 2008)

"Watts calls the people who do 'accidental influentials.'"

Thompson, C. "Is the Tipping Point Toast?" *Fast Company*, February 1, 2008. http://www.fastcompany.com/magazine/122/is-the-tipping-point-toast.html.

"It is an international project known as the Large Hadron Collider."

Before it launched, at least one pair of theoretical physicists predicted doom: "The hypothesized Higgs boson ... might be so abhorrent to nature that its creation would ripple backward through time and stop the collider before it could make one, like a time traveler who goes back in time to kill his grandfather."

"It is a question of timing."

"CERN & Innovation: The Heart of the Matter." *WIPO Magazine*, December 2008. http://www.wipo.int/export/sites/www/pct/en/news/extracts/2008/wipo_magazine_12_2008_cern.pdf.

"The major challenge for Knowledge Transfer organizations is to improve the chances of serendipity by providing appropriate support structures and resources."

Hill, N., Higgons, R., Green, K., and Rafe, D. "Knowledge Transfer from Space Exploration: Prospects and Challenges for the U.K." ABOTTS Report, April 2005. p. 28.

"Not long ago the best place to find a needle was somewhere you knew you could find it, like a pin cushion."

This line was inspired by a blog post by information architect, Mark Baker, "The Best Place to Find a Needle Is a Haystack." http://www.wipo.int/export/sites/www/pct/en/news/extracts/2008/wipo_magazine_12_2008_cern.pdf.

8: Skill: Permeability—Storming the Castle

"The world's handmade marketplace"

"Etsy—About" at http://etsy.com/about.

"A beer cozy made out of a taxidermied squirrel"

Winchell, April. "Chimes and Misdemeanors." http://www.regretsy.com/2010/03/25/chimes-and-misdemeanors/. March 25, 2010.

Winchell, April. "That's Nacho iPod." http://www.regretsy.com/2011/11/06/weekend-flashback-thats-nacho-ipod/. November 6, 2011.

Winchell, April. "A Long Cold One." http://www.regretsy.com/2011/08/17/a-long-cold-one/. August 17, 2011.

Fair warning: You might lose hours of your workday to browsing through the Regretsy archives.

"No one knows how to treat you anymore. No one cares."

Winchell, April. "Sooner or Later, You'll Pay, Pal." http://www.regretsy.com/2011/12/06/sooner-or-later-youll-pay-pal/. December 6, 2011.

"Horror Stories: PayPal Did It!"

The site PayPalSucks.com is the most popular of the sites that make up "The No PayPal Network," including AboutPayPal.org, PayPalWarning.com, and Screw-PayPal.com. You can read PayPalSucks.com forums at http://www.paypalsucks.com/forums/.

"I used to be in customer relationship management."

Nusca, Andrew. "Wendy Lea: Online, 'Customer Service Is the New Marketing,'" http://www.zdnet.com/blog/btl/wendy-lea-online-customer-service-is-the-new-marketing/64098. November 23, 2011.

"Markets are conversations."

Levine, R., Locke, C., Searls, D., and Weinberger, D. *The Cluetrain Manifesto: The End of Business as Usual.* New York: Basic Books, 2001.

Also available in its entirety online at http://www.cluetrain.com/book/.

"Occasionally blossom into full-scale, Web-wide customer revolt"

For a wonderfully detailed study of the how and why behind this phenomenon of decentralized customer revolt, see Clay Shirky's *Here Comes Everybody: The Power of Organizing Without Organizations.* New York: Penguin, 2009.

"Customers everywhere were already scattered around the Web."

As founders, we owe a huge debt of gratitude to the authors of *The Cluetrain Manifesto.* A big part of the founding philosophy that drove the creation of Get Satisfaction, much of which we've laid out in this book, was developing on top of the thinking that the Cluetrain authors put forth. They were the first to grasp just how completely power was shifting from the hands of companies to the hands of consumers, and also the first to suggest that this might be better for companies than their initial responses might indicate.

"Pampers provides good customer service and support as a foundation."

Scott Hirsch, Vice President for Business Development, Get Satisfaction, personal interview with Lane Becker, December 13, 2011.

"Back in 2008, a customer asked a question on the Whole Foods community."

"Wonderful Water Wanted" topic at http://getsatisfaction.com/wholefoods/topics/wonderful_water_wanted.

"We were born in a San Francisco garage."

"Timbuk2—About Us" at http://www.timbuk2.com/wordpress_cms/customer-service/about/.

"One of these moms asked Timbuk2 whether they would ever make a diaper bag."

"Do you guys make a diaper bag?" at http://getsatisfaction.com/timbuk2/topics/do_you_guys_make_a_diaper_bag.

"We always have a choice between love and fear."

Doc Searls, author of *The Cluetrain Manifesto*, personal interview with Lane Becker, December 13, 2011.

"Sickness unfolds in stories."

Charon, Rita. *Narrative Medicine: Honoring the Stories of Illness*. New York: Oxford University Press, 2006.

9: Skill: Attraction—Magnetic Fields

"The opportunities for engaged learning are inversely proportional to the knowability of the outcome."

Gever Tulley, Director, Brightworks, personal interview with Thor Muller, December 1, 2011.

"It was made by four kids ranging in age from seven to nine."

The film's producers were Coke, Evan, Kaia, and Quinn, and their stopmotion video, Zompples, can be viewed on YouTube: http://youtu.be/4MRk5kd2fzU.

"And for that, I apologize."

Talarico, B. "Watch Oprah Winfrey Apologize for Not Hearing His Side." http://www.okmagazine.com/videos/watch-oprah-winfrey-apologize-james-frey-not-hearing-his-side. May 18, 2011.

"Jane ni Dhulchaointigh"

An Irish name pronounced nee-gul-queen-tig.

Jane ni Dhulchaointigh, founder and CEO, Sugru. Personal interview with Thor Muller, December 12, 2011.

"It's what explains the constant influx of photos, videos, and testimonials of ingenious uses by customers that have continued in the years since their initial launch."

http://sugru.com/gallery.

"If people can self-report their location, then it would make it easier for us to meet up."

Dennis Crowley, CEO, Foursquare. Personal interview with Lane Becker and Thor Muller, December 14, 2011.

"It read 'Foursquare Mayor Drinks for Free.'"

http://www.flickr.com/photos/leahculver/3942430314/.

10: Unraveling the Double Bind

"Procter & Gamble mandated in 2000 ..."

Huston, Larry and Sakkab, Nabil. "P&G's New Innovation Model." *Harvard Business Review*. http://hbswk.hbs.edu/archive/5258.html. March 20, 2006.

Acknowledgments

As with any creation, this book is the result of a winding history of relationships stretching back as far as we can see. Countless interactions large and small over many years are as responsible as anything for the ideas layered throughout these pages. Conversations had, books borrowed, stories told, ideas exchanged, introductions made—these are the basis for the good luck that has accumulated and continues to take us to remarkable places. It would be impossible for us to name all of serendipity's agents even if they were possible to track. At one point or another all of us—husbands, wives, sons, daughters, teachers, coworkers, artists, authors—provide a spark to someone else's work. We start by honoring this process and our collective roles within it.

There are, however, a few individuals and organizations without whom this book would definitely not have been possible.

First among them is Wendy Lea, who today leads the company we founded, Get Satisfaction, and who helped galvanize the support of publishers, board members, and indeed the whole company. She has believed in us from the beginning, and has provided essential input along the way. We'd also like to thank the whole team at Get Satisfaction for always having our back and for understanding when we disappeared into book-writing mode, particularly the indefatigable Scott Hirsch,

ACKNOWLEDGMENTS

who sees what others miss; Keith Messick, a true believer who ensured there would be at least one sports anecdote in the book; Andy Wibbels, who's always there for us in a pinch; Jessie Young and Courtney Meehan, for research assistance; and Jonathan Grubb, the fourth cofounder (and fifth Beatle) of Get Satisfaction, for his timely suggestion.

A book is largely the product of the people who help you get through it. Numerous friends offered support—emotional, moral, technical, and otherwise—and in particular: John Hagel, who provided inspiration and intellectual leadership on the subject of serendipity inside organizations; Nick Bilton, who assured us it was possible; Dinah Sanders, who helped us get started; Scott Berkun, who helped us navigate the contract process; Heather Meeker, who provided invaluable legal advice; and Sam and Diana Hunt, for loaning us their beautiful house.

We're incredibly grateful for the critical, serendipitous introductions made by Gabe Vidal, Relly Annett-Baker, Michael Lambie, Ben Casnocha, and Stuart Albert; the valuable insight and feedback provided by Jen Bekman, Steve Glenn, Maya Orbach, Heather Gold, Marina Giampietro, Steve Ng Ming Yeow, and Dave Gray; the conference organizers that allowed us to develop these ideas in front of audiences, and in particular: Anima Sarah LaVoy (TEDxOxbridge), Michael Dila (Business Unfinished, University of Toronto), Brad Smith (Webvisions), Marianne van Leeuwen (Emerce Eday); and the timely catalyst provided by the Overlap 2011 Conference in the early stages of the book.

Most importantly, we'd like to thank our wives, Courtney Skott and Amy Muller (also the third cofounder of Get Satisfaction), who tolerated the lack of a social schedule during the months when we were trying to finish this book, but more importantly, have *always* been willing to provide support for whatever crazy new project we had ahead, up to and including this book. And to Quinn and Tesla, so patient with their distracted daddy: yes, the book is finally done now!

And finally, our editor, Genoveva Llosa. Hard to put into words how important it is to have a good editor, and Genoveva is the best. Without her critical eye and willingness to wield it, this project would never have gotten started, much less come anywhere close to finished. We owe her a huge debt of gratitude.

About the Authors

Thor Muller credits any success he's had as a five-time serial entrepreneur to obsessive curiosity, chance occurrences, and a dangerous willingness to break things. He is the cofounder and former chief technology officer of Get Satisfaction, a groundbreaking online customer engagement platform used by over 65,000 companies. As an early Internet business pioneer, Thor started one of the world's first Web design agencies in 1995, acquired by Frog Design to form its renowned global Internet practice. He is a frequent blogger, invited speaker at conferences and universities, and occasional host of his own sing-along piano bar.

Lane Becker has been working on the Web since it began, from setting up web sites at his university in 1994, to his first failed startup (don't ask) in 1999, and on to more successful ventures: cofounding Adaptive Path, the world's first user-experience design firm, and Get Satisfaction, an online customer engagement platform. At Adaptive Path, Lane worked with numerous clients, including National Public Radio, the United Nations, and Princess Cruises, and aided in the development of Measure Map, a blog analytics tool acquired by Google in 2005. Lane is also an advisor to Freestyle.vc, an early-stage Internet venture capital fund.

Index